| FEB 20 '78 | DATE DUE | | |
|---|---|---|---|
| AUG 25 78 | | | |
| APR 19 '82 | | | |
| JUL 21 '82 | | | |
| JUL 29 '82 | | | |
| AUG 30 '83 | | | |
| MAR 30 '84 | | | |
| FEB 12 '85 | | | |
| JUN 13 1989 | | | |
| JY 23 '92 | | | |
| AG 19 '92 | | | |
| FE 16 '96 | | | |
| MY 14 '96 | | | PRINTED IN U. S. A. |

# Pseudonyms

# Pseudonyms
## The Names
## Behind the Names

JOSEPH F. CLARKE

THOMAS NELSON INC., PUBLISHERS
NASHVILLE                    NEW YORK

All rights reserved under International and Pan-American Conventions. Published by Thomas Nelson Inc., Publishers, Nashville, Tennessee.

**Printed in Great Britain**

*First U.S. edition*

**Library of Congress Cataloging in Publication Data**

Clarke, Joseph F
    Pseudonyms.

    Bibliography: p..
    1.  Anonyms and pseudonyms.  I. Title.
Z1041.C57   1977      929′.4      77-22236
ISBN 0-8407-6567-3

To Nuala

# Contents

★

# Prologue

Arthur Hornblow, Jr., didn't like the name Constance Keane. The first time I was made aware of his feelings on the subject was in his office. He'd summoned me early that morning and I raced to his office assuming he had decided to change his mind. I'd had a long and bitter fight with my mother the night before and had cried a lot. I smeared my puffy eyelids with make-up and tried to look as cheerful as possible when I entered his office.

Mr. Hornblow looked as though he'd been up all night. He had.

'Connie,' he began as I sat nervously on the couch, 'it's pretty well agreed around here that we want a different name for you. "I Wanted Wings" is going to be one of the year's big ones, and it could launch you into a very large and important career. And the name you begin that career with is very crucial.'

'Whatever you think, Mr. Hornblow.'

'Now don't misunderstand me, Connie. Connie Keane is a fine name. It's fine as just a name and as a professional name.'

I smiled.

'It always seemed all right to me, Mr. Hornblow.'

He smiled.

'Of course it's all right. But you do realize how many factors are involved in the making of a star, don't you?'

'I guess I really don't.'

'Well, you'll learn, Connie. But believe me, the right name, a name that the public can latch on to and remember can make all the difference. It isn't just a matter, though, of creating a name that can be remembered. If that were all it took, we'd just name you Maude Mudpie or Tilly Tits or something and they'd remember the name.'

I nodded that I understood.

'No, Connie picking a name involves coming up with something that associates in the fan's mind the person attached to that name. The name has to . . . well, it has to be the person, or at least what the fan thinks that person is. You know what I mean?'

'Yes.' I didn't, but that was irrelevant.

'It has to do with images.'

I nodded.

He sat back in his chair and rubbed his eyes.

'I've been up here all night, Connie, trying to come up with the right name for you. All night. And about five this morning, I knew I had it.'

I sat up straight and came to the edge of the couch. A new name was an exciting thing. It's not an exciting event when your name changes because you lose a father and your mother supplies a new one. But when it's created for you to project a desired image, it's damned exciting.

'Connie, here's how I came to choose your new name. I believe that when people look into those navy blue eyes of yours, they'll see a calm coolness—the calm coolness of a lake.'

The first thing that crossed my mind was that I was going to be named Lake something or other. That doesn't sound very outlandish these days with Tab and Rock, but in those days names stuck closer to the norm.

Arthur Hornblow, Jr., continued.

'And your features, Connie, are classic features. And when I think of classic features, I think of Veronica.'

Lake Veronica?

Oh!

Veronica Lake.

Of course.

And then it hit me. My mother was sometimes called Veronica. Of all the goddam names in the world to choose. I could feel the tears welling up and the lump forming in my throat. I tried so hard to hold everything back but I didn't make it. I broke down and bawled like a baby into the couch cushions.

From *Veronica* by Veronica Lake, W. H. Allen

# Introduction

Pseudonyms have been used by all races and professions ever since men could write their names. They have been adopted for a variety of reasons and chosen by many different methods. In this dictionary, you will find the chosen pen-names, aliases, stage names and titles used by writers, criminals, actors, musicians, politicians, sportsmen and many others. Each entry includes the dates and profession of the individual and, when relevant, any information concerning his or her chosen pseudonym.

Whereas previous compilations have been restricted mainly to pen-names, this dictionary extends the range to include, as far as possible, anyone well known who changed his or her name. Of the 3400 pseudonyms listed, pen-names account for roughly half the collection, stage names a third; the remainder of the entries cover personalities in the various spheres of politics, sport, crime, painting and sculpture, and music. In addition to filling a gap that at present exists on our reference-book shelves, this dictionary should prove a diverting entertainment for all those who are interested in 'image-making'. Ours is an age of celebrity, in which it is possible to achieve an almost instant, and frequently international, reputation by appearing in one film, or a networked television series; by writing one bestselling novel, or enjoying a celebrated season on the football field. When, in Daniel J. Boorstin's phrase, you can be 'known for your well-knownness', having the *right* name is a vital ingredient in maintaining your total image.

It is for this reason that actors, dancers, singers and other entertainers often take names that suggest the nature and/or glamour of their professions. Alicia Markova and Margot Fonteyn sound more like ballerinas than Lilian Marks or Margaret Hookham; Soupy Sales and Fibber McGee seem naturally funnier than Milton Hines or James Edward Jordan; Ty Hardin and Roy Rogers can shoot straighter than Orton Hungerford and Leonard Slye; Hedy Lamarr is more enchanting than Hedwig Kiesler; Troy Donahue, Tab Hunter and Omar Sharif make hearts beat faster than Merle Johnson, Art

Gelian, or Michel Shalouz. Neither Diana Fluck nor Paul Gadd might have got very far in the world of entertainment; as Diana Dors and Gary Glitter, each has achieved a considerable reputation.

Politicians, too, adopt names which they feel have political significance, particularly in the east. Lin Yu-Yung, whose name meant 'fostering demeanour', changed his name while in military school to the more aggressive Lin Piao: 'tiger cat'. Stalin disclaimed the name Dzhugashvili to avoid political persecution, but once he came to power this pseudonym, meaning as it does 'man of steel', gained political significance. Molotov, born Skriabin, tried various alternative names between 1906 and 1917, finally adopting the one which meant 'hammer'.

Just as Molotov, Stalin, Lenin and Trotsky assumed new names to avoid the attentions of the Czarist secret police, so in Nazi Germany one Karl Frahm became Willy Brandt to avoid arrest by the Gestapo. Many of the names included in this volume were born out of a need to conceal one's identity because of persecution or discrimination. Film directors Joseph Losey and Carl Foreman worked as Victor Hanbury and Derek Frye after they were blacklisted during the McCarthy trials in the 1950s. Black Power leaders Elijah Muhammad (Elijah Poole) and Malcolm X (Malcolm Little) altered their names to protest against racial prejudice, and to connect themselves more closely with their African roots. Immigrants often find that they are more easily accepted if they take a name appropriate to their adopted country; Emmanuel Goldenberg was advised when at drama school in the United States to choose an Anglo-Saxon name, and Edward G. Robinson was born; Dino Crocetti tried Dino Martini for a while before he became Dean Martin; and Nathan Weinstein later became famous as the novelist Nathanael West. Before the freedom and tolerance of the twentieth century, women frequently wrote under men's names, notably George Eliot and George Sand. There are fewer instances of men using women's names; at the turn of the century, William Sharp wrote romantic novels as Fiona Macleod. Sharp kept his secret well and even entered Miss Macleod in *Who's Who*.

Writers use pen names for many other reasons, the most frequent being to differentiate between the kinds of books they write, to preserve their anonymity or to keep separate their vocation and avocation. The poet C. Day-Lewis wrote detective novels as Nicholas Blake; Michael Innes is the pen-name of literary historian John Stewart. *Junkie*, an account of American novelist William Burroughs' addiction to morphine, was first published under the name of William Lee. Ellery Queen, the popular American mystery writer, was actually two American lawyers, Manfred Lee and Frederic Dannay.

Often the reason for changing one's name has nothing to do with glamour, or suitability to a chosen career, but is simply to avoid confusion with someone of the same or similar name. In the late 1930s, the British actor James Stewart was bound to use a different screen name, and chose Stewart Granger. Singer Ray Robinson was forced to adopt Ray Charles because one Walker Smith, an American boxer, had already styled himself Sugar Ray Robinson. On the other hand, John Henry Brodribb assumed the stage name of Henry Irving to avoid embarrassing his parents, who were ashamed that their son was an actor.

The methods of creating a pseudonym are as varied as the reasons for doing so. Many people use some sort of variation on their given name, whether they choose to use only one part of it (Colette, Joseph Conrad, Fabian), reverse it (as D. H. Lawrence did, occasionally writing as Lawrence H. Davison), shorten it (Jacques Taticheff to Jacques Tati, Gracie Stansfield to Gracie Fields), alter one name only (Gretchen Young to Loretta Young) or simply change the spelling (Warren Beaty to Warren Beatty). Another favoured method is to employ the name of a relative, and many who choose to do this take their mother's maiden name; Pablo Picasso and Le Corbusier are two examples. Comedian Amos Jacobs got the idea for his pseudonym from his two brothers, Danny and Thomas, and styled himself Danny Thomas.

Until the turn of the century, initials, anagrams, and pompous extravagant names were in fashion, particularly as pen names. Thus Matthew Arnold wrote as both 'A' and A.M., the seventeenth-century German novelist Christoffel von Grimmelshausen rearranged all the letters in his name to become the delightful if bewildering Aceeeffghhillmmnnnoorrssstuv, and as two of his numerous pen names Thackeray chose Frederick Haltamont de Montmorency and George Savage Fitzboodle. Mrs Mary Clarke, a nineteenth-century British novelist, opted for the strange choice of Henry Wandsworth Shortfellow.

Many of the names contained within these pages are witty; some are pure whimsy, and others have been necessitated by unhappy circumstances. The aim in compiling this book has been to be as comprehensive as possible, and to demonstrate the changing fashion in the names we choose to use, for whatever reason. The books listed in the bibliography have been invaluable source material, and the staff of both the Marylebone and Richmond Public Libraries were most helpful. I am also grateful to many friends who have contributed entries, and among these a special note of thanks must go to Juan Arango, Christine Blackett, Colin Bottomley, Anne Chadwick, Mal Clarke, Maarten Coetzee, Barbara Coxwell, Roger Hall, Fred

Hilton, Ian Hunter, Shane Langlois, Matthew McGuinness, Richard Middleton, Fran Munden, Adrian Room, Joan Sanders, Wendy Mook Sang and Geoffrey Todd.

Joseph F. Clarke
November 1976

# List of Pseudonyms

# A

**'A'**
Matthew ARNOLD
1822–1888
English poet and critic. He wrote *The Strayed Reveller and Other Poems* under this pseudonym

**A**
Alexander POPE
1688–1744
English poet

**Dr. A**
Isaac ASIMOV
1920–
American science fiction writer, who was born in Russia and went to the U.S.A. in 1923

**A.A.**
Elizabeth Barrett BROWNING
1806–1861
British poet

**A.A.**
George A.A. WILLIS
1897–
British humorist, better known as Anthony Armstrong who wrote for *Punch*

**A.B.**
Aubrey BEARDSLEY
1872–1898
British illustrator

**A.B.**
Benjamin FRANKLIN
1706–1790
American statesman, scientist and philosopher

**A.B.**
Jonathan SWIFT
1667–1745
Irish writer and satirist

**A.M.**
Matthew ARNOLD
1822–1888
British poet and critic

**A.P.H.**
Sir Alan Patrick HERBERT
1890–1971
British writer, humorist and politician

**A.A. ABBOTT**
Samuel SPEWACK
1898–
Russian-born American author

**Bud ABBOTT**
William ABBOTT
1895–1974
American comedian; the 'straight man' of the Abbott and Costello partnership

**ABRAHAM-A-SANTA-CLARA**
Ulrich MEGERLE
1644–1709
German writer and monk

**Lee ABRAMS**
Leon ABRAMSON
1925–
American jazz drummer

**Ray ABRAMS**
Raymond ABRAMSON
1920–
American jazz saxophonist

3

**Johnny ACE**
John M. ALEXANDER
1932–1954
American rhythm and blues singer.
He died playing Russian roulette

**ACEEEFFGHHIILLMMNNOO
RRSSSTUV**
Christoffel Von
GRIMMELSHAUSEN
1625–1676
German novelist. The pseudonym
is an alphabetical anagram of his
real name

**Uriel ACOSTA**
Gabriel D'ACOSTA
*c*. 1584–1640
Portuguese-born Jewish philosopher. Born in Oporto, he
persuaded his family, who had
been forcibly converted to Roman
Catholicism, to flee to Amsterdam.
Here, after circumcision, he took
the name Uriel

**ACQUANETTA**
Burnu DAVENPORT
1920–
American actress

**Janet Buchanan ADAM SMITH**
Mrs. John CARLETON
1905–
British writer

**Casey ADAMS**
Max SHOWALTER
1917–
American actor. Recently he has
reverted to using his real name

**Don ADAMS**
Donald YARMY
1927–
American actor

**Edie ADAMS**
Edith ENKE
1927–
American singer, widow of Ernie
Kovacs

**Harrison ADAMS**
St George Henry RATHBONE
1854–1928

American writer of dime novels
and boys' books

**Julie ADAMS**
Betty May ADAMS
1926–
American actress

**Maude ADAMS**
Maude KISKADDEN
1872–1953
American stage actress. Adams is
her mother's maiden name

**Moses ADAMS**
George BAGBY
1828–1883
American author, lecturer and
editor

**Nick ADAMS**
Nick ADAMSCHOCK
1932–1968
American actor

**Max ADELER**
Charles CLARK
1847–1915
American humorist, journalist
and author

**Joey ADONIS**
Joseph DOTO
*c*. 1895–
Italian-born American gambler

**Renée ADORÉE**
Jeanne DE LA FONTE
1898–1933
French actress, active in Hollywood during the 1920s

**Iris ADRIAN**
Iris HOSTETTER
1913–
American character actress

**AE**
George RUSSELL
1867–1935
Irish poet and essayist, friend of
W. B. Yeats. AE was originally the
error of a printer who could not
read the pseudonym Aeon

**George Washington AESOP**
George T. LANNIGAN
1815–1874
American journalist

**AFRO**
Afro BASALDELLA
1912–
Italian painter

**Anthony AFTERWIT**
Benjamin FRANKLIN
1706–1790
American statesman, scientist and philosopher

**AGA KHAN III**
Aga Sultan Sir Mohamad SHAH
1877–1957
Indian leader. Head of the Ismailian Moslem sect

**Friar Antonio AGAPIDO**
Washington IRVING
1783–1859
American short story writer and historian

**Shmuel Yosef AGNON**
Shmuel CZACZKES
1888–1970
Israeli writer. He won the Nobel Prize for Literature (1966)

**Georgius AGRICOLA**
Georg BAUER
1494–1555
German physician and mineralogist

**Johann AGRICOLA**
Johannes SCHNEIDER (or SCHNITTER)
1492–1566
German Protestant reform leader

**Martin AGRICOLA**
Martin SORE (or SOHR)
1486–1556
German composer, formerly a farmer, hence the pseudonym

**Rodolphus AGRICOLA**
Roelof HUYSMANN
1443–1485
Dutch philosopher and humanist

**Owen AHERNE**
Ronald CASSILL
1919–
American author

**Ernst AHLGREN**
Victoria BENEDICTSSON
1850–1888
Swedish novelist

**Henry G. AIKMAN**
Harold Hunter ARMSTRONG
1884–
American novelist

**Gustave AIMARD**
Oliver GLOUX
1818–1883
French writer of adventure stories

**Anouk AIMÉE**
Françoise SORYA
1932–
French actress, originally known simply as Anouk

**Walter AIMWELL**
William SIMONDS
1822–1859
American author

**Patricia AINSWORTH**
Patricia BIGG
1932–
Australian writer

**Ruth AINSWORTH**
Ruth GILBERT
1918–
British writer

**Catherine AIRLIE**
Jean McLEOD
1908–
British writer

**Docteur AKAKIA**
François Marie AROUET
1694–1778
French philosopher and writer better known as Voltaire

**AKBAR**
Jelal-ed-din-MOHAMMED
1542–1605
Mogul emperor of India (1556–1605)

**Floyd AKENS**
L. Frank BAUM
1856–1919
American writer of books for boys

**Anna AKHMATOVA**
Anna Andreyevna GORENKO

1888–1966
Russian poet
**AKHNATON I**
**AMENHOTEP IV**
*d.* 1362 B.C.
Egyptian pharaoh from 1397. He
changed his name 6 years later in
honour of Aton, a sun god
**Rabbin AKIB**
François Marie AROUET
1694–1778
French philosopher and writer
better known as Voltaire
**AL**
Albert SMITH
1934–
British author
**ALAIN**
Émile CHARTIER
1868–1951
French essayist and philosopher
**ALAIN-FOURNIER**
Henri Alban FOURNIER
1886–1914
French novelist
**Antony ALBAN**
Antony THOMPSON
1939–
British author
**Don ALBERT**
Albert DOMINIQUE
1908–
American jazz trumpeter
**Eddie ALBERT**
Eddie Albert HEIMBERGER
1908–
American actor. He started as a
singer on a Minneapolis radio
station but when radio announcers
began referring to him as Eddie
'Hamburger' he decided to change
his name
**Martha ALBRAND**
Heidi LOEWENGARD
1913–
German-American novelist. Al-
brand is the name of her Danish
great-grandfather
**Hardy ALBRIGHT**

Hardy ALBRECHT
1903–
American actor, popular during
the 1930s
**ALCIBIADES**
Alfred TENNYSON
1809–1892
English poet
**ALCUINUS**
John CALVIN
1509–1564
French theologian and religious
reformer
**ALCYONE**
Jiddu KRISHNAMURTI
1896–
Indian writer; wrote *At the Feet of
the Master* (1912) under this
pen-name
**Robert ALDA**
Alphonso D'ABRUZZO
1914–
American actor
**Mark Aleksandrovich ALDANOV**
M. A. LANDAU
1886–1957
Russian novelist
**ALDIBORONTIPHOSCOPHOR-
NIO**
James BALLANTYNE
1772–1833
Scottish journalist. This name was
given to him by Sir Walter Scott
in allusion to his pompous manner
**Richard ALDINGTON**
Edward Godfrey ALDINGTON
1892–1962
British writer and critic
**Sholom ALEICHEM**
Solomon RABINOWITZ
1859–1916
American author

**O. ALEIJADINHO**
Antonio DA COSTA
1729–1815
Brazilian sculptor. He was born
deformed, hence his nickname
which means 'Little Cripple'

**Alexander ALEKHINE**
Aleksandr ALOYKHIN
1892–1946
Russian chess player. World champion from 1927 to 1935, and from 1937 to 1946
**ALERTUS**
Norbert N. HERST
1887–
British author
**Tony ALESS**
Anthony ALLESSANDRINI
1921–
American jazz pianist
**Joan ALEXANDER**
Joan PEPPER
1920–
British author
**Grigori ALEXANDROV**
Grigori MORMENKO
1903–
Russian film director
**Willibald ALEXIS**
Georg HÄRING
1798–1817
German writer
**ALFRED**
Samuel ADAMS
1722–1803
American statesman
**ALI BEY**
Samuel KNAPP
1783–1838
American author
**Dave ALLEN**
David O'MAHONEY
1936–
Irish comedian
**Don Bala ALLEN**
Terry Diener ALLEN
1889–
American author
**Elizabeth ALLEN**
Elizabeth GILLEASE
1934–
American actress
**Fred ALLEN**
John F. SULLIVAN
1894–1956

American radio comedian. He started as a juggler in 1915 with the name Fred St. James. Soon after he dropped the St., becoming Fred James. In 1921, tired of telling people he wasn't a member of the James Gang, he changed his name to Allen 'as a tribute to Ethan Allen who had stopped using the name after the revolution'
**Graham ALLEN**
George ARNOLD
1834–1865
American journalist and poet
**James ALLEN**
Paul ADER
1919–
American author
**K. ALLEN**
Ronald RICHARDS
1923–
British author
**Phog ALLEN**
Forrest C. ALLEN
1885–
American baseball coach
**Ronald ALLEN**
Alan AYCKBOURN
1939–
British playwright
**T. D. ALLEN**
Terry and Don ALLEN
*c.* 1907– ; *c.* 1890
American authors
**Woody ALLEN**
Allen Stewart KONIGSBERG
1935–
American comedian
**Alfred ALLENDALE**
Theodore Edward HOOK
1788–1841
English novelist and editor
**Mary ALLERTON**
Mary GOVAN
1897–
American author
**Svetlana ALLILUYEVA**
Svetlana STALINA

1926–
Russian author, daughter of Joseph Stalin. She now uses her mother's maiden name

**Claude ALLISTER**
Claude PALMER
1891–1970
English actor

**June ALLYSON**
Ella GEISMAN
1917–
American actress

**V. ALOF**
Nikolai Vasilievich GOGOL
1809–1852
Russian novelist and dramatist

**ALPHA OF THE PLOUGH**
Alfred George GARDINER
1865–1946
English journalist and essayist. He was editor of the *Daily News* (1902–1919)

**Robert ALTON**
Robert Alton HART
1906–1957
American film director

**Don ALVARADO**
José PAIGE
1900–1967
American actor

**Espriella Manuel ALVAREZ**
Robert SOUTHEY
1774–1843
British poet

**Danny ALVIN**
Daniel VINIELLO
1902–1958
American jazz drummer

**Giuseppe AMATO**
Giuseppe VASATURO
1899–1964
Italian film producer

**AMBER**
Martha HOLDEN
1844–1896
American author

**Richard AMBERLEY**
Paul BOURQUIN
1916–
British writer. He uses this pseudonym for mystery stories

**Simon AMBERLEY**
Peter HOAR
1912–
British author

**An AMERICAN**
Samuel ADAMS
1722–1803
American statesman

**An AMERICAN**
William COBBETT
1763–1835
English political journalist

**An AMERICAN**
James FENIMORE COOPER
1789–1851
American novelist

**An AMERICAN**
Alexander HAMILTON
1757–1804
American lawyer and statesman

**An AMERICAN**
Henry Wadsworth LONGFELLOW
1807–1882
American poet

**An AMERICAN GENTLEMAN**
Washington IRVING
1783–1859
American short story writer and historian

**Junius AMERICANUS**
Charles ENDICOTT
1793–1863
American sea captain and author

**Junius AMERICANUS**
Arthur LEE
1740–1792
American diplomat and author

**Jennifer AMES**
Maysie GREIG
1901–
Australian writer of romantic fiction

**Leon AMES**
Leon WYCOFF
1903–
American actor

**AMICUS**
William ALEXANDER
1768–1841
English Quaker and publisher

**Breton AMIS**
Rayleigh B. A. BEST
1905–
British novelist

**AMOS 'N' ANDY**
Freeman F. GOSDEN and
Charles CORRELL
c. 1900–
American blackface vaudeville act which became the leading comedy show on radio. First appeared as 'Sam 'n' Henry' on station WGN in Chicago in 1925. They changed the names to 'Amos 'n' Andy' in 1926

**Anthony AMPLEGIRTH**
A. A. DENT
1915–
British author

**Daphne ANDERSON**
Daphne SCRUTTON
1922–
British actress

**Ella ANDERSON**
Ellen McLEOD
1924–
British writer

**G. M. ANDERSON**
Max ARONSON
1882–1972
American actor. Known by his nickname 'Bronco Billy' he was one of Hollywood's first Western stars

**Judith ANDERSON**
Frances ANDERSON
1898–
Australian-born American actress

**Joseph ANDREWS**
Henry FIELDING
1707–1754
English novelist

**Julie ANDREWS**
Julie WELLS
1935–
English musical comedy star. She adopted the name Andrews from her mother's second husband, Ted Andrews, a Canadian singer

**Pierre ANDREZEL**
Baroness Karen
BLIXEN-FINECKE
1885–1962
Danish novelist and story-teller. Better known as Isak Dinesen

**Pier ANGELI**
Anna Maria PIERANGELI
1932–1972
Italian actress active in Hollywood during the 1950s

**Fra ANGELICO**
Guido di PIETRI
1387–1455
Italian painter and monk

**Maya ANGELOU**
Marguerite JOHNSON
1928–
American writer and entertainer. Her brother gave her the name Maya. Angelou is the name of her first husband

**Muriel ANGELUS**
Muriel FINDLAY
1909–
British actress; popular during the 1930s

**ANNABELLA**
Suzanne CHARPENTIER
1909–
French actress; active in Hollywood during the 1930s

**ANN-MARGRET**
Ann-Margaret OLSSON
1941–
Swedish-born American actress

**F. ANSTEY**
Thomas Anstey GUTHRIE
1856–1934
British writer. He signed his first work, a serial for *The Cambridge Tatler* (1877), T. Anstey but a printer's error made the 'T' an 'F'

**James ANSTRUTHER**
James A. Maxtone GRAHAM

1924–
British writer
**John ANTHONY**
John A. SABINI
1921–
American writer
**Joseph ANTHONY**
Joseph Anthony DEUSTER
1912–
American film director
**Michael ANTHONY**
John Salkeld TETLEY
1901–
British author
**Ray ANTHONY**
Ray ANTONINI
1922–
American bandleader
**ANTI-CLIMACUS**
Sören KIERKEGAARD
1813–1855
Danish philosopher and theologian
**ANTOINE**
Antek CIERPLIKOWSKI
1884–
Polish-born French hairdresser
**Brother ANTONINUS**
William EVERSON
1912–
American author
**ANTONIO**
Antonio RUIZ SOLER
1921–
Spanish dancer and choreographer,
Director of the Ballets de Madrid
**APE**
Carlo PELLEGRINI
1839–1889
Italian caricaturist. His portraits
appeared in *Vanity Fair* from 1869
**Guillaume APOLLINAIRE**
Wilhelm Apollinaris de
KOSTROWITSKY
1880–1918
French poet and art critic of
Polish descent
**APOTH**
Alexander POPE

1688–1744
English poet
**Johnny APPLESEED**
John CHAPMAN
c. 1775–1847
American frontier character in
Ohio who devoted his life to the
planting of apple seed
**John ARCHER**
Ralph BOWMAN
1915–
American actor
**Clive ARDEN**
Lily NUTT
1888–
British author
**Elizabeth ARDEN**
Florence GRAHAM
1890–
Canadian cosmetician. Born in
Toronto to a Scottish father and
English mother. Left for New
York where she started her first
beauty salon in 1909, under the
name 'Elizabeth Arden'. The name
was inspired by the book *Elizabeth
and Her German Garden* and
Tennyson's *Enoch Arden*
**Eve ARDEN**
Eunice QUEDENS
1912–
American comedienne. She acted
from 1928 to 1934 under her own
name and then took the name Eve
Arden which is a combination of
'Evening in Paris' and 'Elizabeth
Arden'
**Mavis ARETA**
Mavis WINDER
1907–
New Zealand author
**ARION**
G. K. CHESTERTON
1874–1936
British critic, novelist and poet
**ARISTEAS**
Henry MEECHAM
1886–
British author

**The ARISTO OF THE NORTH**
Sir Walter SCOTT
1771–1832
Scottish poet and novelist

**Buddy ARNOLD**
Arnold GRISHAVER
1926–
American jazz musician. He played the clarinet and tenor sax

**Harry ARNOLD**
Harry Arnold PERSSON
1920–
Swedish jazz musician

**Peleg ARKWRIGHT**
David Law PROUDFIT
1842–1897
American author

**Harold ARLEN**
Hymen ARLUCK
1905–
American composer of popular songs

**Michael ARLEN**
Dikran KUYUMJIAN
1895–1956
British novelist, born in Bulgaria of Armenian parents. He changed his name by deed poll in 1913 when he began writing

**Richard ARLEN**
Cornelius VAN MATTEMORE
1898–1976
American actor. Hero of many B films in the thirties and forties

**ARLETTY**
Arlette-Leónie BATHIAT
1898–
French film and stage actress

**George ARLISS**
George ANDREWS
1868–1946
British actor. His film career began in 1920. He won an Academy Award in 1930 for *Disraeli*

**Jacobus ARMINIUS**
Jakob HARMENSEN
1560–1609
Dutch Protestant theologian

**Anthony ARMSTRONG**
George A. A. WILLIS
1897–
British humorist who wrote for *Punch*

**Henry ARMSTRONG**
Henry JACKSON
1912–
American boxer. The only professional boxer to hold three world championships simultaneously

**Robert ARMSTRONG**
Donald R. SMITH
1890–1973
American actor. He played the part of the film producer in *King Kong* (1933)

**Sybil ARMSTRONG**
Sybil EDMONDSON
1898–
British author

**James ARNESS**
James AURNESS
1923–
American actor, who played Marshall Dillon in TV series *Gunsmoke*. Brother of Peter Graves

**Peter ARNO**
Curtis Arnoux PETERS
1904–1968
American cartoonist

**Sig ARNO**
Siegfried ARON
1895–
German comic actor. He was in Hollywood from 1932

**Birch ARNOLD**
Alice BARTLETT
1848–1930
American author

**Edward ARNOLD**
Gunther SCHNEIDER
1890–1957
American actor who began his film career in the early thirties

**Françoise ARNOUL**
Françoise GAUTCH
1931–

French actress, popular during the 1950s

**Sidney J. ARODIN**
Sidney J. ARNONDRIN
1901–1948
American jazz musician

**AROUET**
Joseph B. LADD
1764–1786
American author

**George K. ARTHUR**
George K. A. BREST
1899–
British actor

**Gladys ARTHUR**
Dorothy OSBORNE
1917–
British author

**Jean ARTHUR**
Gladys GREENE
1905–
American actress, in many films during the thirties and forties

**Robert ARTHUR**
Robert ARTHAUD
1925–
American actor

**Robert ARTHUR**
Robert A. FEDER
1909–
American film producer

**Marvin ASH**
Marvin ASHBAUGH
1914–
American jazz pianist

**Gordon ASHE**
John CREASEY
1908–1973
English writer. The Toff, an aristocratic private eye, starred in 45 detective novels that Creasey wrote under this pseudonym

**Martin ASHE**
Julien NEIL
1904–
British author

**Tom ASHE**
Jonathan SWIFT
1667–1745

Irish writer and satirist

**Renee ASHERSON**
Renee ASCHERSON
1920–
British actress

**Edward ASHLEY**
Edward Ashley COOPER
1904–
British actor

**Francis ASKHAM**
Julia GREENWOOD
1910–
British author

**Grégoire ASLAN**
Kridor ASLANIAN
1908–
French-Turkish character actor

**ASSIAC**
Heinrich FRAENKEL
1897–
British writer of German origin

**Fred ASTAIRE**
Fred AUSTERLITZ
1899–
American dancer and actor. Son of Frederic and Ann (Gelius) Austerlitz who legally changed their name to Astaire in 1901

**Bob ASTOR**
Bob DADE
1915–
American jazz musician

**Mary ASTOR**
Lucille LANGEHANKE
1906–
American film actress. She made her debut in *The Beggar's Maid* (1920). She became Mary Astor in 1923 as a result of a joint decision by Jesse Lasky, Louella Parsons and Walter Wanger – they disliked her German sounding name

**Kemal ATATÜRK**
Mustafa Kemal PASHA
1881–1938
Turkish military and political leader. He ruled as dictator (1932–1938)

**William ATHELING**
Ezra POUND
1885–1972
American poet. He used this pseudonym when music critic for the magazine *New Age* (1917–21)

**ATHENAGORAS**
Aristokles SPIROU
1886–
Greek churchman

**Charles ATKIN**
Frank GRIFFIN
1911–
British author

**M. D. ATKINS**
Ezra POUND
1885–1972
American poet. He used this pseudonym for a magazine article (1919)

**Charles ATLAS**
Angelo SICILIANO
1893–1973
American strong man, born in Acri, Italy. He won the contest for the 'World's Most Perfectly Developed Man' in 1922. In 1930 he started a correspondence school teaching 'Dynamic Tension' a system of physical development similar to isometrics

**Cécile AUBRY**
Anne-José BENARD
1929–
French actress

**Dorothy AUCHTERLONIE**
Dorothy GREEN
1915–
Australian author

**Mischa AUER**
Mischa OUNSKOWSKY
1905–1967
Russian-born actor, popular in Hollywood during the thirties and forties

**AUGUR**
William BLAKE
1757–1827
English painter, poet and mystic. He used this pen-name for *America; a prophecy* (1793)

**Georgie AULD**
John ALTWERGER
1919–
Canadian jazz musician. He played sax with Bunny Berigan, Artie Shaw, Benny Goodman, etc. and later formed his own band

**Jean-Pierre AUMONT**
Jean-Pierre SALOMONS
1909–
French romantic actor. He went to Hollywood in 1941

**AUNT FANNY**
Frances BARROW
1822–1894
American writer of children's books

**Lovie AUSTIN**
Cora CALHOUN
1887–
American jazz pianist

**The AUTOCRAT OF THE BREAKFAST TABLE**
Oliver Wendell HOLMES
1809–1894
American writer and physician

**Frankie AVALON**
Francis AVALLONE
1939–
American pop singer and actor

**Al AVERY**
Rutherford MONTGOMERY
1896–
American author

**Lynn AVERY**
Lois Dwight COLE
*c.* 1910–
American author

**Margaret AVON**
Sheila KEATLEY
1912–
British writer

**AXIS SALLY**
Mildred Gillars SISK
*c.* 1918–
American traitor, born in Portland, Maine. She worked as an

actress in New York and Europe during the thirties and broadcast from Berlin during the Second World War when she received her G.I. nickname. In 1947 she returned to the United States, was convicted of treason and served a ten year prison sentence

**Felix AYLMER**
Felix JONES
1889–
English film and stage actor

**Agnes AYRES**
Agnes HINKLE
1896–1940
American star of silent films. She played opposite Rudolf Valentino in *The Sheik* (1921)

**Lew AYRES**
Lewis AYER
1908–
American actor; star of *All Quiet on the Western Front* (1930)

**Charles AZNAVOUR**
Charles AZNAVURJAN
1924–
French singer and actor

**AZORÍN**
José MARTINEZ RUIZ
1873–1967
Spanish essayist, novelist and critic

# B

**B.B.**
D. J. WATKINS-PITCHFORD
1905–
British writer of children's books

**BAAL-SCHEM-TOV**
Israel BEN ELIEZER
*c.* 1700–1760
Russian Jewish leader, founded Hasidim sect

**BAB**
William Schwenck GILBERT
1836–1911
British librettist of the 'Gilbert and Sullivan' light operas. He used this pen-name for his first literary work *Bab Ballads* (1869)

**BABER**
Zahir ed-din MOHAMMED
*c.* 1482–1530
Indian emperor

**BABY SANDY**
Sandra Lee HENVILLE
1938–
American child film actress

**Lauren BACALL**
Betty Joan PERSKE
1924–
American actress born in New York, daughter of William Perske and Natalie Weinstein, a New Yorker of German–Rumanian parentage. When her parents divorced in 1930 her mother adopted the name Bacal which is Rumanian for Weinstein. Miss Bacall added the second 'L' to stop people rhyming her name with cackle. Lauren is a Hollywood acquisition which she dislikes

**BADGERY**
Suzanne HUNT
1942–
Australian author

**Buddy BAER**
Jacob BAER
1915–
American heavyweight boxer and actor

**Enid BAGNOLD**
Lady JONES
1899–
British novelist and playwright

**Mildred BAILEY**
Mildred RINKER

1907–1951
American singer
**Frank BAKER, D.O.N.**
Sir Richard BURTON
1829–1890
British explorer. He wrote a poem
'Stone Talk' (1867) under this pen-
name
**Léon BAKST**
Lev ROSENBERG
1866–1924
Russian painter. Designed sets for
Diaghilev's Ballets Russes
**George BALANCHINE**
Georgi BALANCHIVADZE
1904–
Russian-born American chore-
ographer. Name changed by Sergei
Diaghilev in 1924. He founded the
School of American Ballet in 1934
**Enid BALDRY**
Enid CITOVICH
1902–
British author
**Ina BALIN**
Ina ROSENBERG
1937–
American actress
**Zachary BALL**
Kelly R. MASTERS
1897–
American author
**Kaye BALLARD**
Catherine BALOTTA
1926–
American singer-comedienne
**Peter BAMM**
Kurt EMRICH
1897–
German novelist
**Anne BANCROFT**
Anne ITALIANO
1931–
American stage and screen actress.
She acted under the name of Ann
Marno before selecting the name
Anne Bancroft from a list sub-
mitted to her by Darryl F. Zanuck
when she made her first film

*Don't Bother to Knock* (1952). She
won an Academy Award for *The
Miracle Worker* (1962)
**Hastings BANDA**
Kamuzu BANDA
*c.* 1902–
Malawi statesman. His parents
gave him the name Kamuzu (the
little root), because root herbs,
prescribed by a medicine man,
were believed to have cured his
mother's barrenness. He later
adopted as his first name the sur-
name of a missionary friend John
Hastings
**Monty BANKS**
Mario BIANCHI
1897–1950
Italian comic dancer, lived in
Britain from 1930. Former hus-
band of Gracie Fields
**Vilma BANKY**
Vilma LONCHIT
1902–
Austro-Hungarian star of Ameri-
can silent films
**Angela BANNER**
Angela MADISON
1923–
British author
**Mark BANNERMAN**
Anthony C. LEWING
1933–
British author
**Peter BANNON**
Paul DURST
1921–
American author
**Theda BARA**
Theodosia GOODMAN
1890–1955
American actress, the original
'vamp' – because of her vampish
appearance. Her pseudonym is an
anagram of Arab Death
**Antonia BARBER**
Barbara ANTHONY
1932–
British author

**Jay BARBETTE**
Bart SPICER
1918–
American author
**BARD OF RYDAL MOUNT**
William WORDSWORTH
1770–1850
English poet
**Lynn BARI**
Marjorie BITZER
1915–
American actress
**Jack BARKER**
Michael J. BARKER
1915–
American author
**Captain Robert BARNACLE**
Charles NEWELL
1821–c. 1900
American novelist
**A. M. BARNARD**
Louisa May ALCOTT
1832–1888
American writer. Name used for
thrillers
**Binnie BARNES**
Gitelle BARNES
1905–
English actress. She went to
Hollywood in 1934
**Nancy BARNES**
Helen ADAMS
1897–
American author
**Esdras BARNIVELT**
Alexander POPE
1688–1744
English poet
**David BARON**
Harold PINTER
1930–
English playwright. When acting
he uses the name David Baron
**Amanda BARRIE**
Amanda BRODBENT
1939–
British actress
**Jane BARRIE**
Irene WOODFORD

1913–
British author
**Mona BARRIE**
Mona SMITH
1909–
American actress
**Wendy BARRIE**
Wendy JENKINS
1912–
British actress. She went to Holly-
wood in 1934
**Maurice BARRINGTON**
Denis BROGAN
1900–1974
British author
**Ann BARRY**
Amy BYERS
1906–
British author
**Don BARRY**
Donald Barry D'ACOSTA
1912–
American actor
**Gene BARRY**
Eugene KLASS
1921–
American actor, popular on TV
as Bat Masterson
**John BARRY**
Barry PRENDERGAST
1935–
British pop musician
**Margaret BARRY**
Ida HIGMAN
1910–
Australian author
**Ethel BARRYMORE**
Ethel BLYTHE
1879–1959
American stage and screen actress.
Sister of John and Lionel Barry-
more
**Georgina BARRYMORE**
Emma DREW
1856–1893
American actress. Mother of
Ethel, John and Lionel Barrymore
**John BARRYMORE**
John Blythe

1882–1942
American film actor, brother of
Ethel and Lionel Barrymore. Ro-
mantic idol of the 1920s

**Lionel BARRYMORE**
Lionel BLYTHE
1878–1954
American stage and screen actor,
brother of Ethel and John Barrymore. Played Dr. Gillespie in the
original Dr. Kildare series

**Maurice BARRYMORE**
Herbert BLYTHE
1847–1905
American actor. Father of Ethel,
John and Lionel Barrymore

**Lionel BART**
Lionel BEGLEITER
1930–
British composer, lyricist and
playwright

**Freddie BARTHOLOMEW**
Frederick Llewellyn
1924–
British child actor who went to
Hollywood in 1935

**Nancy BARTLETT**
Charles STRONG
1906–
American novelist

**Sy BARTLETT**
Sacha BARABIEV
1909–
American film producer

**Eva BARTOK**
Eva SJOKE
1926–
Hungarian actress in international
films

**Fra BARTOLOMEO**
Bartolomeo della PORTA
1475–1517
Italian painter

**Florence BATES**
Florence RABE
1888–1954
American actress. Her first part
was as Mrs. Van Hopper in
Hitchcock's *Rebecca* (1940)

**Felix BATTLE**
Bernard LEVIN
1928–
British journalist

**Paul BAULAT**
Frederic VALMAIN
1931–
French writer

**Vicki BAUM**
Mrs. Richard LERT
1896–1960
German novelist

**Mary BAWN**
Mary Wright
1917–
American writer

**Beryl BAXTER**
Beryl IVORY
1926–
British actress

**George Owen BAXTER**
Frederick FAUST
1892–1944
American novelist

**Gillian BAXTER**
Gillian HIRST
1938–
British author

**Jane BAXTER**
Feodora FORDE
1909–
British actress

**John BAXTER**
E. Howard HUNT
1923–
American novelist. Ex-C.I.A.
agent who was involved in the
Watergate affair

**Olive BAXTER**
Helen EASTWOOD
1892–
British novelist

**Valerie BAXTER**
Laurence MEYNELL
1899–
British novelist

**Nora BAYES**
Dora GOLDBERG

1868–1928
American vaudeville singer
**BEACHCOMBER**
J. B. MORTON
1893–
British journalist. He wrote for the *Daily Express* from 1924 to 1975 when he retired
**BEAKITORIUS**
Benjamin DISRAELI
1804–1881
British statesman and novelist
**John BEAL**
Alexander BLIEDUNG
1909–
American actor
**Orson BEAN**
Dallas BURROWS
1925–
American actor and comedian. Started in show business in 1948 as a magician and chose the most incongruous name he could think of
**Bullen BEAR**
Augustine DONNELLY
1923–
Australian writer on financial topics
**Baden BEATTY**
Frederick CASSON
1910–
British psychiatrist and author
**Warren BEATTY**
Warren BEATY
1937–
American film actor. He added the extra 't' when he started acting. He is the brother of Shirley Maclaine
**Philip BEAUCHAMP**
Jeremy BENTHAM
1748–1832
English philosopher and legal reformer
**BEAUMARCHAIS**
Pierre Augustin CARON
1732–1799
French dramatist

**Susan BEAUMONT**
Susan BLACK
1936–
British film actress
**A BEAUTIFUL AND UNFORTUNATE YOUNG LADY**
Thomas T. WHALLEY
1746–1828
English clergyman and poet
**Gilbert BÉCAUD**
François SILLY
1925–
French singer
**Lillian BECKWITH**
Lillian COMBER
1916–
British writer
**Ann BEDFORD**
Joan REES
1927–
British author
**Sidney BEDFORD**
Lawrence MEYNELL
1899–
British novelist
**Janet BEECHER**
Janet Beecher MEYSENBURG
1884–1955
American actress
**Francis BEEDING**
John Leslie PALMER and Hilary St. George SAUNDERS
1885–1944 and 1898–1951
British writers of adventure stories. Palmer and Saunders began working together in 1920 and preserved their anonymity until 1925 when Saunders gave a talk as Francis Beeding on 'his' method of work. Palmer heckled him from the audience until Saunders, in seeming desperation, invited him to the platform, where all was revealed
**Maurice BEJART**
Maurice Jean de BERGER
1927–
Belgian ballet dancer and choreographer

**Barbara BEL GEDDES**
Barbara Geddes LEWIS
1922–
American actress

**BELGIAN HARE**
Lord Alfred DOUGLAS
1870–1945
British poet

**BELITA**
Gladys JEPSON-TURNER
1924–
British ice-skater

**Acton BELL**
Anne BRONTË
1820–1849
English novelist, the youngest of
the Brontë sisters

**Currer BELL**
Charlotte BRONTË
1816–1855
English novelist

**Ellis BELL**
Emily Jane BRONTË
1818–1848
English poet and novelist. In
choosing their pseudonyms the
Brontë sisters retained their initials

**John BELL**
Victor Hugo JOHNSON
1912–
American author

**Josephine BELL**
Doris Bell BALL
1897–
British writer of detective novels

**Marie BELL**
Marie BELLON-DOWNEY
1900–
French actress

**Rex BELL**
George F. BELDAM
1905–1962
American cowboy actor of the
1930s

**George BELLAIRS**
Harold BLUNDELL
1902–
British author

**Une BELLE DAME**
François Marie AROUET
1694–1778
French philosopher and writer
better known as Voltaire

**Walter BELLMAN**
Hugh G. BARRETT
1917–
British writer on farming topics

**Louis BELLSON**
Louis BELASSONI
1924–
American jazz drummer

**Richard BENEDICT**
Riccard BENEDETTO
1916–
American actor

**Un BÉNÉDICTIN**
François Marie AROUET
1694–1778
French philosopher and writer
better known as Voltaire

**David BEN-GURION**
David GREEN
1886–1973
Israeli statesman, born in Plonsk,
Poland. He emigrated to Palestine
in 1906, and was the first premier
of Israel (1949–53 and 1955–63).
'Ben-Gurion' was originally a pen-
name chosen for its biblical flavour

**Bruce BENNETT**
Herman BRIX
1909–
American actor. Played Tarzan in
films (1935). He changed his German name in 1940

**Dwight BENNETT**
D. B. NEWTON
1916–
American writer of cowboy stories

**Tony BENNETT**
Anthony BENEDETTO
1926–
American popular singer

**Jack BENNY**
Benjamin KUBELSKY
1894–1974
American comedian. His original

stage name was Ben K. Benny, but because he was often confused with Ben Bernie, another comedian, he took the name Jack Benny

**Stella BENSON**
Mrs. J. C. O'G. ANDERSON
1892–1933
British novelist

**John BENYON**
John WYNDHAM
1930–
British science fiction writer

**Gertrude BERG**
Gertrude EDELSTEIN
1899–1966
American TV and radio actress. Famous on TV as Molly of the Goldberg family

**Polly BERGEN**
Nellie Paulina BURGIN
1930–
American actress and singer

**Ludwig BERGER**
Ludwig BAMBERGER
1892–1969
German film director

**Elisabeth BERGNER**
Elizabeth ETTEL
1898–
German actress. She played in British films during the 1930s

**Anthony BERKELEY**
Anthony Berkeley COX
1893–1971
British detective story writer. Also used the pen-name Francis Iles

**Busby BERKELEY**
William Berkeley ENOS
1895–1976
American dance director, made 75 film musicals between 1930 and 1953. Amy Busby, a leading lady with the Frawley stock company, of which his father was director, was the origin of Busby

**Tom BERKLEY**
Clifford GREEN
1891–
British author

**Milton BERLE**
Milton BERLINGER
1908–
American comedian, popular on TV during the 1950s

**Irving BERLIN**
Israel BALINE
1888–
American composer of popular music. Born in Temun, a village in Eastern Russia, his family emigrated to U.S.A. in 1893 to avoid the pogroms and settled in New York. His first big hit was 'Alexander's Ragtime Band' (1911)

**Paul BERN**
Paul LEVY
1889–1932
American film director. He committed suicide soon after marriage to Jean Harlow

**Robert BERNARD**
Robert B. MARTIN
1918–
American author

**Sarah BERNHARDT**
Sara BERNARD
1844–1923
French actress. Illegitimate daughter of Judith Van Hard, a Dutch prostitute, and Édouard Bernard, a French law student

**Claude BERRI**
Claude LANGMANN
1934–
French film director

**Judith M. BERRISFORD**
Clifford and Mary LEWIS
1912–; 1921–
British authors

**Jules BERRY**
Jules PAUFICHET
1883–1951
French character actor

**Matilda BERRY**
Kathleen Middleton Murry
1888–1923
English short story writer, born in New Zealand

**Isaiah BERSHADSKY**
Isaiah DOMACHEVITSKY
1872–1910
Polish-Hebrew writer

**Anne BETTERIDGE**
Margaret POTTER
1926–
British writer

**Don BETTERIDGE**
Bernard NEWMAN
1897–1968
English author and lecturer. He used this pseudonym for detective and spy stories

**Billy BEVAN**
William B. HARRIS
1887–1957
British-born American comic actor

**Isaac BICKERSTAFF**
Richard Steele
1672–1729
Irish-born English playwright and essayist. He was the first editor of *The Tatler* (1709–1711) using this pseudonym which he borrowed from Swift

**Isaac BICKERSTAFF**
Jonathan SWIFT
1667–1745
Irish writer and satirist. He used this pseudonym in 1708 to silence John Partridge, an almanac maker, who had gained something of a reputation as a prophet. Swift published an almanac *Predictions for the ensuing year by Isaac Bickerstaff* in which he predicted Partridge's death on 29 March. On 30 March Swift published an account of it in 'An Elegy of Mr. Partridge'. The hoax was a success despite Partridge's protests that he was still alive

**BIG BOPPER**
Jape RICHARDSON
1938–1959
American rock and roll singer. He was killed in air crash with Buddy Holly and Ritchie Valens in February 1959

**Cantell A. BIGLEY**
George Washington PECK
1817–1859
American journalist and music critic

**Hosea BIGLOW**
James Russell LOWELL
1819–1891
American poet and diplomat

**Josh BILLINGS**
Henry Wheeler SHAW
1818–1885
American humorist

**BILLY THE KID**
William H. BONNEY
1859–1881
American outlaw

**Zenobia BIRD**
Laura LEFEVRE
*c.* 1900–
American author

**Tala BIRELL**
Natalie BIERLE
1908–1959
Austrian actress who went to the U.S.A. in the thirties

**George A. BIRMINGHAM**
Reverend James Owen HANNAY
1865–1950
Irish novelist

**Joey BISHOP**
Joseph GOTTLIEB
1919–
American comedian. He started in show business in 1938 when he adopted the surname of his roadie, Glenn Bishop

**Georges BIZET**
Alexandre César Léopold BIZET
1838–1875
French composer

**Cilla BLACK**
Priscilla WHITE
1943–
British pop singer

**Gavin BLACK**
Oswald WYND
1913–
British author
**Kitty BLACK**
Dorothy BLACK
1914–
British writer
**Lionel BLACK**
Dudley BARKER
1910–
British author
**Veronica BLACK**
Maureen PETERS
1935–
British author
**BLACKBEARD**
Edward TEACH
*d.* 1718
British pirate
**Hereth BLACKER**
Herbert CHALKE
1897–
British author
**Malcolm BLACKLIN**
Aiden CHAMBERS
1934–
British author
**John BLACKWELL**
Edwin COLLINGS
1913–
British author
**Vivian BLAINE**
Vivienne STAPLETON
1921–
American actress and singer
**Betsy BLAIR**
Elizabeth BOGER
1923–
American actress
**David BLAIR**
David BUTTERFIELD
1932–
English ballet dancer
**Janet BLAIR**
Martha LAFFERTY
1921–
American actress
**Jacqueline BLAIRMAN**

Jacqueline H. PINTO
1927–
British writer
**Anne BLAISDELL**
Elizabeth LININGTON
1921–
American author
**Amanda BLAKE**
Beverly NEILL
1929–
American actress, in films and TV
**Andrea BLAKE**
Anne WEALE
1929–
British author
**Cameron BLAKE**
Michael MASON
1900–
British author
**Jerry BLAKE**
Jacinto CHABANIA
1908–1961
American jazz musician
**Justin BLAKE**
John BOWEN and Jeremy BULLMORE
1924– ; dates unknown
British writers of children's books
**Monica BLAKE**
Marie MUIR
1904–
British author
**Nicholas BLAKE**
C. DAY-LEWIS
1904–1972
English poet. He wrote detective novels under this pseudonym. Created Poet Laureate in 1968. Blake is one of his mother's family names and Nicholas is the name of his younger son
**Robert BLAKE**
Michael GUBITOSI
1934–
American actor. Former child actor
**Vanessa BLAKE**
Mary BROWN

22

1913–
British author
**Sally BLANE**
Elizabeth YOUNG
1910–
American actress. Sister of Loretta
Young
**Oliver BLEECK**
Ross THOMAS
1926–
American author
**Sonia BLEEKER**
Sonia ZIM
1919–
American author
**Vicesimus BLENKINSOP**
Theodore Edward HOOK
1788–1841
English novelist and editor
**Reginald BLISS**
H. G. WELLS
1866–1946
British writer. He used this pen-
name for the book *Boon* (1915)
**Claire BLOOM**
Claire BLUME
1931–
English actress. In 1943 she won a
scholarship to the Guildhall School
of Music and Drama. Her mother
changed Claire's name to Bloom
in 1944
**Ben BLUE**
Benjamin BERNSTEIN
1900–
American vaudeville comedian;
also appeared in films
**David BLUE**
S. David COHEN
1941–
American pop singer-composer.
Pseudonym supplied by Bob Dylan
**Harry BLUFF**
Mathew Fontaine MAURY
1806–1873
American naval officer and author
**Nellie BLY**
Elizabeth SEAMAN
1867–1922

American journalist and traveller
**John BLYTH**
John HIBBS
1925–
British author
**Betty BLYTHE**
Elizabeth SLAUGHTER
1893–1972
American star of silent films
**BOB OF LYM**
Sir Robert WALPOLE
1676–1745
English statesman
**BODFAN**
John ANWYL
1875–
British author
**Budd BOETTICHER**
Oscar BOETTICHER
1916–
American film director
**Dirk BOGARDE**
Derek Jules Gaspard Ulric Niven
VAN DEN BOGAERDE
1921–
British actor
**Hilarius BOGBINDER**
Sören KIERKEGAARD
1813–1855
Danish philosopher and theologian
**Tom BOGGS**
William KING
1663–1712
English writer
**Charles BOGLE**
William Claude DUKINFIELD
1879–1946
American comedian. He used this
pseudonym for screen plays, but is
better known as W. C. Fields
**Willy BOJAN**
Dr. Wilhelm STEKEL
1868–1940
Austrian psychiatrist. Bojan was
his home town
**Kooshti BOK**
George MAIR
1914–
British author

**Marc BOLAN**
Marc FELD
1943–
English pop singer. The first notice he had that his name had been changed was when he saw the label of his first record which read 'Marc Bowland'. Decca informed him that they did not think Marc Feld was 'suitable'. It was later shortened to Bolan

**Ralph BOLD**
Charles GRIFFITHS
1919–
British author

**Milord BOLINGBROCKE**
François Marie AROUET
1694–1778
French philosopher and writer better known as Voltaire

**Ray D. BOLITHO**
Dorothy BLAIR
1913–
South African author

**Evelyn BOLSTER**
Sister Mary Angela BOLSTER
1925–
Irish author

**Beulah BONDI**
Beulah BONDY
1892–
American actress

**Gary U.S. BONDS**
Gary ANDERSON
1939–
American pop singer

**Emery BONETT**
Felicity COULSON
1906–
British author

**John BONETT**
John COULSON
1906–
British author

**Sherwood BONNER**
Katherine McDOWELL
1849–1894
American novelist and secretary to Henry Wadsworth Longfellow

**Daniel BOONE**
Peter Lee STRINGER
1943–
American pop singer

**Pat BOONE**
Charles Eugene BOONE
1934–
American pop singer

**Edwina BOOTH**
Josephine WOODRUFF
1909–
American actress of the silent film era

**Shirley BOOTH**
Thelma Booth FORD
1907–
American stage and screen actress. She won an Academy Award for *Come Back Little Sheba* (1951)

**Bob BOOTY**
Sir Robert WALPOLE
1676–1745
English statesman

**Cornell BORCHERS**
Cornelia BRUCH
1925–
German actress, who played in international films

**Lee BORDEN**
Borden DEAL
1922–
American author

**Mary Cathart BORER**
Mary Cathart MYERS
1906–
British actress

**Victor BORGE**
Borge ROSENBAUM
1909–
Danish comedian and pianist. Made his debut in 1932 and was the best paid Danish entertainer of the thirties. Changed his name in 1940 when he emigrated to America

**Ernest BORGNINE**
Ermes BORGNINE
1917–

American actor. He won an Academy Award for *Marty* (1955)

**Ludwig BORNE**
Lob BARUCH
1786–1837
German journalist of Jewish descent

**The BOSTON BARD**
Robert Stevenson COFFIN
1797–1827
American poet

**A BOSTONIAN**
Edgar POE
1809–1849
American poet and short-story writer. He wrote his first book *Tamerlane and other Poems* (1829) under this pseudonym. He is better known as Edgar Allan Poe

**Elizabeth BOTT**
Elizabeth SPILLIUS
1924–
British author

**Sandro BOTTICELLI**
Alessandro FILIPEPI
*c.* 1444–1510
Florentine painter, the son of a tanner. His pseudonym derives from Botticello, the nickname of his elder brother Giovanni, a broker. His finest painting is 'The Birth of Venus'

**Chili BOUCHIER**
Dorothy BOUCHIER
1909–
British actress

**Houri BOUMEDIENNE**
Mohammed BOUKHAROUBA
1928–
Algerian politician

**BOURVIL**
André RAIMBOURG
1917–1970
French comic actor

**Bartholomew BOUVERIE**
William Ewart GLADSTONE
1809–1898
British statesman

**Jim BOWDEN**
William SPENCE
1923–
British author

**Elizabeth BOWEN**
Mrs. Alan CAMERON
1899–1973
Anglo-Irish novelist and short-story writer

**Marjorie BOWEN**
Margaret CAMPBELL
1888–1952
British novelist. Also used the names George R. Preedy, and Joseph Shearing. She married Zefferino Costanzo in 1912; he died in 1916 and in the following year she married Arthur Long

**David BOWIE**
David JONES
1948–
British pop singer whose first hit was 'Space Oddity' (1969)

**Barbara BOYD**
Agnes BURR
1905–
American journalist

**Martin BOYD**
Martin MILLS
1893–
Australian novelist. He used this pen-name for his three novels; *Love Gods* (1925), *Brangame* (1926) and *The Montforts* (1928)

**Nancy BOYD**
Edna St. Vincent MILLAY
1892–1950
American poet

**Stephen BOYD**
William MILLER
1928–1977
Irish-born American actor

**Catherine BOYLE**
Caterina di FRANCAVILLA
1929–
British TV personality

**Peter BOYLSTON**
George Ticknor CURTIS
1812–1894
American lawyer and author

**BOZ**
Charles DICKENS
1812–1870
British novelist. *Sketches by Boz* appeared in 1836. 'Boz,' he tells us 'was the nickname of a pet child, a younger brother, whom I had dubbed Moses, in honour of "The Vicar of Wakefield" which, being pronounced Bozes got shortened to Boz'

**Timothy BRACE**
Theodore PRATT
1901–
American author, he wrote mystery stories under this pseudonym

**E. S. BRADBURNE**
Elizabeth S. LAWRENCE
1915–
British author

**Will BRADLEY**
Wilbur SCHWICHTENBERG
1912–
American jazz trombonist

**Scott BRADY**
Gerald TIERNEY
1924–
American actor

**Ernest BRAMAH**
Ernest Bramah SMITH
1867–1942
British writer

**Max BRAND**
Frederick FAUST
1892–1944
American writer of westerns

**Mona BRAND**
Mona FOX
1915–
Australian author

**Marc BRANDEL**
Marcus BERESFORD
1919–
British author

**Henry BRANDON**
Henry KLEINBACH
1910–
American actor

**Sheila BRANDON**
Claire RAYNER
1931–
British writer

**Willy BRANDT**
Karl Herbert FRAHM
1913–
German political leader. In 1933, Frahm, then leader of a youth organisation, unsuccessfully appealed to the trade unions for a general strike. Threatened with arrest by the Gestapo, he left Germany for Norway under the name Willy Brandt

**Joseph BRANT**
THAYENDANEGEA
1742–1807
American Indian chief

**BRASSAI**
Gyula HALASZ
1899–
French photographer, famous for his photographs of Paris night life. His pseudonym derives from his birthplace, Brasso, Transylvania

**Wellman BRAUD**
Wellman BREAUX
1891–1966
American jazz bass player

**Vivian BRECK**
Vivian BRECKENFELD
*c*. 1920–
American author

**Calvin BRENT**
John HORNBY
1913–
British author

**Evelyn BRENT**
Mary RIGGS
1899–
American film star during the silent era

**George BRENT**
George B. NOLAN
1904–
Irish-born American actor, in films from 1930

**Nigel BRENT**
Cecil WIMHURST
1905–
British author

**Romney BRENT**
Romulo LARRALDE
1902–
Mexican actor. He acted in British films during the 1930s

**Edmund BREON**
Edmund McLAVERTY
1882–1951
British actor

**Jeremy BRETT**
Jeremy HUGGINS
1935–
British actor

**Eliot BREWSTER**
James N. GIFFORD
1896–1957
American author

**Fanny BRICE**
Fanny BORACH
1891–1951
American actress and singer. Changed her name when she went on stage because she was tired of being called 'More-Ache' and 'Bore-Act' by her friends. She shortened her first name in the thirties

**Ann BRIDGE**
Lady O'MALLEY
1889–1974
British author

**Madeline BRIDGES**
Mary DE VERE
c. 1850–1932
American poet

**James BRIDIE**
Osborne Henry MAVOR
1888–1951
Scottish playwright

**Mary BRIEN**
Louise DANTZLER
1908–
American film star of the silent screen

**Raley BRIEN**
Johnston McCULLEY
1883–
Canadian author and playwright

**Carl BRISSON**
Carl PEDERSON
1895–1958
Danish singer and actor, who came to Britain in 1921

**A BRITISH OFFICER IN THE SERVICE OF THE CZAR**
Daniel FOE
1660–1731
English journalist and novelist; called Daniel Defoe

**May BRITT**
Maybritt WILKENS
1933–
Swedish actress

**Barbara BRITTON**
Barbara CZUKOR
1920–
American actress, popular during the forties in Hollywood

**Colonel BRITTON**
Douglas RITCHIE
1905–
British broadcaster to German occupied countries during the Second World War. His identity was a carefully guarded secret until after the war

**Steve BRODIE**
John STEVENS
1919–
American actor

**Charles BRONSON**
Charles BUCHINSKI
1922–
American film actor. He changed his name at the time of the McCarthy trials in order to sound more American

**Pat BRONX**
Peter SCHILPEROORT
1919–
Dutch jazz musician

**Clive BROOK**
Clifford BROOK

1887–
British actor, popular in Hollywood during the twenties
**Hillary BROOKE**
Beatrice PETERSON
1916–
American actress
**Clark BROOKER**
Kenneth FOWLER
1900–
American author
**Chatty BROOKS**
Rosella RICE
1827–*c.* 1900
American author
**Elkie BROOKS**
Elaine BOOKBINDER
1948–
British pop singer
**Geraldine BROOKS**
Geraldine STROOCK
1925–
American actress
**Jonathan BROOKS**
John Calvin MELLETT
1888–
American author
**Leslie BROOKS**
Leslie GETTMAN
1922–
American actress
**Mel BROOKS**
Melvyn KAMINSKY
1926–
American film director. He started out as a drummer and changed his name to avoid being confused with Max Kaminsky, the trumpet player
**Phyllis BROOKS**
Phyllis WEILER
1914–
American actress
**A BROTHER OF THE BIRCH**
William COBBETT
1763–1835
English political journalist
**Caroline BROWN**
Caroline KROUT

1853–1931
American author
**Georgia BROWN**
Lillian KLOT
1933–
British singer
**Irving BROWN**
William Taylor ADAMS
1822–1897
American writer of travel books
**Jamieson BROWN**
W. J. C. BROWN
1910–
Australian author
**Mr. BROWN**
William Makepeace THACKERAY
1811–1863
British author
**Thomas BROWN**
Thomas MOORE
1779–1852
Irish poet
**Vanessa BROWN**
Smylla BRIND
1928–
American juvenile actress who made a few films in the forties
**Will C. BROWN**
C. S. BOYLES
1905–
American author of Western stories
**Septimus BROWNE**
H. G. WELLS
1866–1946
British writer. He used this pen-name for articles in *Science Schools Journal* (1887–89)
**David BRUCE**
Marden McBROOM
1914–1976
American actor
**Virginia BRUCE**
Helen Virginia BRIGGS
1910–
American actress
**Beau BRUMMELL**
George BRUMMELL

1778–1840
English Regency dandy
**Georg BRUNIS**
George BRUNIES
1900–
American jazz trombonist
**Lucius Junius BRUTUS**
William CRANCH
1769–1855
American jurist
**Dora BRYAN**
Dora BROADBENT
1923–
English actress. Originally chose
the stage name Bryant from the
match manufacturers 'Bryant and
May' but when the programme
came back from the printers the
last letter had been left out so she
settled for Dora Bryan
**Jane BRYAN**
Jane O'BRIEN
1918–
American actress
**Yul BRYNNER**
Taidje KHAN, Jr.
1916–
American stage and screen actor.
Claims his real name is Taidje
Khan, Jr., but nobody has been
able to find out for sure who he
really is – not even his wives
**Belle Z. BUBB**
Samuel BECKNER
1820–1861
American editor
**BUBBA FREE JOHN**
Franklin Albert JONES
1943–
American guru
**Henrietta BUCKMASTER**
Henrietta HENKLE
1909–
American author
**BUCKSKIN SAM**
Samuel HALL
1878–
American dime novelist

**BUDDHA**
Siddhartha GAUTAMA
c. 560–c. 484 B.C.
Indian founder of Buddhism.
Buddha is a title meaning 'the
enlightened one'
**Jasper BUDDLE**
Albert SMITH
1816–1860
English comic writer
**BUFFALO BILL**
William Frederick Cody
1846–1917
American showman born in Iowa.
He was given this nickname after
killing nearly 5,000 buffalo in 18
months, to supply the workers on
the Kansas Pacific Railway with
meat
**Ned BUNTLINE**
Edward JUDSON
1820–1886
American writer, first of the dime
novelists. He used the character
Buffalo Bill in some of his novels
**Austin C. BURDICK**
Sylvanus COBB
1821–1877
American writer of adventure
stories
**G. A. L. BURGEON**
Arthur Owen BARFIELD
1898–
British writer
**Anthony BURGESS**
John Burgess WILSON
1917–
British novelist
**Leda BURKE**
David GARNETT
1892–
British writer. He wrote his first
novel *Dope Darling* under this
pen-name
**Marie BURKE**
Marie HOLT
1894–
British actress

**Shifty BURKE**
  Peggie BENTON
  1906–
  British author
**Vinnie BURKE**
  Vincent BUCCI
  1921–
  American jazz bass player
**George BURNS**
  Nathan BIRNBAUM
  1896–
  American radio and TV comedian
**Richard BURTON**
  Richard JENKINS
  1925–
  British actor. In 1943 he adopted
  the surname of his drama teacher
  in Port Talbot, Philip Burton
**Thomas BURTON**
  Stephen LONGSTREET
  1907–
  American author
**BURTON JUNIOR**
  Charles LAMB
  1775–1834

English essayist
**Sir Alexander BUSTAMANTE**
  William CLARKE
  1884–
  Jamaican politician, the first Prime
  Minister of Jamaica (1962–1967)
**The BUSYBODY**
  Benjamin FRANKLIN
  1706–1790
  American philosopher, scientist
  and statesman
**Red BUTTONS**
  Aaron CHWATT
  1919–
  American actor. In 1935, when he
  worked as a bellboy at Dinty
  Moore's tavern in the Bronx, the
  red-haired boy wore a uniform
  with forty-eight buttons, and cus-
  tomers named him Red Buttons
**Edd BYRNES**
  Edward BREITENBERGER
  1933–
  American juvenile actor of the
  fifties

# C

**C.**
  Samuel Taylor COLERIDGE
  1772–1834
  English poet
**C.3.3.3.**
  Oscar WILDE
  1854–1900
  Irish playwright, poet and wit. He
  used this pseudonym to write
  *The Ballad of Reading Gaol* (1898).
  The pseudonym means – Cell 3,
  Landing 3, Galley 3
**C.L.I.O.**
  Joseph ADDISON
  1672–1719
  English essayist. The initials stand
  for the names of the places where
  he wrote – Chelsea, London,

Islington and the office
**Fernán CABALLERO**
  Cecilia de FABER
  1797–1877
  Spanish novelist
**CABBY WITH A CAMERA**
  Maxwell GREEN
  1929–
  British author
**Bruce CABOT**
  Etienne DE BUJAC
  1904–1972
  American actor
**Michael CACOYANNIS**
  Michaelis CACOGHIANNIS
  1922–
  Greek Cypriot film director

**Alexander CADE**
Kenneth W. METHOLD
1931–
British author

**CADMUS and HARMONIA**
John and Susan BUCHAN
1875–1940; 1883–
British writers

**Michael CAINE**
Maurice Micklewhite
1933–
British actor. After playing a few bit parts he changed his first name to his nickname Mike and his second name to Caine from the film *The Caine Mutiny*

**Elinor CALDWELL**
Clare BRETON-SMITH
1906–
British author

**Taylor CALDWELL**
Janet Taylor CALDWELL
1900–
American novelist. She was born Manchester, England but has lived in the U.S.A. since 1907

**The CALEDONIAN COMET**
Sir Walter SCOTT
1771–1832
Scottish poet and novelist

**Louis CALHERN**
Carl Henry VOGT
1895–1956
American actor, born in Brooklyn. In 1901 the family moved to St. Louis, Missouri. In 1912 he decided to become an actor and under pressure from his uncle, who regarded having an actor in the family as a disgrace, chose a pseudonym. Calhern is a contraction of Carl Henry, and Louis derives from the city of St. Louis

**Rory CALHOUN**
Francis DURGIN
1922–
American actor, popular in Hollywood in the fifties

**CALIBAN**
John Cowie REID
1916–
New Zealand author

**Michael CALLAN**
Martin CALINIFF
1935–
American actor

**Theo CALLAS**
Desmond CORY
1928–
British author

**Joseph CALLEIA**
Joseph SPURIN-CALLEJA
1897–
American actor, born in Malta

**Michael CALLUM**
Michael GREAVES
1941–
British author

**Phyllis CALVERT**
Phyllis BICKLE
1915–
British actress

**V. F. CALVERTON**
George GOETZ
1900–
American author

**Corinne CALVET**
Corinne DIBOS
1925–
French actress. Acted in Hollywood during the 1950s

**Henry CALVIN**
Clifford HANLEY
1922–
Scottish novelist. He writes detective stories under this pen-name

**Margaret CAMERON**
Kathleen LINDSAY
1903–
British author

**Rod CAMERON**
Nathan COX
1910–
Canadian actor. He made many films in Hollywood from 1940

**CAMILLUS**
Alexander HAMILTON

1757–1804
American lawyer and statesman
**Judith CAMPBELL**
Marion PARES
1914–
British author
**Judy CAMPBELL**
Judy GAMBLE
1916–
British stage and TV actress
**Mrs. Patrick CAMPBELL**
Beatrice TANNER
1865–1940
English stage actress
**Scott CAMPBELL**
Frederick W. DAVIS
1858–1933
American dime novelist
**CAMPEADOR**
Rodrigo DIAZ DE VIVAR
c. 1040–1099
Spanish national hero, better known as 'El Cid'
**CANALETTO**
Antonio CANALE
1697–1768
Italian painter
**CANDIDO**
Candido CAMERO
1921–
Cuban jazz musician
**CANDIDO**
José MARTINEZ RUIZ
1873–1967
Spanish essayist, novelist and critic. He wrote his first book under this pseudonym, but was better known as 'Azorín'
**Edward CANDY**
Barbara NEVILLE
1925–
British author
**Dennis CANNAN**
Denis PULLEIN-THOMPSON
1919–
British actor
**John CANNE**
Samuel BUTLER

1612–1680
English poet and satirist
**Dyan CANNON**
Samile Diane FRIESEN
1938–
American actress
**CANTINFLAS**
Mario MORENO
1911–
Mexican comedian. His stage name, which is meaningless, was given him by one of his fans
**Eddie CANTOR**
Edward Israel ISKOWITZ
1893–1964
American comedian. In 1908, he tried his talents at Miner's Bowery Theatre Amateur Night. He won the $5 prize and changed his name to Edward Cantor. He starred in the Ziegfeld Follies (1917–1920)
**Truman CAPOTE**
Truman PERSONS
1924–
American writer. He adopted the name of his stepfather, Joseph Capote, a textile businessman
**Al CAPP**
Alfred Gerald CAPLIN
1909–
American cartoonist
**CAPTAIN BEEFHEART**
Donald VAN VLIET
1945–
American rock singer
**CAPTAIN TOM**
Daniel FOE
1660–1731
English journalist and novelist; called Daniel Defoe
**CAPUCINE**
Germaine LEFEBVRE
1933–
French actress, former model
**CARACALLA**
Marcus Aurelius ANTONINUS
A.D. 188–217
Roman emperor (211–217). He was assassinated by Macrinus

**James CAREY**
Harold James CAREW-SLATER
1909–
British author

**Joyce CAREY**
Joyce LAWRENCE
1898–
British stage actress

**Catherine CARFAX**
Eleanor FAIRBURN
1928–
Irish author

**Richard CARGOE**
Robert PAYNE
1911–
English author

**Captain George CARLETON**
Daniel FOE
1660–1731
English journalist and novelist; called Daniel Defoe

**William CARLETON**
William F. BARTLETT
1876–
American novelist

**Kitty CARLISLE**
Catherine HOLZMAN
1915–
American opera singer

**CARLO-RIM**
Jean-Marius RICHARD
1905–
French film director

**John Roy CARLSON**
Avodis DEROUNIAN
1909–
American author

**Ann CARMICHAEL**
Margaret H. McALPINE
1907–
British author

**Harry CARMICHAEL**
Leo H. OGNALL
1908–
British author

**Sacha CARNEGIE**
Raymond CARNEGIE

1920–
British author

**Martine CAROL**
Maryse MOURER
1922–1967
French actress

**Sue CAROL**
Evelyn LEDERER
1907–
American actress

**Glyn CARR**
Frank SHOWELL STYLES
1908–
British author

**Jane CARR**
Rita BRUNSTROM
1909–
British actress

**Joe Fingers CARR**
Louis BUSH
1910–
American pianist

**Roberta CARR**
Irene ROBERTS
1929–
British author

**Emma CARRA**
Avis S. SPENCER
*c.* 1820–1870
American novelist

**John CARRADINE**
Richmond CARRADINE
1906–
American actor. He used the stage name John Peter Richmond from 1930 to 1935 then changed to John Carradine under which name he had great success in Hollywood during the thirties and forties

**Edward CARRICK**
Edward CRAIG
1905–
British theatrical designer, son of Edward Gordon Craig

**John CARRICK**
Hugh P. CROSBIE
1912–
British author

**Dorothy CARRINGTON**
Lady Dorothy ROSE
1910–
British author

**Michael CARRINGTON**
Meurig WILLIAMS
1925–
British author

**Barbara CARROLL**
Barbara Carole COPPERSMITH
1925–
American jazz pianist

**Consolata CARROLL**
Sister Mary CONSOLATA
1892–
American author and nun

**Diahann CARROLL**
Carol Diahann JOHNSON
1935–
American singer and actress

**Joan CARROLL**
Joan FELT
1932–
American child actress, who acted
under her own name until 1940,
then changed to Carroll because it
sounded musical

**John CARROLL**
Julian LA FAYE
1908–
American film actor and singer,
popular during the forties

**Lewis CARROLL**
Charles Lutwidge DODGSON
1832–1898
English writer of books for
children. He wrote *Alice's Adventures
in Wonderland* (1865). First
used his pseudonym in 1856 when
he wrote the poem 'Solitude', and
continued to use the name for all
his non-academic works. Dodgson
created it by taking his own names
Charles Lutwidge, translating them
into Latin as Carolus Ludovicus,
then reversing and translating
them into English

**Madeleine CARROLL**

**Marie M. O'CARROLL**
1906–
British stage and screen actress,
who acted in Hollywood during
the thirties and forties

**Martin CARROLL**
Margaret CARR
1935–
British author

**Nancy CARROLL**
Ann LA HIFF
1905–1965
American film actress of the
thirties

**Jeannie CARSON**
Jean SHUFFLEBOTTOM
1928–
British actress

**Netta CARSTENS**
Christine LAFFEATY
1932–
British author

**Bob CARTER**
Bob KAHAKALAU
1922–
American jazz bass player

**Helena CARTER**
Helen RICKERTS
1923–
American film actress of the
forties

**James CARTER**
Frederic VALMAIN
1931–
French author

**Janis CARTER**
Janis DREMANN
1921–
American radio and film actress
of the 1940s

**Nicholas CARTER**
Frederick W. DAVIS
1858–1933
American dime novelist

**Nicholas CARTER**
Frederick DEY
1865–1922
American dime novelist

**Nick CARTER**
  Bryan CARTER
  1917–
  British author
**Nick CARTER**
  John Russell CORYELL
  1852–1924
  American dime novelist
**Nick CARTER**
  George C. JENKS
  1850–1929
  English-born American novelist
**Barbara CARTLAND**
  Barbara McCORQUODALE
  1904–
  British author
**Maria CASARES**
  Maria C. QUIROGA
  1922–
  French actress
**Justin CASE**
  Rupert GLEADOW
  1909–
  British lawyer and writer on legal matters
**Edwin CASKODEN**
  Charles MAJOR
  1856–1913
  American novelist and lawyer
**Mama CASS**
  Ellen COHEN
  1942–1974
  American pop singer. Formerly known as Cass Elliott when a member of the group 'Mamas and Papas'
**CASSANDRA**
  Sir William CONNOR
  1909–1967
  British journalist. He used this pen-name from 1935 in the *Daily Mirror*
**Butch CASSIDY**
  Robert Le Roy PARKER
  1866–1909
  American bank robber. His nickname originated from the fact that he worked for a time as a butcher when on the run from the law. In 1907, when things became too hot in the United States, he left for South America with the Sundance Kid where they resumed their careers as bank robbers. Cassidy shot himself when cornered by the Bolivian army

**Igor CASSINI**
  Igor LOIEWSKI
  1915–
  Russian-born American gossip columnist. He wrote under the pen-name Cholly Knickerbocker
**CASSIUS**
  Michael FOOT
  1913–
  British politician. He used this pen-name when he was political columnist of the *Daily Herald* (1955–60)
**Lee CASTLE**
  Lee CASTALDO
  1915–
  American jazz trumpeter
**Stanley CASTLE**
  Rilma BROWNE
  *c.* 1895–
  American author
**Vernon CASTLE**
  Vernon BLYTHE
  1885–1918
  British dancer, popular in the U.S.A. with his partner Irene Castle until his death in an air crash
**William CASTLE**
  William SCHLOSS
  1914–
  American film director
**Harry CASTLEMON**
  Charles FOSDICK
  1842–1915
  American author
**The CAT**
  Mathilde CARRÉ
  1910–
  French spy
**CATO**
  Alexander HAMILTON

1757–1804
American lawyer and statesman
**Christopher CAULDWELL**
Christopher St. John SPRIGG
1907–
British author
**CAVENDISH**
Henry JONES
1831–1899
English physician and card game expert who invented whist
**Paul CELAN**
Paul ANTSCHEL
1920–
German poet
**Gabriel CELAYA**
Rafael MUGICA
1911–
Spanish poet
**The CELEBRATED COMMONER**
William PITT
1708–1778
English statesman
**CELTICUS**
Aneurin BEVAN
1897–1960
British politician
**Blaise CENDRARS**
Frederic SAUSER
1887–1961
French writer
**C. W. CERAM**
Kurt W. MAREK
1915–
American author
**Allen CHALMERS**
Edward UPWARD
1903–
British author
**Jon CHALON**
John S. CHALONER
1924–
British author
**CHAMPFLEURY**
Jules HUSSON
1821–1889
French novelist
**Jeff CHANDLER**

Ira GROSSEL
1918–1961
American film actor
**Lon CHANEY, Jr.**
Creighton CHANEY
1906–1973
American film actor
**Maristan CHAPMAN**
John and Mary CHAPMAN
1891– ; 1865–
English-born American novelists
**Cyd CHARISSE**
Tula FINKLEA
1924–
American dancer and actress. She came to use the name Cyd as a child, when her baby brother called her Sid in trying to say sister. Charisse is the name of her first husband, Nico Charisse, whom she married in 1939
**Frederick CHARLES**
Frederick Charles ASHFORD
1909–
British industrial designer
**Joan CHARLES**
Charlotte UNDERWOOD
1914–
American author and translator
**Mark CHARLES**
Richard BICKERS
1917–
British author
**Ray CHARLES**
Ray Charles ROBINSON
1932–
American singer, pianist, composer and bandleader
**Richard CHARLES**
Richard Charles AWDRY
1929–
British author
**Robert CHARLES**
Robert Charles SMITH
1938–
British author
**Teddy CHARLES**
Theodore Charles COHEN
1928–

American jazz musician, plays vibes

**Leslie CHARTERIS**
Leslie Charles YIN
1907–
British detective story writer, who created 'The Saint'. He was born in Singapore

**Charlie CHASE**
Charles PARROTT
1893–1940
American film comedian and director of the 1920s and 1930s

**James Hadley CHASE**
René RAYMOND
1906–
British author of crime and adventure fiction. He wrote *No Orchids for Miss Blandish* (1939)

**CHASMINDO**
Simon DACH
1605–1659
German poet

**Robert CHATTAN**
Robert SMITH
1914–
British author

**A CHATTERER**
Samuel ADAMS
1722–1803
American statesman

**Paddy CHAYEFSKY**
Sidney CHAYEFSKY
1923–
American playwright and scriptwriter. Wrote *Marty* (1955) and *Paint Your Wagon* (1969)

**Chubby CHECKER**
Ernest EVANS
1941–
American pop singer and dancer

**Tomo CHEEKI**
Philip FRENEAU
1752–1832
American sailor and poet

**Pierre CHENAL**
Pierre COHEN
1903–
French film director

**Marie CHER**
Marie SCHERR
*c.* 1900–
American author

**A. E. CHERRYMAN**
Bernard LEVIN
1928–
British journalist

**Peter CHESTER**
Dennis PHILLIPS
1924–
British author

**Walter CHIARI**
Walter ANNICHIARICO
1924–
Italian film actor

**CHIEF THUNDERCLOUD**
Victor DANIELS
1900–1955
American Indian actor

**CHI LIEN**
Elizabeth WONG
1937–
Hong Kong author

**Robert Orr CHIPPERFIELD**
Isabel OSTRANDER
1885–1924
American novelist

**Jill CHRISTIAN**
Noreen DILCOCK
1907–
British author

**Linda CHRISTIAN**
Blanca Rosa WELTER
1923–
Mexican actress

**Paul CHRISTIAN**
Paul HUBSCHMID
1917–
German actor. He uses this pseudonym in the U.S.A.

**CHRISTIAN-JAQUE**
Christian MAUDET
1904–
French film director

**Agatha CHRISTIE**
Lady MALLOWAN
1891–1975
English writer of detective stories,

née Miller. She married Archibald Christie in 1914. They were divorced in 1928 and in 1930 she married Max (now Sir Max) Mallowan, the archaeologist

**CHU FENG**
John BLOFELD
1913–
British writer who lives in Thailand

**Korney CHUKOVSKY**
N. I. KORNEICHUK
1882–
Russian writer

**CICERO**
Elias BASNA
c. 1900–1970
German spy. An Albanian, he was valet to the British Ambassador in Ankara. He photographed confidential documents, including war plans and sold them to the Germans who paid him £300,000 in forged British banknotes

**El CID**
Rodrigo DIAZ DE VIVAR
c. 1040–1099
Spanish national hero; also called 'Campeador'

**CID HAMET BENENGELI**
Thomas Babington MACAULAY
1800–1859
British historian

**Giovanni CIMABUE**
Cenni Di PEPO
c. 1240–1302
Italian painter

**The CITIZEN OF THE WORLD**
Oliver GOLDSMITH
1728–1774
Irish playwright, novelist and poet

**Riccard CITTAFINO**
Richard BICKERS
1917–
British author

**René CLAIR**
René CHOMETTE
1898–
French film director. He took this

pseudonym when he first played a part in a film in 1920

**Ina CLAIRE**
Ina FAGAN
1895–
American actress

**Ada CLARE**
Jane McELHENEY
1836–1874
American novelist and poet

**Helen CLARE**
Pauline CLARKE
c. 1925–
British author

**Fitzroy CLARENCE**
William Makepeace THACKERAY
1811–1863
British author

**CLARÍN**
Leopoldo ALAS
1852–1901
Spanish novelist and literary critic. Clarín means 'bugle'

**Dane CLARK**
Bernard ZANVILLE
1913–
American film actor

**Kenny CLARKE**
Liaquat Ali SALAAM
1914–
American jazz musician

**CLAUDE LORRAINE**
Claude GELLÉE
1600–1682
French landscape painter

**James CLAUGHTON-JAMES**
James W. BENTLEY
1914–
British author

**Mrs. Mary CLAVERS**
Caroline KIRKLAND
1801–1864
American author

**Bertha M. CLAY**
John Russell CORYELL
1852–1924
American dime novelist

**Charles M. CLAY**
Charlotte M. CLARK
*c.* 1850–1935
American author

**Jedediah CLEISHBOTHAM**
Sir Walter SCOTT
1771–1832
Scottish poet and novelist

**CLEMENT OF ALEXANDRIA**
Titus Flavius CLEMENS
*c.* A.D. 152–*c.* 214
Greek theologian

**John CLEVEDON**
Ernest PLUMLEY
1909–
British author

**Charles CLIFFORD**
William Henry IRELAND
1777–1835
English literary forger

**John CLIFFORD**
John BAYLISS
1919–
British author

**Colin CLIVE**
Clive GREIG
1898–1937
English actor in Hollywood from 1930

**Stuart CLOETE**
St. Edward S. GRAHAM
1897–
British writer

**Upton CLOSE**
Josef HALL
1894–1960
American lecturer

**Yvonne CLOUD**
Yvonne KAPP
1903–
British author

**Capt. CLUTTERBUCK**
Sir Walter SCOTT
1771–1832
Scottish poet and novelist

**Dorothy CLYDE**
Fay HAMMERTON
1894–1973

British stage actress who became better known by her second pseudonym: Fay Holden

**Kit CLYDE**
Luis Philip SENARENS
1863–1939
American dime novelist

**Pierre COALFLEET**
Frank Cyril DAVISON
1893–
American author

**Arnett COBB**
Arnette COBBS
1918–
American jazz tenor sax player

**John COBB**
John Cobb COOPER III
1921–
American novelist

**Lee J. COBB**
Lee JACOBY
1911–1976
American stage and film actor

**Charles COBORN**
Colin McCALLUM
1852–1945
British music-hall entertainer famous for his rendering of 'The Man who Broke the Bank at Monte Carlo'

**Steve COCHRAN**
Robert COCHRAN
1917–1965
American film actor

**Corinna COCHRANE**
Corinna PETERSON
1923–
British author

**Pindar COCKLOFT, Esq.**
William IRVING
1766–1821
American humorist, brother of Washington Irving

**Lew CODY**
Louis COTE
1884–1934
American film actor of the silent era.

**Geoffrey COFFIN**
F. Van Wyck MASON and Helen
BRAWNER
1897– ; 1902–
American authors of mystery
stories
**Joshua COFFIN**
Henry Wadsworth
LONGFELLOW
1807–1882
American poet
**Junior COGHLAN**
Frank COGHLAN
1916–
American actor
**Two Gun COHEN**
Morris COHEN
1889–
Born in the East End of London,
he went to China in 1922 as an
arms dealer but became involved
in the Republican cause; was made
a general in the Chinese Army in
1928
**Émile COHL**
Émile COURTE
1857–1938
French film cartoonist, who made
many films between 1908–1920
**Claudette COLBERT**
Lily Claudette CHAUCHOIN
1905–
American actress, born in Paris.
Her family emigrated to the
U.S.A. in 1910. She changed her
name in 1923, when she started
acting
**Henry COLCRAFT**
Henry SCHOOLCRAFT
1793–1864
American author and explorer
**Nat King COLE**
Nathaniel Adams COLES
1917–1965
American negro pianist and singer.
He dropped the 's' when the King
Cole Trio was formed in 1937
**Cy COLEMAN**
Seymour KAUFMAN

1929–
American pianist
**COLETTE**
Sidonie Gabrielle COLETTE
1873–1954
French writer
**Bonar COLLEANO**
Bonar SULLIVAN
1924–1958
American actor, popular in Britain
during the 1940s
**Constance COLLIER**
Laura HARDIE
1878–1955
British actress in Hollywood from
1935
**Hunt COLLING**
Evan LOMBINO
1926–
American novelist, better known
as Evan Hunter and Ed McBain
**Geoffrey COLLINS**
Greg JEFFERIES
1938–
British author
**Joan COLLINS**
Mildred COLLINS
1921–
American author
**Michael COLLINS**
Dennis LYNDS
1924–
American author
**Doric COLLYER**
Dorothy HUNT
1896–
British author
**June COLLYER**
Dorothy HEERMANCE
1907–
American actress
**Russ COLUMBO**
Ruggiero COLUMBO
1903–1934
American pop singer
**Chris COLUMBUS**
Joseph Christopher Columbus
MORRIS

1903–
American jazz drummer
**James COLVIN**
Michael MOORCOCK
1932–
British writer of science fiction.
He used his pen-name for contributions to *New Worlds*
**Betty COMDEN**
Elizabeth COHEN
1918–
American writer
**COMENIUS**
Jan Amos KOMENSKÝ
1592–1670
Czech writer and educational reformer
**Perry COMO**
Pierno COMO
1913–
American singer
**Francis Snow COMPTON**
Henry Brooks ADAMS
1838–1918
American historian and essayist.
He wrote *Esther* (1881) under this pseudonym
**Joyce COMPTON**
Eleanor HUNT
1907–
American actress
**COMUS**
R. M. BALLANTYNE
1825–1894
Scottish author of boys' books
**CONFUCIUS**
K'UNG FU-TZU
*c.* 550–480 B.C.
Chinese philosopher and social reformer. Confucius is a latinized form of K'ung Fu-Tzu
**Chester CONKLIN**
Jules COWLES
1888–1971
American film comedian. He played for Mack Sennett and Charlie Chaplin
**Sean CONNERY**
Thomas CONNER

1930–
British actor
**J. J. CONNINGTON**
Alfred Walter STEWART
1880–1947
British scientist who wrote detective stories under this pen-name
**Chuck CONNORS**
Kevin CONNOR
1921–
American actor
**Michael CONNORS**
Kreker OHANIAN
1925–
American film actor, formerly known as Touch Connors
**Joseph CONRAD**
Teodor Jozef Konrad KORZENIOWSKI
1857–1924
Polish-born English novelist
**Robert CONRAD**
Conrad FALK
1935–
American television actor
**Robert CONROY**
Robert Goldston
1927–
American author
**Michael CONSTANTINE**
Constantine JOANIDES
1927–
American actor
**Constantin CONSTANTIUS**
Sören KIERKEGAARD
1813–1855
Danish philosopher and theologian
**Paul CONSTANTIUS**
John HUS
*c.* 1370–1415
Czech theologian and religious reformer
**Richard CONTE**
Nicholas CONTE
1914–1975
American film actor
**Gary CONWAY**
Gareth CARMODY

1938–
American actor
**Tom CONWAY**
Thomas SANDERS
1904–1967
British actor, the brother of George Sanders
**Robin COOK**
Robert COOK
1931–
British author
**Alice COOPER**
Vince FURNIER
1948–
American pop singer, who became famous in 1973 for his sadistic stage act. He chose this name because it sounded like a healthy, normal, blonde folk-singer
**Gary COOPER**
Frank COOPER
1901–1961
American film star
**Jackie COOPER**
John BIGELOW
1922–
American child actor of the thirties
**COQUELIN AÎNÉ**
Benoît Constant COQUELIN
1841–1909
French actor
**Christopher CORAM**
Peter WALKER
1936–
British author
**Le CORBUSIER**
Charles Édouard JEANNERET
1887–1965
Swiss architect, pioneer of modern architectural movement. In 1921 he adopted his mother's maiden name as his architectural pseudonym, reserving the name Jeanneret for his paintings
**Ellen CORBY**
Ellen HANSEN
1913–
American actress

**Alex CORD**
Alexander VIESPI
1931–
American actor
**Mara CORDAY**
Marilyn WATTS
1932–
American film actress
**Rita CORDAY**
Paula CORDAY
1924–
British actress, in Hollywood from 1942
**El CORDOBÉS**
Manuel BENITEZ
c. 1936–
Spanish bullfighter. *El Cordobés* means 'the man from Cordoba'
**Raymond CORDY**
Raymond CORDIAUX
1898–1956
French comic actor of the thirties
**A.L.A. CORENANDA**
Allen NUMANO
1908–
Japanese author
**CORIOLANUS**
James McMILLAN
1925–
British author
**Joyce I. CORLETT**
Joyce I. KIRKWOOD
1912–
British author
**Adrienne CORRI**
Adrienne RICCOBONI
1930–
British actress
**Ray 'Crash' CORRIGAN**
Ray BENARD
1907–1976
American cowboy actor of the thirties
**Ricardo CORTEZ**
Jacob KRANTZ
1898–
American actor. Played the Latin lover in silent movies

**Stanley CORTEZ**
Stanley KRANTZ
1908–
American cinematographer, brother of Ricardo Cortez

**Baron CORVO**
Frederick William Serafino Austin Lewis Mary ROLFE
1860–1913
English writer. Rolfe claimed that the title, Baron Corvo, had been bestowed upon him by the Duchess Sforza-Cesarini, whom he had met in Italy and who adopted him as a grandson

**Ulysses COSMOPOLITE**
George BERKELEY
1684–1753
Irish bishop and philosopher. He used this pen-name for his articles to the *Guardian* in 1713

**Frank COSTELLO**
Francesco CASTIGLIA
1891–1973
Italian-born New York gambler

**Lou COSTELLO**
Louis Francis CRISTILLO
1906–1959
American comedian, the fat half of the Abbott and Costello comedy team

**Nicole COURCEL**
Nicole ANDRIEUX
1930–
French actress

**COUSIN ALICE**
Mary BRADLEY
1835–1898
American novelist and poet

**COUSIN CICELY**
Sarah BRADFORD
1818–1875
American author

**Egbert Augustus COWSLIP, Esq.**
Benjamin BARKER
*c.* 1820–*c.* 1870
American novelist

**Buster CRABBE**
Clarence CRABBE
1907–
American actor. He was seventh in the line of screen Tarzan's in 1933

**Jane CRABTREE**
H. G. WELLS
1866–1946
British writer. He used this pen-name for 'Hints on visiting the Academy, addressed to a young lady' in *Pall Mall Budget* (1894)

**A. A. CRAIG**
Poul ANDERSON
*c.* 1924–
American science fiction writer

**David CRAIG**
James TUCKER
1929–
British writer

**Georgia CRAIG**
Peggy DERN
1896–
American novelist

**Henry Edward Gordon CRAIG**
Edward GODWIN
1872–1966
English actor, producer and stage designer. Illegitimate son of Ellen Terry, the actress, and Edwin Godwin, an architect. He used the name Edward Godwin until his mother's marriage to the actor Charles Wardell in 1877, when he became known as Edward Wardell. In 1887 his mother decided to give him a new name – Henry Edward Gordon Craig. Henry was in tribute to Henry Irving, Gordon after her friend Lady Gordon and Craig after the island Ailsa Craig in Scotland whose name appealed to her – 'what a magnificent name for an actress!'

**James CRAIG**
James MEADOR
1912–
American actor

**Jennifer CRAIG**
Ailsa BRAMBLEBY

1915–
British author
**Michael CRAIG**
Michael GREGSON
1928–
British film actor. He changed his name to avoid confusion with John Gregson
**Lucius CRASSUS**
Alexander HAMILTON
1757–1804
American lawyer and statesman
**Anne CRAWFORD**
Imelda CRAWFORD
1920–1956
British actress
**Joan CRAWFORD**
Lucille LE SUEUR
1908–1977
American actress. In 1923 she auditioned for the chorus of a revue and when she gave her name the director said 'Well, honey, you certainly picked a fancy one.' She went to Hollywood in 1925 when she made a few films under her own name. Then the studio sponsored a contest to find her a new one and to her dismay she was renamed Joan Crawford, she thought it sounded like 'crawfish'
**Michael CRAWFORD**
Michael DUMBLE-SMITH
1942–
British comic actor
**Robert CRAWFORD**
Hugh C. RAE
1935–
British author
**Port CRAYON**
David STROTHER
1816–1888
American soldier, illustrator and author
**Joseph CREHAN**
Charles WILSON
1884–1966
American film actor

**Tom CRIB**
Thomas MOORE
1779–1852
Irish poet
**Otis CRIBLECOBLIS**
William Claude DUKINFIELD
1879–1946
American comedian, better known as W. C. Fields. This was one of the pseudonyms he used to write screen plays
**CRICKETER**
Neville CARDUS
1889–1974
British journalist
**CRISPIE**
S. E. CRISP
1906–
British author
**Edmund CRISPIN**
Robert B. MARSHALL
1921–
British author
**Linda CRISTAL**
Victoria MAYA
1936–
Mexican actress
**CRITO**
Charles LAMB
1775–1834
English essayist
**David CROCKETT**
Augustus S. CLAYTON
1783–1839
American author
**Chrystal CROFTANGRY**
Sir Walter SCOTT
1771–1832
Scottish poet and novelist
**Richmal CROMPTON**
Richmal C. LAMBURN
1890–1969
British writer of books for boys. She created the schoolboy character, 'William'
**Richard CROMWELL**
Roy RADEBAUGH
1910–1960
American actor

**Hume CRONYN**
Hume BLAKE
1911–
Canadian actor, in Hollywood from 1943

**Provan CROSBIE**
Hugh P. CROSBIE
1912–
British author

**Bing CROSBY**
Harry Lillis CROSBY
1901–
American singer and actor, called Bing after an early cartoon character

**James CROSS**
Hugh Jones PARRY
1916–
British author

**Christopher CROWFIELD**
Harriet Beecher STOWE
1811–1896
American novelist – author of *Uncle Tom's Cabin* (1852). Wrote *House and Home Papers*, a book about gracious living, under this pseudonym

**Robinson CRUSOE**
Daniel FOE
1660–1731
English writer, better known as Daniel Defoe. Used this pseudonym for the first and greatest of his novels, *The Life and Strange Surprizing Adventures of Robinson Crusoe of York, Mariner* (1720)

**James CRUZE**
Jez Cruz BOSEN
1884–1942
American silent film director

**The CUMERLAND POET**
William WORDSWORTH
1770–1850
English poet

**Constance CUMMINGS**
Constance HALVERSTADT
1910–
American stage and screen actress, she acted in Britain from 1940

**E. V. CUNNINGHAM**
Howard FAST
1914–
American novelist. In 1947 he was imprisoned for refusing to co-operate with the House Committee on Un-American Activities, and afterwards wrote under this pseudonym

**Tyman CURRIO**
John Russell CORYELL
1852–1924
American dime novelist

**Phyllis CURTIN**
Phyllis SMITH
1927–
American singer. She retained the name of her first husband for professional reasons

**Alan CURTIS**
Harold NEBERROTH
1909–1953
American actor

**Tony CURTIS**
Bernard SCHWARTZ
1925–
American actor, born in New York, son of Hungarian-Jewish immigrant parents. His name was changed by Hollywood producer, Bob Goldstein, who said to him 'Schwartz ain't a name to get you into the big time – not even George Bernard Schwartz'

**Michael CURTIZ**
Mihaly KERTÉSZ
1888–1962
American film director

**CYNAN**
Albert EVANS-JONES
1895–
Welsh author and bard

# D

**D.E.D.I.**
W. B. YEATS
1865–1939
Irish poet and dramatist. He used these initials for an article in the *Irish Theosophist*, 'Invoking the Irish Fairies' (1892) and for a pamphlet *Is the Order of R.R. & A.C. to Remain a Magical Order?* (1901). The Order Rubidae Rosae and Aureae Crucis was a branch of the Order of the Golden Dawn, a mystical society which Yeats joined. D.E.D.I. are the initials of his adopted motto: *Daemon Est Deus Inversus*

**D.P.**
H. G. WELLS
1866–1946
British writer. He used these initials for a series of articles on science and politics in *The Times* (1916)

**Morton DA COSTA**
Morton TECOSKY
1914–
American theatrical director

**Lil DAGOVER**
Marta LILETTS
1897–
German actress

**Alan DALE**
Alfred COHEN
1861–1928
English-born American drama critic and novelist

**Jack DALE**
Joe HOLLIDAY
1910–
Canadian author

**Cass DALEY**
Catherine DAILEY
1915–
American comedienne

**DALIDA**
Jolanda GIGLIOTTI
1933–
French actress

**John DALL**
John THOMPSON
1918–
American actor

**Hugh D'ALLENGER**
John H. D. KERSHAW
1931–
British writer

**Lili DAMITA**
Lilliane CARRÉ
1901–
French actress

**Stuart DAMON**
Stuart ZONIS
1937–
American actor

**Vic DAMONE**
Vito FARINOLA
1929–
American pop singer

**Claude DAMPIER**
Claude COWAN
1885–1955
British comedian

**Viola DANA**
Violet FLUGRATH
1897–
American actress

**Clemence DANE**
Winifred ASHTON
1888–1965
English playwright and novelist. She adopted name of a well known church in the Strand, London

**Karl DANE**
Karl DAEN
1886–1934
Danish actor, in Hollywood during the twenties

**Paul M. DANFORTH**
John E. ALLEN
1921–
British writer on aeronautics

**DANIEL THE PROPHET**
Daniel FOE
1660–1731
English journalist and novelist;
called Daniel Defoe
**Bebe DANIELS**
Virginia DANIELS
1901–1971
American film actress
**John S. DANIELS**
Wayne D. OVERHOLSTER
*c.* 1915–
American novelist
**Gabriele D'ANNUNZIO**
Gabriele RAPAGNETTA
1863–1938
Italian writer. His father legally
changed his name to D'Annunzio
**DANTE**
Durante ALIGHIERI
1265–1321
Italian poet
**Michael DANTE**
Ralph VITTI
1931–
American actor
**Jack DANVERS**
Camille Auguste Marie
CASELEYR
1909–
Australian author
**J. N. DARBY**
Mary GOVAN
1897–
American author
**John DARBY**
James GARRETSON
1825–1895
American author and physician
**Kim DARBY**
Zerby DENBY
1937–
American actress
**Denise DARCEL**
Denise BILLECARD
1925–
French actress
**Alex D'ARCY**
Alexander SARRUF

1908–
Egyptian actor in international
films
**Phyllis DARE**
Phyllis DONES
1890–1975
British actress
**Zena DARE**
Florence Hariette Zena DONES
1887–1975
British actress. With her sister
Phyllis, she was one of the four
leading postcard beauties of
Edwardian England
**Bobby DARIN**
Walden Robert CASSOTTO
1936–1973
American pop singer. He picked
the name Darin from a telephone
directory
**Hope DARING**
Anna JOHNSON
1860–1945
American author
**Rubén DARÍO**
Felix Rubén GARCÍA
SARMIENTO
1867–1916
Nicaraguan poet
**Linda DARNELL**
Manetta DARNELL
1921–1965
American actress
**James DARREN**
James ERCOLANI
1936–
American actor
**Frankie DARRO**
Frank JOHNSON
1917–
American actor
**Rufus DART II**
Burton KLINE
*c.* 1870–1952
American journalist
**Bella DARVI**
Bayla WEGIER
1927–1971

Polish actress, in Hollywood during the fifties

**Jane DARWELL**
Patti WOODWARD
1880–1967
American character actress. Won an Academy Award for her playing of Ma Joad in *The Grapes of Wrath* (1940). She chose her stage name from a character in fiction

**Frei Antonio DAS CHAGAS**
Antonio da Fonseca SOARES
1631–1682
Portuguese poet and Franciscan monk

**Sylvanus DASHWOOD**
George S. HILLARD
1808–1879
American writer

**Howard DA SILVA**
Harold SILVERBLATT
1909–
American actor

**Henri DAUGE**
Henrietta HAMMOND
1854–1883
American novelist

**Claude DAUPHIN**
Claude FRANC-NOHAIN
1903–
French actor

**L. H. DAVIDSON**
D. H. LAWRENCE
1885–1930
British poet and novelist. He used this pen-name for a review of *The Book of Revelation* by Dr. J. Oman in the *Adelphi* (1924)

**Louise DAVIES**
Louise GOLDING
1923–
British author

**Marion DAVIES**
Marian DOURAS
1897–1961
American actress

**Bette DAVIS**
Ruth Elizabeth DAVIS
1908–
American actress

**Gordon DAVIS**
E. Howard HUNT
1923–
American author. Ex-C.I.A. agent who was involved in the Watergate affair

**Lawrence H. DAVISON**
D. H. LAWRENCE
1885–1930
British poet and novelist. He wrote *Movements in European History* under this pseudonym

**Hazel DAWN**
Hazel LETOUT
*c.* 1890–
American actress and singer. Studied acting in London, where the theatrical producer, Paul Rubens, changed her name. In 1911 she starred in the Broadway musical *The Pink Lady* which was so popular that she became known as The Pink Lady and a new cocktail was named in her honour

**Jonathan DAWPLUCKER, Esq.**
John BARCLAY
1756–1826
Scottish physician

**Jane DAWSON**
Dorothy CRITCHLOW
1904–
British author

**Doris DAY**
Doris KAPPELHOFF
1924–
American singer and actress. In 1940 she was offered a job by Barney Rapp, a Cincinnati band leader, who advised her to change her name. She suggested Doris La Ponselle, but Rapp arbitrarily christened her Day after hearing her sing 'Day After Day'

**Irene DAY**
Eve ORME
1894–
British author

**Laraine DAY**
La Raine JOHNSON
1920–
American actress. She made five films under her own name before adopting the surname of her drama teacher Elias Day, manager of the Players Guild at Long Beach, California

**Eddie DEAN**
Edgar GLOSSUP
1907–
American actor

**Isabel DEAN**
Isabel HODGKINSON
1918–
British actress

**Sonia DEAN**
Gwendoline SOUTAR
1921–
Australian author

**Vinnie DEAN**
Vincent DI VITTORIO
1929–
American jazz musician. Plays alto sax

**Norman DEANE**
John CREASEY
1908–1973
English writer. Creasey wrote 21 suspense stories under this pseudonym

**Yvonne DE CARLO**
Peggy MIDDLETON
1922–
American actress

**DECIMUS**
Thomas CHATTERTON
1752–1780
English poet

**Peter DECKER**
Malcolm DECKER
c. 1900–
American author

**Arturo DE CORDOVA**
Arturo GARCIA
1908–1973
Mexican actor

**Sir Roger DE COVERLEY**
Jonathan SEWALL
1728–1796
American lawyer and author

**Frances DEE**
Jean DEE
1907–
American actress

**Kiki DEE**
Pauline MATTHEWS
1947–
British pop singer

**Ruby DEE**
Ruby WALLACE
1925–
American actress

**Sandra DEE**
Alexandra ZUCK
1942–
American model and actress

**Simon DEE**
Carl HENTY-DODD
1934–
British disc-jockey

**DEEP WILL**
William PITT, the Younger
1759–1806
English statesman; he used this pen-name for *A Political Dictionary for the Guinea-less Pigs* (1790)

**Daniel DEFOE**
Daniel FOE
1660–1731
English writer, son of James Foe, a London tallow chandler. He changed his name to Defoe in 1703. Author of *Robinson Crusoe* (1720)

**Buddy DE FRANCO**
Boniface Ferdinand Leonardo DE FRANCO
1923–
American jazz clarinettist

**Carl DEKKER**
John LAFFIN
1922–
British author

**Bella DELAMARE**
Matilda Wood

1870–1922
English music hall entertainer,
better known as Marie Lloyd

**Denis DELANEY**
Peter GREEN
1924–
British writer. He wrote a novel,
*Cat in Gloves* (1956), under this
pen-name

**Bernard DELFONT**
Bernard WINOGRADSKY
1909–
Russian-born English theatrical
impresario. His parents emigrated
to England in 1911. Brother of
Lew Grade

**Danièle DELORME**
Gabrielle GIRARD
1926–
French actress

**Victoria DE LOS ANGELES**
Victoria GAMEZ
1923–
Spanish soprano noted in opera
and recital

**Dolores DEL RIO**
Dolores ASÚNSOLO
MARTINEZ
1905–
Mexican actress

**Andrea DEL SARTO**
Andrea d'AGNOLO
1486–1531
Florentine painter, he was called
del Sarto because he was the son
of a tailor

**Doug DEMAREST**
Will BARKER
1913–
American writer on natural history

**Katherine DE MILLE**
Katherine LESTER
1911–
American actress

**Kirk DEMING**
Harry Sinclair DRAGO
1888–
American writer of cowboy stories

**Frederick Haltamont DE
MONTMORENCY**
William Makepeace
THACKERAY
1811–1863
British author

**Gérard DE NERVAL**
Gérard LABRUNIE
1808–1855
French poet and novelist

**Catherine DENEUVE**
Catherine DORLÉAC
1943–
French actress

**Richard DENNING**
Louis DENNINGER
1914–
American actor

**Patrick DENNIS**
Edward Everett TANNER, III
1921–
American author. He wrote best-
seller *Auntie Mame* under this
pseudonym

**Reginald DENNY**
Reginald DAYMORE
1891–1967
British actor

**Teixeira DE PASCOAIS**
Joaquim DE VASCONCELOS
1877–1952
Portuguese poet

**Thomas DE QUINCEY**
Thomas QUINCEY
1785–1859
English writer. The aristocratic
'De' was added by himself and he
claimed descent from a Norman
family. Wrote *Confessions of an
English Opium-Eater* (1821)

**John DEREK**
Derek HARRIS
1926–
American actor

**Stephen DERMOTT**
Parnell BRADBURY
1904–
British writer

**DERVENTIO**
Walter D. HUGHES
1918–
British writer

**Jean DE SAINT LUC**
John GLASSCO
1909–
Canadian erotic novelist

**Johannes DE SILENTIO**
Sören KIERKEGAARD
1813–1855
Danish philosopher and theologian

**Florence DESMOND**
Florence DAWSON
1905–
English dancer and impersonator. Her first appearance on stage was as a child dancer in *The Babes in the Wood* at the Strand Theatre, London in 1915. The matron in charge of the child dancers suggested the name Desmond

**Emmy DESTINN**
Emmy KITTL
1878–
Czech opera singer

**DETERMINATUS**
Samuel ADAMS
1722–1803
American statesman

**Dame Ninette DE VALOIS**
Edris STANNUS
1898–
British prima ballerina and choreographer

**Jane DE VERE**
Julia WATSON
1943–
British author

**Justin DE VILLENEUVE**
Nigel DAVIES
1939–
British manager of Twiggy, the fashion model and actress

**James DEWEY**
Mildred McNEILLY
1910–
American writer of mystery stories

**Billy DE WOLFE**

William JONES
1907–
American actor

**Marquis DE XIMENEZ**
François Marie AROUET
1694–1778
French philosopher and writer better known as Voltaire

**Anthony DEXTER**
Walter FLEISCHMANN
1919–
American actor

**Robert DHERY**
Robert FOULLCY
1921–
French comedian

**B. H. DIAS**
Ezra POUND
1885–1972
American poet. He used this penname when art critic for the magazine *New Age* (1917–20)

**Corno DI BASSETTO**
George Bernard SHAW
1856–1950
Irish dramatist, essayist, critic and pamphleteer. He wrote musical criticism for the *Star* in the 1880s under this pseudonym

**Margaret DICKINSON**
Margaret E. MUGGESON
1942–
British author

**Bo DIDDLEY**
Ellas McDANIEL
1928–
American rock and roll singer

**Marlene DIETRICH**
Maria Magdalena DIETRICH
1902–
German actress and singer

**Robert DIETRICH**
E. Howard HUNT
1923–
American author. Ex-C.I.A. agent who was involved in the Watergate affair

**Phyllis DILLER**
Phyllis DRIVER

1917–
American comedienne
**Isak DINESEN**
Baroness Karen
BLIXEN-FINECKE
1885–1962
Danish novelist and story-teller
**Julio DINIS**
Joaquim COELHO
1839–1871
Portuguese novelist
**DIOGENES**
Sir Max BEERBOHM
1872–1956
British essayist and caricaturist.
He used this pen-name for a letter
to *The Carthusian* (1886)
**DION**
Dion DI MUCCI
1940–
American pop singer
**DIOTIMA and AMANDA**
Esme WYNN-TYSON
1898–
British author
**Dick DISTICH**
Alexander POPE
1688–1744
English poet
**Richard DIX**
Ernest BRIMMER
1894–1949
American actor
**DIZZY SAL**
Edward SALDANHA
1934–
American jazz musician
**DJANIRA**
Djanira PAIVA
1914–
Brazilian painter
**Q. K. Philander DOESTICKS**
Mortimer THOMPSON
1831–1875
American author and humorist
**Barnaby DOGBOLT**
Herbert SILVETTE
1907–
American author

**Silence DOGWOOD**
Benjamin FRANKLIN
1706–1790
American statesman, scientist,
philosopher and author. Used this
pseudonym for his 'Dogwood
Papers' in the *New England
Courant* in 1722
**Alexander DOHLBERG**
David BURG
1933–
British author
**Anton DOLIN**
Patrick HEALEY-KAY
1904–
British ballet dancer and choreo-
grapher. Changed his name in
1923 to Anton, which he borrowed
from a character in a Chekhov
play, and Dolin which was
suggested by a fellow student
**Marcus J. DOLLEY**
Bernard WATNEY
1922–
British author
**Kwesi DOMPO**
Frank PARKES
1932–
Ghanaian writer
**Troy DONAHUE**
Merle JOHNSON
1936–
American actor
**Vivian DONALD**
Charles McKINNON
1924–
British author
**DONATELLO**
Donato di Betto BARDI
*c.* 1385–1466
Italian painter and sculptor
**DONOVAN**
Donovan LEITCH
1943–
British pop singer
**DON QUIXOTE, Jr.**
James TYTLER
1747–1804
American author

**Dolores DORN**
Dolores DORN-HEFT
1935–
American actress
**Philip DORN**
Fritz VAN DUNGEN
1905–
Dutch actor. He was in Hollywood during the forties
**Marie DORO**
Marie STEWART
1882–1956
American actress, in silent films
**Diana DORS**
Diana FLUCK
1931–
British actress
**Gabrielle DORZIAT**
Gabrielle MOPPERT
1880–
French actress
**Donald DOUGLAS**
Donald KINLEYSIDE
1905–1945
American actor
**Kirk DOUGLAS**
Issur Danielovitch DEMSKY
1916–
American film star. Born in New York to Russian-Jewish parents, he won a scholarship to the American Academy of Dramatic Arts in 1940. In 1941 he decided that his name was not likely to help his career so chose Douglas, because of his admiration for Douglas Fairbanks Jr., and Kirk because it sounded 'snazzy'
**Melvyn DOUGLAS**
Melvyn HESSELBERG
1901–
American actor
**Mike DOUGLAS**
Michael Delaney DOWD, Jr.
c. 1923–
American television personality
**Robert DOUGLAS**
Robert Douglas FINLAYSON
1909–

British actor, who acted in Hollywood from 1947
**Shane DOUGLAS**
Richard WILKES-HUNTER
1906–
Australian author
**Kent DOUGLASS**
Robert D. MONTGOMERY
1908–
American actor
**Billie DOVE**
Lilian BOHNY
1900–
American actress of the twenties
**Peggy DOW**
Peggy VARNADOW
1928–
American actress
**Eddie DOWLING**
Joseph GOUCHER
1894–
American theatrical producer. He used his mother's maiden name as his stage name
**J. DOWNING**
Charles Augustus DAVIS
1795–1867
American author
**John DOYLE**
Robert GRAVES
1895–
British poet and novelist
**Lynn DOYLE**
Leslie A. MONTGOMERY
1837–1935
Irish author
**Alfred DRAKE**
Alfredo CAPURRO
1914–
American singer and dancer
**Charles DRAKE**
Charles RUPPERT
1914–
American actor
**Charlie DRAKE**
Charles SPRINGALL
1925–
British comedian

**Dona DRAKE**
Rita NOVELLA
1920–
Mexican singer and dancer

**Fabia DRAKE**
Fabia Drake McGLINCHY
1904–
British stage and screen character actress

**Tom DRAKE**
Alfred ALDERDICE
1919–
American actor

**M. B. DRAPIER**
Jonathan SWIFT
1667–1745
Irish writer and satirist. He wrote *A Letter to the People of Ireland* (1724) under this pseudonym

**George DRAYNE**
Johnston McCULLEY
1883–
Canadian author and playwright

**Alfred DRAYTON**
Alfred VARICK
1881–1949
British actor

**Lillian R. DRAYTON**
John Russell CORYELL
1852–1924
American dime novelist

**Sonia DRESDEL**
Lois OBEE
1909–1976
British actress

**Louise DRESSER**
Louise KERLIN
1881–1965
American character actress of the thirties

**Marie DRESSLER**
Lelia VON KOERBER
1869–1934
American actress and comedienne

**Ellen DREW**
Terry RAY
1915–
American actress

**Mary DREWERY**
Mary SMITH
1918–
British author

**Edward DRIVER**
Brian GRITT
1938–
British author

**DROCH**
Robert BRIDGES
1858–1941
American poet

**Joanne DRU**
Joanne LA COCK
1923–
American actress. She called herself Joanne Marshall during her brief stage career, then she was discovered by Howard Hawks, the film director, who said she needed a new name. She chose Dru after a Welsh ancestor

**Ivor DRUMMOND**
Roger LONGRIGG
1929–
British author

**The Rev. Dr. DRYASDUST**
Sir Walter SCOTT
1771–1832
Scottish poet and novelist

**Bide DUDLEY**
Walter DUDLEY
1877–1944
American drama critic and playwright

**Nancy DUDLEY**
Lois Dwight COLE
*c.* 1910–
American author

**Pete DUEL**
Peter DEUEL
1940–1971
American actor

**Eileen-Marie DUELL**
Rhonda PETRIE
1922–
British author

**Dionysius DUGGAN**
William MAGINN

1794–1842
Irish journalist
**Georges DUHAMEL**
Denis THEVENIN
1884–1966
French writer
**Philip DUKES**
Richard BICKERS
1917–
British author
**Germaine DULAC**
Germaine
SAISSET-SCHNEIDER
1882–1942
French film director of silent films
**Steffi DUNA**
Stephanie BERINDEY
1913–
Hungarian-American actress and
dancer
**Duke DUNCAN**
St. George Henry RATHBONE
1854–1928
American writer of dime novels
and boys' books
**Walter B. DUNLAP**
Sylvanus COBB
1821–1877
American writer of adventure
stories
**Michael DUNN**
Gary MILLER
1935–1973
American dwarf actor
**Desmond DUNNE**
James LEE-RICHARDSON
1913–
British author
**Deanna DURBIN**

Edna Mae DURBIN
1921–
Canadian singer, was in Holly-
wood during the late thirties. Her
name was changed to Deanna by
MGM in 1935
**Junior DURKIN**
Trent DURKIN
1915–1935
American actor
**George DURYEA**
Tom KEENE
1896–
American actor
**Charles DUSTIN**
John GIESY
1877–1947
American novelist
**Ann DVORAK**
Ann McKIM
1912–
American actress. She used her
mother's maiden name as a stage
name
**Allan DWIGHT**
Lois Dwight COLE
c. 1910–
American author
**Jack DYKES**
Jack OWEN
1929–
British author
**Bob DYLAN**
Robert ZIMMERMAN
1941–
American singer, poet and com-
poser. He officially changed his
name to Bob Dylan on 9 August
1962 in honour of Dylan Thomas

# E

Ronald EADIE
Duncan GLEN
1933–
British author

John Prescott EARL
Beth GILCHRIST
1879–1957
American author, who wrote stories for boys under this pseudonym

W. J. EARLE
Luis Philip SENARENS
1863–1939
American dime novelist

Hargis EARLYWINE
Clark KINNAIRD
1901–
American author

Packey EAST
Leslie Townes HOPE
1903–
American comedian. This pseudonym was used during a short-lived boxing career

Charles EASTMAN
OHIYESA
1851–1939
American Sioux Indian physician and author

Leone EBREO
Judah ABRAVANEL
1460–1525
Jewish philosopher

Buddy EBSEN
Christian EBSEN
1908–
American actor-dancer of the thirties

Billy ECKSTINE
William ECKSTEIN
1914–
American singer

EDAX
Charles LAMB
1775–1834
English essayist

Barbara EDEN
Barbara HUFFMAN
1934–
American actress

Icarus Walter EDGAR
Stanley BISHOP
1906–
British writer on pigeon racing

Josephine EDGAR
Mary MUSSI
1907–
British author

Charles EDMONDS
Charles Edmund CARRINGTON
1897–
British author

Stephen EDWARD
Simon S. PALESTRANT
1907–
American author

Vince EDWARD
Vincent Edward ZORRIO
1928–
American film actor

Agnes EDWARDS
Agnes ROTHERY
1888–1954
American author

Bertram EDWARDS
Herbert C. EDWARDS
1912–
British author

Blake EDWARDS
William Blake McEDWARDS
1922–
American film director

John Milton EDWARDS
William COOK
1867–1933
American author. He wrote *The Fiction Factory* (1912) under this pen-name

Julia EDWARDS
John Russell CORYELL
1852–1924
American dime novelist

**Leonard EDWARDS**
Reginald WILD
1912–
British writer
**Lesley EGAN**
Elizabeth LININGTON
1921–
American author
**Denise EGERTON**
Denise DUGGAN
1930–
British author
**Florence ELDRIDGE**
Florence McKECHNIE
1901–
American stage and film actress
**ELIA**
Charles LAMB
1775–1834
English essayist, poet and letter writer. He wrote essays signed Elia for the *London Magazine* (1820–23), these were later collected and published as the *Essays of Elia* (1823)
**ELIN PELIN**
Dimitar IVANOV
1878–1949
Bulgarian writer
**George ELIOT**
Mary Ann EVANS
1819–1880
English novelist. She took George from George Henry Lewes, a literary editor with whom she was living. Eliot has no special significance
**Filinto ELISIO**
Padre Manuel DO NASCIMENTO
1734–1819
Portuguese poet
**ELIZABETH**
Mary Annette BEAUCHAMP
1866–1941
British novelist. Her best known book is *Elizabeth and her German Garden* (1898)
**Duke ELLINGTON**
Edward Kennedy ELLINGTON
1899–1974
American jazz musician and composer. Acquired the nickname Duke in high school because of his smart appearance
**Don ELLIOTT**
Don HELFMAN
1926–
American jazz musician
**Wild Bill ELLIOTT**
Gordon ELLIOTT
1906–1965
American film actor
**Mary ELLIS**
Mary ELSAS
1900–
American actress and singer
**Patricia ELLIS**
Patricia O'BRIEN
1916–1970
American film actress, popular in the thirties
**James ELLISON**
James Ellison SMITH
1910–
American film actor
**Ziggy ELMAN**
Harry FINKLEMAN
1914–1968
American jazz musician
**ELMWOOD**
James Russell LOWELL
1819–1891
American diplomat and poet
**Francis ELPHINSTONE**
Vincent POWELL-SMITH
1939–
British author
**Isobel ELSOM**
Isobel REED
1893–
British stage and film actress
**Willem ELSSCHOT**
Alfons DE RIDER
1882–1960
Belgian novelist
**John ELSWORTH**
John Salkeld TETLEY

1901–
British writer
**Julian ELTINGE**
William DALTON
1883–1941
American female impersonator in silent films
**Paul ÉLUARD**
Eugène GRINDAL
1895–1952
French surrealist poet
**Maurice ELVEY**
William FOLKARD
1887–1967
British film director
**Odysseus ELYTIS**
Odysseus ALEPOUDELIS
1912–
Greek poet
**Gilbert EMERY**
Gilbert Emery Bensley POTTLE
1875–1945
British actor, in Hollywood from the early thirties
**An EMINENT HAND**
Alexander POPE
1688–1744
English poet
**EMIN PASHA**
Eduard SCHNITZER
1840–1892
German doctor and explorer who explored the Nile. He replaced Gordon as Governor of Equatoria (Sudan)
**Clare EMSLEY**
Clare PLUMMER
1912–
British author
**An ENEMY OF THE PEACE**
Jonathan SWIFT
1667–1745
Irish writer and satirist
**Norman ENGLAND**
Godfrey WEBB
1914–
British author
**Goliah ENGLISH**
John BOYLE

(Earl of Cork and of Orrery)
1707–1762
Irish writer
**Mark EPERNAY**
John Kenneth GALBRAITH
1908–
Canadian economist. Mark was chosen in honour of Mark Twain and Epernay taken from the champagne. He wrote *The McLandress Dimension* (1964)
**Thomas ERASTUS**
Thomas LIEBER
1524–1583
Swiss physician and theologian
**Victor EREMITA**
Sören KIERKEGAARD
1813–1855
Danish philosopher and theologian
**Lief ERICKSON**
William ANDERSON
1911–
American film actor
**Walter ERIKSON**
Howard FAST
1914–
American novelist
**John ERICSON**
Joseph MEIBES
1927–
American actor, born in Germany
**Will ERMINE**
Harry Sinclair DRAGO
1888–
American writer of cowboy stories
**Rosalind ERSKINE**
Roger LONGRIGG
1929–
British author
**Levi ESHKOL**
Levi SHKOLNIK
1895–1969
Russian-born Israeli statesman. When he emigrated to Palestine in 1923 he hebraicized his family name to Eshkol (meaning 'cluster of grapes'). Succeeded Ben-Gurion as Prime Minister in 1963

**Aurora ESMERALDA**
Ella MIGHELS
1853–1934
American author
**Carl ESMOND**
Willy EICHBERGER
1905–
Austrian actor, in international films
**Henry ESMOND, Esq.**
William Makepeace THACKERAY
1811–1863
British author
**Dr. ESPERANTO**
Lazar Ludwik ZAMENHOF
1859–1917
Polish oculist and philologist who devised the artificial language Esperanto
**David ESSEX**
David COOK
1945–
British actor and singer
**Frank ESSEX**
Mike SIMMONDS
1934–
British author
**Jon ESSEX**
Joel WATFORD
1906–
British author
**Tom ESTERBROOK**
Lafayette Ronald HUBBARD
1911–
American writer and founder of Scientology. He used this penname for articles on Scientology
**John ESTEVEN**
Samuel SHELLABARGER
1888–1954
American educator and author of mystery stories
**Robert ETON**
Lawrence MEYNELL
1899–
British author
**ETONIAN**
William Ewart GLADSTONE

1809–1898
British statesman
**Dale EVANS**
Frances Octavia SMITH
1912–
American actress and singer
**Gil EVANS**
Ian GREEN
1912–
Canadian jazz composer
**Humphrey ap EVANS**
Humphrey DRUMMOND
1922–
British author
**Joan EVANS**
Joan EUNSON
1934–
American actress who played teenage roles in the early fifties
**Judith EVELYN**
J. E. ALLEN
1913–1967
American stage actress
**Kenny EVERETT**
Maurice COLE
1943–
British disc-jockey
**Wade EVERETT**
Will COOK
1921–
American author
**Anthony EVERGREEN**
Washington IRVING
1783–1859
American short story writer and historian
**Tom EWELL**
S. Yewell TOMPKINS
1909–
American comic actor
**An EYE-WITNESS**
Charles LAMB
1775–1834
English essayist
**An EYE-WITNESS**
Alexander POPE
1688–1744
English poet

# F

**F.P.A.**
Franklin P. ADAMS
1881–1960
American journalist and poet
**FABIAN**
Fabian FORTE
1942–
American pop singer
**Nanette FABRAY**
Nanette FABARES
1922–
American comedy actress and singer
**A. A. FAIR**
Erle Stanley GARDNER
1889–1970
American writer of detective stories
**Douglas FAIRBANKS**
Douglas Elton Thomas ULMAN
1883–1939
American star of the silent screen. He was the son of Hezakiah Charles Ulman and Ella Adelaide Marsh. When his parents divorced in 1884 his mother resumed the name of her first husband, John Fairbanks, which her son subsequently used and, in 1900, took legally
**Clarence FAIRCHILD**
Edwin Ross CHAMPLIN
1854–1928
American editor and poet
**L. FAIRFAX**
Celia Logan CONNELLY
1837–1904
American journalist and novelist
**Michael FAIRLESS**
Margaret Fairless BARBER
1869–1901
British mystic, who wrote *The Roadmender* (1902), a devotional work
**Oliver FAIRPLAY**
Thomas JEFFERSON

1743–1826
American statesman and president (1809–1813)
**Adam FAITH**
Terence NELHAMS
1940–
British pop singer
**Jinx FALKENBURG**
Eugenia FALKENBURG
1919–
American actress
**Hans FALLADA**
Rudolf DITZEN
1893–1947
German writer
**Georgie FAME**
Clive POWELL
1942–
British pop singer
**Alison FARELY**
Dorothy POLAND
1937–
British author
**Chris FARLOWE**
John DEIGHTON
1940–
British pop singer
**Ella FARMAN**
Eliza PRATT
1837–1907
American author
**Martha FARQUHARSON**
Martha FINLEY
1826–1909
American author
**Suzanne FARRELL**
Roberta FICKER
1945–
American ballerina
**FATHER ABRAHAM**
Benjamin FRANKLIN
1706–1790
American philosopher, scientist and statesman
**George FATTY**
Franz PRESSLER

1927–
Austrian jazz clarinettist

**Catherine FAWCETT**
Catherine COOKSON
1906–
British author

**Guy FAWKES**
Robert BENCHLEY
1889–1945
American humorist

**Alice FAYE**
Alice LEPPERT
1912–
American actress, popular during the thirties

**Irving FAZOLA**
Irving PRESTOPNIK
1912–1949
American jazz clarinettist. His name derives from three notes of the tonic-sol-fa: FA-SOH-LA

**FEAR CHANAIDH**
John Lorne CAMPBELL
1906–
Scottish author

**FEARDANA**
Robert Dwyer JOYCE
1836–1883
Irish poet and physician

**Stepin FECHIT**
Lincoln PERRY
1898–
American negro comedian

**Feike FEIKEMA**
Frederick Feike MANFRED
1912–
American novelist

**Charles K. FELDMAN**
Charles GOULD
1904–1968
American film producer

**Shane FENTON**
Bernard JEWRY
1943–
British pop singer. He changed his name again in 1972, to Alvin Stardust

**Peter FENWICK**
Peter Fenwick HOLMES

1932–
British author

**FERNANDEL**
Fernand CONTANDIN
1903–1971
French comic actor. This name was given to him by his mother-in-law who always referred to him as her daughter's Fernand, or *Fernand d'elle*

**Gul FERRAR**
William J. T. SMITH
1920–
British author

**FERREX**
Ezra POUND
1885–1972
American poet. He used this pen-name for a magazine article in 1914

**Tom FERRIS**
Peter WALKER
1936–
British author

**Gabriele FERZETTI**
Pasquale FERZETTI
1925–
Italian actor

**Edwige FEUILLÈRE**
Edwige CUNATI
1907–
French actress, a leading member of the Comédie Française

**Jacques FEYDER**
Jacques FRÉDÉRIX
1888–1948
French film director

**Padraic FIAAC**
Patrick J. O'CONNOR
1924–
Irish author

**Ferdinando FIDGET**
Alexander CHALMERS
1759–1835
Scottish author

**Virginia FIELD**
Margaret FIELD
1917–

British actress, second lead of Hollywood films in the forties

**Gabriel FIELDING**
Alan Gabriel BARNSLEY
1916–
British novelist

**Henry FIELDING**
William Henry IRELAND
1777–1835
English literary forger

**Jerry FIELDING**
Gerald FELDMAN
1922–
American jazz musician and composer

**Gracie FIELDS**
Grace STANSFIELD
1898–
English singer and comedienne. Her name was shortened by her mother on the advice of a theatrical agent, who said the name Stansfield was too long to appear in large letters on a theatre

**Stanley FIELDS**
Walter L. AGNEW
1884–1941
American character actor, former prizefighter and vaudevillian

**W. C. FIELDS**
William Claude DUKINFIELD
1879–1946
American comedian. His parents addressed their son as Claude, a name he detested all his life; the villains in his films were often called Claude. Started his career as a boy juggler in 1891. At first he called himself 'Whitey, the Wonder Boy' and his first performance as W. C. Fields was at Fortescue's Pier, Atlantic City in 1893

**FIGARO**
Henry CLAPP
1814–1875
American journalist

**FILIA**
Sarah DORSEY

1829–1879
American author

**Matthew FINCH**
Merton FINK
1921–
British author

**Peter FINCH**
Peter INGLE-FINCH
1916–1977
British actor

**Paddy FINUCANE**
Brendan FINUCANE
1920–1942
British fighter pilot in World War II

**FIRDAUSI**
ABÚ-'L KÁSIM MANSÚR
c. A.D. 940–c. 1020
Persian poet. He wrote the *Shah Náma*, the Book of Kings

**Clay FISHER**
Henry ALLEN
1912–
American author

**Cyrus FISHER**
Darwin TEILHET
1904–
American author

**Arnold FISHKIN**
Arnold FISHKIND
1919–
American jazz bass player

**Ensign Clarke FITCH, U.S.N.**
Upton SINCLAIR
1878–1968
American novelist. While still a teenager, he wrote about two million words a year of juvenile pulp fiction, using many pseudonyms. *Cliff Faraday in Command, or, the Fight of His Life* (1897) was written under this one

**Adam FITZADAM**
Philip Dormer Stanhope, Earl of CHESTERFIELD
1694–1773
English statesman and writer

**Roger FITZALAN**
Elleston TREVOR

1920–
British author

**George Savage FITZBOODLE, Esq.**
William Makepeace
THACKERAY
1811–1863
British author

**Barry FITZGERALD**
William SHIELDS
1888–1961
Irish actor, who acted in Hollywood from 1936. From 1906 to 1926 he played the dual role of civil servant by day and actor by night, and adopted the name Barry Fitzgerald for fear of losing his civil service job

**Walter FITZGERALD**
Walter BOND
1896–
British character actor on both stage and screen

**FITZNOODLE**
Benjamin VALLENTINE
1843–1926
American author. He wrote for *Puck*, a comic magazine, under this pen-name (1877–1884)

**Blaise FITZTRAVESTY**
William MAGINN
1794–1842
Irish journalist

**John FITZVICTOR**
Percy Bysshe SHELLEY
1792–1822
English poet

**Reginald FITZWORM**
John BOYLE
(Earl of Cork and of Orrery)
1707–1762
Irish writer

**Paul FIX**
Paul Fix MORRISON
1902–
American film actor

**Viktor FLAMBEAU**
Gertrude BRIGHAM

*c.* 1890–
American writer

**Bud FLANAGAN**
Chaim Reuben WEINTROP
1896–1968
English music hall comedian, part of the comedy-singing team, Flanagan and Allen. He changed his name to Flanagan to revenge himself upon an Irish Sergeant-major with anti-semetic views, whom he had met during the 1914–1918 war. He intended to make sure that the name would always be ridiculed. Ironically, his first break in show business was given to him by Florrie Forde, whose original name was Flanagan

**Marty FLAX**
Martin FLACHSENHARR
1924–
American jazz saxophonist

**George FLEMING**
Julia FLETCHER
1858–1939
American novelist

**Geraldine FLEMING**
John Russell CORYELL
1852–1924
American dime novelist

**Rhonda FLEMING**
Marilyn LOUIS
1922–
American film actress, popular during the forties and fifties

**FLIMNAP, the Lilliputian Premier**
Sir Robert WALPOLE
1676–1745
English statesman

**FLORIO**
James G. BROOKS
1808–1841
American poet

**Julius FLORUS**
William PITT
1759–1806
English statesman. Before reporters were authorised to publish

the proceedings of Parliament, Pitt reported as Julius Florus

**FLOTSAM**
B. C. HILLIAM
1890–1968
English singer; one half of the comic song duo, Flotsam and Jetsam, popular in the 1930s

**FLYING OFFICER X**
H. E. BATES
1905–1973
English short-story writer and novelist. During the Second World War he was a Squadron-Leader in the R.A.F. and wrote stories of service life under this pseudonym

**Joan FONTAINE**
Joan DE HAVILLAND
1917–
American actress, born in Japan of British parentage, and sister of Olivia de Havilland. She acted bit parts in films under the names Joan Burford and Joan St. John before settling, in 1937, on the name Joan Fontaine, after her stepfather, George M. Fontaine

**Margot FONTEYN**
Margaret HOOKHAM
1919–
English ballerina. Margot is derived from Margaret and Fonteyn from her (Brazilian) mother's maiden name Fontes

**Dick FORAN**
Nicholas FORAN
1910–
American film actor who played leading parts in light comedies and westerns in the early forties

**Aleck FORBES**
St. George Henry RATHBONE
1854–1928
American writer of dime novels and boys' books

**Bryan FORBES**
John CLARKE
1926–
British actor, scriptwriter and film director

**Kathryn FORBES**
Kathryn ANDERSON
1909–
American author. She took the surname of her paternal grandmother

**Meriel FORBES**
Merial FORBES-ROBERTSON
1913–
British stage actress

**Ford Madox FORD**
Ford Madox HUEFFER
1873–1939
English writer. Changed his name by deed poll in 1919. The possession of a German surname had been embarrassing during the war and he had suffered because of it.

**Francis FORD**
Francis O'FEENEY
1883–1953
American actor. Brother of film director, John Ford

**Gerald FORD**
Leslie KING, Jr.
1913–
American politician. He became President of the United States on the retirement of Richard M. Nixon on 9 August 1974. When he was an infant his parents were divorced. His mother later married Gerald Ford, Sr., who adopted the boy and gave him his name

**Glenn FORD**
Gwyllyn FORD
1916–
Canadian-born film star of Hollywood dramas

**John FORD**
Sean O'FEENEY
1895–1973
American film director. He went to Hollywood in 1914 and started as a property man at Universal City under the name John Ford

**Leslie FORD**
Zenith J. BROWN
1898–
American novelist

**Mary FORD**
Colleen SUMMERS
1924–
American singer and guitarist who worked with Les Paul during the fifties

**Wallace FORD**
Sam GRUNDY
1897–1966
British actor who went to Hollywood in the early thirties

**Florrie FORDE**
Florence FLANAGAN
1876–1940
Australian singer; toured British music halls

**Nicholas FORDE**
Arthur ELLIOTT-CANNON
1919–
British author

**Walter FORDE**
Thomas SEYMOUR
1896–
British film director of the thirties and forties

**Mark FOREST**
Lou DEGNI
1933–
American actor and gymnast

**Frank FORESTER**
Henry W. HERBERT
1807–1858
American novelist

**Felix C. FORREST**
Paul LINEBARGER
1913–
American author

**Sally FORREST**
Katherine FEENEY
1928–
American film actress who played leading parts in the early fifties

**Steve FORREST**
William Forrest ANDREWS
1924–
American actor, brother of Dana Andrews

**Mary FORRESTER**
Elsie HUMPHRIES
1905–
British author

**John FORSYTHE**
John FREUND
1918–
American stage and film actor

**Robert FORSYTHE**
Kyle Samuel CRICHTON
1896–1960
American author

**Alfred FOSSE**
Oliver JELLY
1909–
British author

**Dianne FOSTER**
Dianne LARUSKA
1928–
Canadian actress who had made British and American films

**Fanny FOSTER**
Emily JUDSON
1817–1854
American author

**George FOSTER**
Major Jock HASWELL
1919–
British author

**Norman FOSTER**
Norman HOEFFER
1900–1976
American film actor and director

**Susanna FOSTER**
Suzan LARSEN
1924–
American actress and operatic singer

**Larry FOTINE**
Lawrence FOTINAKIS
1911–
American jazz pianist

**FOUGASSE**
Cyril Kenneth BIRD
1887–
British cartoonist; was editor of *Punch* 1949–53

**Gene FOWLER**
Gene DEVLAN
1890–
American journalist. He adopted the name of his mother's second husband, Frank Fowler

**David FOX**
Isabel OSTRANDER
1885–1924
American novelist

**Petronella FOX**
Penelope BALOGH
1916–
British writer on psychiatric subjects

**William FOX**
William FRIEDMAN
1879–1952
Hungarian-American movie mogul, the Fox of 20th Century Fox

**Redd FOXX**
James Elroy SANFORD
1922–
American TV comedian. In 1940, when he was known by the nickname Chicago Red, he altered his name by adding an extra 'd' and Foxx, in honour of the baseball player, Jimmy Foxx

**FRA DIAVOLO**
Michele PEZZA
1771–1806
Italian brigand

**Anatole FRANCE**
Anatole François THIBAULT
1844–1924
French writer

**Anthony FRANCIOSA**
Anthony PAPALEO
1928–
Italian-American actor. He was given his mother's maiden name after the separation of his parents in 1929

**Arlene FRANCIS**
Arline KAZANJIAN
1908–
American television personality and film actress

**C. D. E. FRANCIS**
Patrick HOWARTH
1916–
British author

**Connie FRANCIS**
Concetta FRANCONERA
1938–
American pop singer. She used her stage name for the first time on Arthur Godfrey's *Talent Scouts* show in 1950

**Kay FRANCIS**
Katherine GIBBS
1899–1968
American film actress popular in the thirties

**Harry FRANCO**
Charles F. BRIGGS
1804–1877
American author

**Rose FRANKEN**
Mrs. W. B. MELONEY
1898–
American author

**Charles FRANKLIN**
Frank USHER
1896–
British author

**Jay FRANKLIN**
John F. CARTER
1897–
American author

**Alex FRASER**
Henry BRINTON
1901–
British author

**Jane FRASER**
Rosamunde PILCHER
1924–
British author

**Pisanus FRAXI**
Henry Spencer ASHBEE
c. 1840–1900
British author. Reputed to be the author of the erotic *My Secret Life*

**Jane FRAZEE**
Mary Jane FRAHSE
1918–
American singer and actress of
the forties
**Dr. Frank FREDERICKS**
Dr. Frederick SIGFRED
1909–
American author
**Edmund FREEBETTER**
Nathan DABOLL
1750–1818
American almanac maker. He
published the *New England Alman-*
*ack* from 1776–92 under this
pen-name
**Arthur FREED**
Arthur GROSSMAN
1894–1973
American songwriter and film
producer
**Mona FREEMAN**
Monica FREEMAN
1926–
American film actress
**Paul FRENCH**
Isaac ASIMOV
1920–
American science fiction writer
who was born in Russia and
went to the U.S.A. in 1923. He
used this pen-name for juvenile
science fiction
**Jack FRENCHMAN**
Jonathan SWIFT
1667–1745
Irish writer and satirist
**Pierre FRESNAY**
Pierre Jules LAUDENBACH
1897–1974
French actor and director
**Austin FRIARS**
Frederick DANIELS
1908–
British author
**T. FRIBBLE**
Jonathan SWIFT
1667–1745
Irish writer and satirist

**Fred W. FRIENDLY**
Fred WACHENHEIMER
1915–
American television producer. He
adopted his mother's maiden
name as a pseudonym
**David FROME**
Zenith J. BROWN
1898–
American novelist
**Harold FROY**
Guy DEGHY
1912–
British author
**Derek FRYE**
Carl FOREMAN
1914–
American writer-producer-director
Carl Foreman was blacklisted by
the Hollywood studios after the
McCarthy witch-hunt. Since then
he has worked in Britain and this
is the pseudonym he used in 1954
when making the film *The Silver*
*Tiger*
**Sonia FUCHS**
Sonia SEEDO
1906–
British author
**Blind Boy FULLER**
Fuller ALLEN
1903–1940
American blues singer
**Jerry FULLER**
Eric NELSON
1940–
American pop singer. He used this
name early in his career, then
changed to Ricky Nelson under
which name he became famous.
In 1969 he dropped the 'y'
becoming Rick Nelson
**Joseph FUME**
William Andrew CHATTO
1800–1864
British author
**Rigdum FUNNIDUS**
Horace and Henry MAYHEW
and Robert BROUGH

1816–1872; 1812–1887; 1828–1860
British editors of Cruikshank's
*Comic Almanac*
**Ronald FURMINGER**
Ronald BIGGS
1930–
English criminal, one of the
Great Train Robbers. Biggs used
this alias when on the run in
Australia in 1974
**Betty FURNESS**
Betty CHOATE
1916–

American television personality
**Billy FURY**
Ronald WYCHERLEY
1941–
English pop singer. He was
discovered in 1959 by the pro-
moter, Larry Parnes, who changed
his name
**T. I. FYTTON-ARMSTRONG**
John GAWSWORTH
1912–
British author

# G

**Percival G**
Peter IRVING
1771–1838
American author; brother of
Washington Irving. He wrote
*Giovanni Sbogarro: A Venetian
Tale* (1820)
**Franceska GAAL**
Fanny ZILVERITCH
1909–
Hungarian actress who played in
Hollywood in the thirties
**Gridiron GABBLE, Gent., Godson
to Mother Goose**
Joseph HASLEWOOD
1759–1833
English editor
**Clarke GABEL**
Clark GABLE
1901–1960
American film actor. He used his
pseudonym for a short period at
the beginning of his career before
reverting to his real name
**Jean GABIN**
Alexis MONCOURGE
1904–1976
French actor. Starred in *La
Grande Illusion* (1937) and *Le Jour
Se Lève* (1939)

**Zsa Zsa GABOR**
Sari GABOR
1919–
Hungarian-born Hollywood actress
**GAKI**
AKUTAGAWA RYUNOSUKE
1892–1927
Japanese writer. His story *Rasho-
mon* (1915) was made into a film
in 1951
**Skeets GALLAGHER**
Richard GALLAGHER
1891–1955
American vaudeville star
**Amelita GALLI-CURCI**
Amelita GALLI
1889–1963
Italian coloratura soprano
**GANCONAGH**
W. B. YEATS
1865–1939
Irish poet and dramatist
**Sir Gregory GANDER, Kt.**
George ELLIS
1753–1815
English satirist and poet
**Greta GARBO**
Greta GUSTAFSON
1905–
Swedish actress, went to Holly-

wood in 1926. As the name Gustafson filled several pages of the Stockholm telephone directory, her director Mauritz Stiller decided that something more unusual was required for his protégée. After a short spell as Mona Gabor, she finally became Greta Garbo in November 1923. Among those who have been credited with choosing her name are: Stiller, his scriptwriter, the vicar who confirmed her, and her friend Mimi Pollak. The origin of the name is either Gabor, the Hungarian royal name, or Darbo, after Erica Darbo, a popular Norwegian operatta singer of the day

**John GARDEN**
Harry FLETCHER
1902–
British author

**John GARFIELD**
Julius GARFINKLE
1913–1952
American stage and screen actor

**Ralph GARI**
Ralph GAROFALO
1927–
American jazz musician

**Beverly GARLAND**
Beverly FESSENDEN
1926–
American actress, leading lady in some Hollywood fifties films

**Judy GARLAND**
Frances GUMM
1922–1969
American singer and actress on stage and screen. On stage from the age of five. In 1931, George Jessel suggested that she should change her name to Garland, after his friend, Robert Garland, drama critic of the New York *World-Telegram*. In 1932 she changed her first name to Judy

because it sounded 'peppy'. She was in films from 1936

**James GARNER**
James BAUMGARNER
1928–
American film actor

**John GARY**
John Gary STRADER
1937–
American singer

**Romain GARY**
Romain KACEW
1926–
American writer

**Jane GASKELL**
Jane Gaskell DENVIL
1941–
British author

**Michael GAUNT**
James ROBERTSHAW
1911–
British author

**James GAVIN**
John GOLENOR
1928–
American film actor. His name was changed to Gavin by Universal International Studio, Hollywood

**Amelia GAY**
Grace HOGARTH
1905–
American author

**Mr. Joseph GAY**
Alexander POPE
1688–1744
English poet

**Glance GAYLORD**
Warren BRADLEY
1847–1868
American author

**Janet GAYNOR**
Laura GAINER
1906–
American actress; a Hollywood star of the 1930s

**Mitzi GAYNOR**
Francesca Mitzi VON GERBER
1930–

American singer, dancer and actress
**Eunice GAYSON**
Elizabeth GRAYSON
1933–
British actress
**Clara GAZUL**
Prosper MÉRIMÉE
1803–1870
French writer
**Will GEERLINK**
Pim HOFDORP
1912–
Dutch author
**GEMELLUS**
François Marie AROUET
1694–1778
French philosopher and writer better known as Voltaire
**GENET**
Janet FLANNER
1892–
American journalist
**A GENTLEMAN OF OXFORD**
Percy Bysshe SHELLEY
1792–1822
English poet
**A GENTLEMAN OF THE UNIVERSITY OF OXFORD**
Percy Bysshe SHELLEY
1792–1822
English poet. He wrote *St. Irvyne; or the Rosicrucian: A Romance* under this pseudonym
**GEOFFREY**
Madelyn PALMER
1910–
British author
**Theodate GEOFFREY**
Dorothy WAYMAN
1893–
American author
**David GEORGE**
David VOGENITZ
1930–
American author
**Gaston GEORGE**
Geoffrey OSTERGAARD
1926–

British author
**Jonathan GEORGE**
John F. BURKE
1922–
British author
**Manfred GEORGE**
Manfred GEORG
1893–
German author
**Sidney GEORGE**
Sammy GREENFIELD
1878–1945
American vaudeville comedian
**Uncle GEORGE**
Increase Niles TARBOX
1815–*c.* 1890
American clergyman and author
**Jim GERALD**
Jacques GUÉNOD
1889–1958
French stage and screen actor
**GERALDO**
Gerald BRIGHT
1904–1974
British bandleader
**Steve GERAY**
Stefan GYERGYAY
1904–
Hungarian character actor; acted in British and American films
**The GERMAN MILTON**
Friedrich Gottlieb KLOPSTOCK
1724–1803
German poet
**Gene GERRARD**
Eugene O'SULLIVAN
1892–1971
British music hall comedian
**Domenico GHIRLANDAIO**
Domenico BIGORDI
1449–1494
Florentine painter
**Lewis Grassic GIBBON**
James MITCHELL
1901–
British author
**Terry GIBBS**
Julius GUBENKO
1924–

American jazz musician; plays
vibes, piano and drums
**Helen GIBSON**
Rose WENGER
1892–1962
American actress of the silent era.
Married to Hoot Gibson
**Hoot GIBSON**
Edward GIBSON
1892–1962
American actor of silent screen;
played cowboy heroes. Married to
Helen Gibson
**Frank GIFFIN**
Ernest Frank CARTER
1899–
British writer on model railways
**Marinx GIJSEN**
Joannes GORIS
1899–
Flemish author
**John GILBERT**
John PRINGLE
1895–1936
American film actor
**Paul GILBERT**
Paul MacMAHON
1924–
American comic dancer and film
actor
**Great GILDERSLEEVE**
Hal PEARY
*c.* 1900–
American radio comedian of the
thirties and forties
**Ann GILLIS**
Alma O'CONNOR
1927–
American child film actress
**Virginia GILMORE**
Sherman POOLE
1919–
American film actress of the 1940s
**GIORGIONE**
Giorgio BARBARELLI
*c.* 1478–*c.* 1510
Venetian painter
**Dorothy GISH**
Dorothy DE GUICHE

1898–1968
American film star of the silent era
**Lillian GISH**
Lillian DE GUICHE
1896–
American film star of the silent era.
Sister of Dorothy Gish
**GLADIOLUS**
William Ewart GLADSTONE
1809–1898
British statesman
**Gary GLITTER**
Paul GADD
1935–
British pop singer. Formerly
known as Paul Raven a night-club
blues singer. In 1971, on the
advice of his manager, he decided
to change his whole image. This,
of course, included a change of
name – Paul Raven to Gary
Glitter (Glitter was a former
nickname). He also used the name
Paul Monday for one single
'Here Comes the Sun' (1967)
**Walker GLOCKENHAMMER**
H. G. WELLS
1866–1946
British writer. He used this pen-
name for 'Mammon' in *Science
Schools Journal* (1887)
**GNATHO**
Alexander POPE
1688–1744
English poet
**GOD**
Armand GODET
1832–1902
French draughtsman
**Paulette GODDARD**
Marion LEVY
1911–
American film actress
**Charles GODFREY**
Godfrey WEBB
1914–
British author
**Michael GOLD**
Irving GRANICH

1896–
American author
**Harry GOLDEN**
Harry GOLDENHURST
1902–
American publisher
**Don GOLDIE**
Don GOLDFIELD
1930–
American jazz musician
**Samuel GOLDWYN**
Samuel GELBFISCH
1882–1974
Polish-born American film producer. Arrived in America at the age of 13. Goldwyn is a combination of Goldfish, the immigration authorities' translation of his original Polish name, and Selwyn, the name of his two partners, Arch and Edgar, Broadway producers who formed Goldwyn Pictures Corporation with him in 1917. He legally changed his name from Goldfish to Goldwyn in 1919. In 1923, after his departure to set up his own company, Goldwyn Pictures Corporation tried, unsuccessfully to prevent him from using the name Goldwyn. The judge found in his favour, provided he added 'not connected with Goldwyn Pictures Corporation' in all public announcements. On granting permission to use the name the judge said 'a self-made man may prefer a self-made name'
**Will B. GOOD**
Roscoe 'Fatty' ARBUCKLE
1887–1933
American slapstick comedian whose career was ruined in 1921 by his involvement in a scandal in which a girl died. He afterwards directed films under this name and that of William Goodrich
**Le Docteur GOODHEART**
François Marie AROUET

1694–1778
French philosopher and writer better known as Voltaire
**William GOODRICH**
Roscoe 'Fatty' ARBUCKLE
1887–1933
American slapstick comedian whose career was ruined in 1921 by his involvement in a scandal in which a girl died. He afterwards directed films under this name and that of Will B. Good
**Godek GOODWILL**
Horace GREELEY
1811–1872
American editor and politician
**Alex GORDON**
Gordon COTLER
c. 1935–
American author
**Glenda GORDON**
Gwyneth G. BEADEL
1908–
British author
**Ian GORDON**
Ian FELLOWES-GORDON
1921–
British author
**Keith GORDON**
Gordon BAILEY
1936–
British journalist
**Ray GORDON**
Gordon WAINWRIGHT
1937–
British author
**Ruth GORDON**
Ruth Gordon JONES
1896–
American stage actress
**Maxim GORKY**
Aleksei Maksimovich PESHKOV
1868–1936
Russian writer
**Veronica GOSLING**
Veronica HENRIQUES
1931–
British author
**Jeremias GOTTHELF**

Albert BITZIUS
1797–1854
Swiss clergyman and writer
**Elliott GOULD**
Elliot GOLDSTEIN
1938–
American film actor. Began to appear on children's TV programmes in 1948 when his mother changed his name to Gould – she thought it sounded better
**Joseph GRACE**
John HORNBY
1913–
British author
**Charlie GRACIE**
Charles GRACI
1936–
American pop singer
**Lew GRADE**
Lewis WINOGRADSKY
1906–
Russian-born English impresario. His parents emigrated to England in 1911. Brother of Bernard Delfont
**A GRADUATE OF OXFORD**
John RUSKIN
1819–1900
English art critic and author
**Roderick GRAEME**
Roderick Graeme JEFFRIES
1926–
British author
**Gwethalyn GRAHAM**
Gwethalyn G. BROWN
c. 1920–
American novelist
**Johnston GRAHAM**
David SMITH
1899–
British author
**Kenny GRAHAM**
Kenneth SKINGLE
1924–
British jazz musician
**Sheilah GRAHAM**
Lily SHEIL
c. 1908–

British-born American journalist, Hollywood gossip columnist. She married Major John Graham Gillam in 1927. He encouraged her to go on the stage and after three months study at the Royal Academy of Dramatic Art she auditioned for a musical comedy under the stage name of Sheilah Graham. She went to Hollywood in the 1930s. Of her original name she has said 'the name Lily Sheil, to this day, horrifies me to a degree impossible to explain'
**Tom GRAHAM**
Sinclair LEWIS
1885–1951
American novelist. He used this pseudonym to write his first book *Hike and the Aeroplane* (1912), a boy's book about flying machines
**Virginia GRAHAM**
Virginia KOMISS
1913–
American radio and television personality
**Gloria GRAHAME**
Gloria HALLWARD
1924–
American film actress
**GRAMMATICUS**
Edward BLAIKLOCK
1903–
British author
**Peter GRANGE**
Christopher NICOLE
1930–
British author
**Stewart GRANGER**
James STEWART
1913–
British actor. He changed his name to avoid confusion with James Stewart
**Cary GRANT**
Archibald LEACH
1904–
English actor. He went to America in 1920 and acted on the New York

stage. In 1932 he went to Hollywood, where B. P. Schulberg of Paramount Pictures offered him a contract. When asked to change his name to something more suitable he chose Cary from his role in *Nikki* a musical comedy he had appeared in in New York, and Grant from a list of names suggested by the studio which wanted to build him up as a competitor to Gary Cooper

**Charles GRANT**
William LENCEL
1888–
American editor and writer

**Kathryn GRANT**
Katherine GRANDSTAFF
1933–
American film actress

**Kirby GRANT**
Kirby HORN
1914–
American film actor

**Lee GRANT**
Lyova ROSENTHAL
1929–
American stage and film actress

**Margaret GRANT**
John Russell CORYELL
1852–1924
American dime novelist

**Margaret GRANT**
William B. MELONEY
1903–
American author

**GRANTORTO**
D. H. LAWRENCE
1885–1930
British poet and novelist. He used this pen-name for 'Whistling of Birds' in the *Athenaeum* (1919). The editor, John Middleton Murry decided that it would be best to use a pseudonym because of Lawrence's reputation

**Peter GRAVES**
Peter AURNESS
1925–
American film actor; brother of James Arness (Aurness)

**Fernand GRAVET**
Fernand MARTENS
1904–1970
French actor

**Berry GRAY**
Robert B. COFFIN
1826–1886
American author

**Charles GRAY**
Donald GRAY
1928–
British stage, TV and film actor

**Colleen GRAY**
Doris JENSEN
1922–
American film actress

**Dulcie GRAY**
Dulcie BAILEY
1919–
British actress

**Gilda GRAY**
Marianna MICHALSKA
1901–1959
Polish-born American dancer. She invented the shimmy

**Glen GRAY**
Glen G. KNOBLAUGH
1906–1963
American jazz saxophone player

**Louise GRAY**
Naomi CHANDOR
1915–
British author

**Nadia GRAY**
Nadia KUJNIR-HERESCU
1923–
Russian-Rumanian actress who has acted in European and British films

**Sally GRAY**
Constance STEVENS
1916–
British film actress of the 1930s and 1940s

**David GRAYSON**
Ray S. BAKER
1870–1946
American biographer and essayist

**Eldred GRAYSON**
Robert HARE
1781–1858
American chemist and novelist

**Kathryn GRAYSON**
Zelma HEDRICK
1922–
American singer; in Hollywood from 1940

**The GREAT CHAM OF LITERATURE**
Dr. Samuel JOHNSON
1709–1784
English lexicographer, critic and poet

**The GREAT MAGICIAN**
Sir Walter SCOTT
1771–1832
Scottish poet and novelist

**The GREAT MAN**
William PITT
1708–1778
English statesman

**The GREAT MERLINI**
Clayton RAWSON
1906–
American author

**The GREAT UNKNOWN**
Sir Walter SCOTT
1771–1832
Scottish poet and novelist

**Richard GREAVES**
George Barr McCUTCHEON
1866–1928
American novelist. He wrote *Brewster's Millions* (1902) under this pseudonym

**Ronnie GREB**
Ronald GRABOWSKI
1938–
American jazz drummer

**El GRECO**
Domenikos THEOTOCOPOULOS
1541–1614
Spanish painter born in Crete

**Henry GREEN**
Henry YORKE

1905–1973
British author

**Mitzi GREEN**
Elizabeth KENO
1920–1969
American child film actress of the thirties

**Olive GREEN**
Myrtle REED
1874–1911
American author

**Gregory GREENDRAKE**
Joseph COAD
*c.* 1790–*c.* 1860
Irish journalist

**Lorne GREENE**
Lorne GREEN
1915–
Canadian character actor, who became famous as Ben Cartwright in the TV series *Bonanza* (1959–1969)

**Max GREENE**
Mutz GREENBAUM
1896–1968
German-born cinematographer. He worked mainly in Britain

**Grace GREENWOOD**
Sara LIPPENCOTT
1823–1904
American author

**Lady GREGORY**
Isabella Augusta PERSSE
1852–1932
Irish playwright

**Paul GREGORY**
Jason Gregory LENHART
1920–
American theatrical director

**Stephen GRENDON**
August DERLETH
1920–
American novelist

**Mr. GRESHAM**
William Ewart GLADSTONE
1809–1898
British statesman

**Joel GREY**
Joel KATZ

1932–
American-actor-singer-dancer
**Nan GREY**
Eschal MILLER
1918–
American film actress
**GREY OWL**
Archie BELANEY
1888–1938
An Englishman, born in Hastings, Belaney spent most of his life living with a tribe of Canadian Indians. He returned to England during the 1930s and passed himself off as a genuine Indian. He gave a successful lecture tour and was introduced to George V. His true identity was discovered only after his death
**Peter GRIEVOUS, Esq., A.B.C.D.E.**
Joseph HOPKINSON
1770–1842
American jurist
**Ethel GRIFFIES**
Ethel WOOD
1878–
English-born American character actress
**David GRIFFIN**
Robin MAUGHAM
1916–
British novelist
**Jack GRIFFITH**
Rev. Jack GRIFFITHS
1902–
British author
**GRIFFITHS**
Helen SANTOS
1939–
British author
**Dod GRILE**
Ambrose BIERCE
1842–1914
American author. He wrote *The Fiend's Delight* (1872) under this pen-name
**Giles GRINAGAIN**
William HOGARTH

1697–1764
English painter
**Juan GRIS**
José Victoriano GONZÁLEZ
1887–1927
Spanish cubist painter
**GROCK**
Karl Adrian WETTACH
1880–1959
Swiss clown. He changed his name in 1903 when he began working with a clown named Brick. They were billed as 'Brick and Grock'
**Anton GROT**
Antocz GROSZEWSKI
1884–
Polish film director; in Hollywood from 1920
**Albertus GROTUS**
Albertus MAGNUS
*c.* 1206–1280
Dominican teacher
**Victor GRUEN**
Victor GRUENBAUM
1903–
Austrian-born American architect. He shortened his name during the Second World War
**Anthony GRUMBLER, Esq. of Grumbleton Hall**
David HOFFMAN
1784–1852
American lawyer, Professor of Law at the University of Maryland
**Anastasius GRÜN**
Anton Alexander Graf von AUERSPERG
1806–1876
Austrian poet
**Matthias GRÜNEWALD**
Mathis GOTHARDT
*c.* 1480–1528
German painter
**Tobias GUARNERIUS**
Charles DIMITRY
1837–1910
American journalist

**Hilde GUEDEN**
Hilde GEIRINGER
1923–
Austrian opera singer
**Georges GUETARY**
Lambros WORLOOU
1915–
Greek/Egyptian singer popular in French cabaret and musical comedy
**Robert GUILLAUME**
Robert W. SNEDDON
1880–
Scottish author
**Slim GUITAR**
Eddie Jones
1926–
American jazz musician
**Lemuel GULLIVER**

Jonathan SWIFT
1667–1745
Irish author and satirist. His *Gulliver's Travels* appeared in 1726
**Sigrid GURIE**
Sigrid Gurie HAUKELID
1911–1969
American/Norwegian actress, in Hollywood during the 1940s
**Anne GWYNNE**
Marguerite Gwynne TRICE
1918–
American film actress; popular during the 1940s
**Greta GYNT**
Greta WOXHOLT
1916–
Norwegian actress; in British films during the forties

# H

**H. D.**
Hilda DOOLITTLE
1886–1961
American poet
**H. H.**
Helen Hunt JACKSON
1830–1885
American novelist and poet
**H. H.**
Sören KIERKEGAARD
1813–1855
Danish philosopher and theologian
**H.U.O.**
Henry Ustick ONDERDONK
1789–1858
American clergyman
**H***** W*****
Horace WALPOLE
1717–1797
English writer
**The Hon. Mr. H – – CE W – – LE**
Horace WALPOLE
1717–1797

English writer
**Achad HAAM**
Asher GINZBERG
1856–1927
Russian-born Jewish philosopher
**Hans HABE**
Jean BEKESSY
1911–
Hungarian author; in U.S.A. from 1940. In 1932, when working as a journalist in Vienna, he discovered and published Hitler's original family name, Schickelgrüber. 'My report was published in the middle of Hitler's campaign for election against Hindenberg, and thousands of copies were sent to Germany where it made the Nazis very angry. Afterwards, my editor and I were shot at in a Vienna cafe'
**Buddy HACKETT**
Leonard HACKER
1924–
American comedian and actor

**Peter HADDON**
Peter TILDSLEY
1898–1962
British actor

**Shafi HADI**
Curtis PORTER
1929–
American jazz musician

**Lelia HADLEY**
Mrs. Eliot-Burton SMITTER
1926–
American author

**Reed HADLEY**
Reed HERRING
1911–
American author

**HÁFIZ**
SHAMS ED-DÍN MUHAMMED
d. *c.* 1388
Persian poet

**Jean HAGEN**
Jean VERHAGEN
1924–
American film actress and comedienne

**Paul HAGGARD**
Stephen LONGSTREET
1907–
American author

**Sadik HAKIM**
Argonne THORNTON
1921–
American jazz musician

**Alan HALE**
Rufus Alan McKAHAN
1892–1950
American film actor; in Hollywood from 1911

**Binnie HALE**
Bernice Hale MONRO
1899–
British comedienne

**Creighton HALE**
Patrick FITZGERALD
1882–1965
American film actor, popular during the twenties

**Jonathan HALE**
Jonathan HATLEY
1892–1966
American character actor

**Sonnie HALE**
Robert Hale MONRO
1902–1959
British comedian, brother of Binnie Hale

**Joyce HALES**
Joyce COOMBS
1906–
British writer

**Adam HALL**
Elleston TREVOR
1920–
British author

**Holworthy HALL**
Harold PORTER
1867–1936
American author

**Huntz HALL**
Henry HALL
1920–
American film actor

**James HALL**
James BROWN
1900–1940
American film actor

**Jarvis HALL**
Helen F. BAGG
*c.* 1895–
American novelist and playwright

**Jon HALL**
Charles LOCHER
1913–
American film actor

**Patrick HALL**
Frederick HALL
1932–
British author

**Jay HALLAM**
Joan RICE
1919–
British author

**Brett HALLIDAY**
Davis DRESSER
1904–
American detective story writer. In his first novel the detective was named Halliday but the publisher

disliked it and had it changed to Burke. Later, after his first Michael Shayne novel had been accepted by another publisher (having been turned down by the first), he decided he needed a pen-name. For his surname he used Halliday and for his first name he chose Brett, the name of his original publisher who had rejected the name Halliday

**James HALLIDAY**
David SYMINGTON
1904–
British author

**Michael HALLIDAY**
John CREASEY
1908–1973
English writer. Creasey wrote 42 suspense stories under this pseudonym

**Harry HALYARD**
(unknown)
c. 1820–c. 1890
American novelist

**Avigdor HAMEIRI**
Emil FEURSTEIN
1886–
Hungarian Hebrew poet

**Betsy HAMILTON**
Idora MOORE
1843–1929
American author

**Julia HAMILTON**
Julia WATSON
1943–
British author

**Paul HAMILTON**
Harold DENNIS-JONES
1915–
British author

**Rufus HAMILTON**
Rufus Hamilton GILMORE
1879–1935
American novelist

**W. J. HAMILTON**
Charles CLARK
c. 1830–1892

American writer of adventure stories

**Hans HAMMERGAFFERSTEIN**
Henry Wadsworth LONGFELLOW
1807–1882
American poet

**Kay HAMMOND**
Dorothy STANDING
1909–
English actress, acted mainly on the stage but made a few films

**Ralph HAMMOND**
Hammond INNES
1913–
British novelist. He uses this pen-name for juvenile fiction

**Walter HAMPDEN**
Walter Hampden DOUGHERTY
1879–1955
American stage and film actor

**Victor HANBURY**
Joseph LOSEY
1909–
As a result of the McCarthy witch-hunt, the American film director Joseph Losey was forced to leave the United States and to seek work in Britain. He used pseudonyms between 1953 and 1957, Victor Hanbury being the one he used for making *The Sleeping Tiger* (1954)

**George HANDY**
George HENDLEMAN
1920–
American jazz pianist and composer

**Pamela HANSFORD JOHNSON**
Lady SNOW
1912–
British novelist

**Robert HARBINSON**
Robert BRYANS
1928–
British author

**Clement HARDIN**
D. B. NEWTON

1916–
American writer of cowboy stories
**Ty HARDIN**
Orton HUNGERFORD
1930–
American actor. Played Bronco Lane on TV
**Ann HARDING**
Dorothy GATLEY
1902–
American actress
**George HARDING**
George RAUBENHEIMER
1923–
British author
**Bobby HARDY**
Marjorie HARDY
1913–
Australian author
**John HARDY, Mariner**
Isaac Israel HAYES
1832–1881
American Arctic explorer
**Elizabeth HARLE**
Irene ROBERTS
1929–
British author
**Jean HARLOW**
Harlean CARPENTIER
1911–1937
American film star, nicknamed the 'Platinum Blonde'
**Ralf HAROLDE**
Ralf Harold WIGGER
1899–1974
American film actor
**Slim HARPO**
James MOORE
1926–1972
American blues singer
**John Benyon HARRIS**
John WYNDHAM
1930–
British science fiction writer
**Peter HARRIS**
William Peter HARRIS
1923–
South African author

**Dolores HART**
Dolores HICKS
1938–
American stage and screen actress
**Don HARTMAN**
Samuel HARTMAN
1901–1958
American writer
**Roger HARTMAN**
Rustam MENTA
1912–
Indian author
**HARTMANN**
Henry SEYMOUR
1931–
British writer
**Laurence HARVEY**
Larushka Mischa SKIKNE
1928–1973
Lithuanian-born British film actor
**Paul HARVEY**
Paul H. AURANDT
1918–
American columnist and news analyst
**Gina HARWOOD**
Esther G. BATTISCOMBE
1905–
British writer
**Signe HASSO**
Signe LARSSON
1910–
Swedish actress, in Hollywood during the forties
**Owen HATTERAS**
H. L. MENCKEN and George Jean NATHAN
1880–1956; 1882–1956
American literary and dramatic critics. They wrote *Pistols for Two* under this pseudonym
**Virgilius HAUFNIENSIS**
Sören KIERKEGAARD
1813–1855
Danish philosopher and theologian
**June HAVER**
June STOVENOUR
1926–

American film actress of the forties

**HAVINGTON**
Elaine HEIGHINGTON
1951–
British fashion model

**June HAVOC**
June HOVICK
1916–
American film actress; sister of Gypsy Rose Lee

**Henry HAWKINS**
Ezra POUND
1885–1972
American poet. He used this pen-name for an article on Cockney slang (1914). It is a pun on Henry Higgins

**John HAWKINS**
Stetia HAGAN
1908–
British author

**Screamin' Jay HAWKINS**
Jelacy HAWKINS
1929–
American rock and roll singer of the late fifties

**Lord HAW-HAW**
William JOYCE
1906–1946
British Fascist and traitor

**Charles HAWTREY**
Charles HARTRE
1914–
British comic actor

**Elezy HAY**
Eliza ANDREWS
1840–1910
American novelist and botanist

**Ian HAY**
Maj.-Gen. John Hay BEITH
1876–1952
British novelist

**John HAY**
John and Barbara
DALRYMPLE-HAY
1928– ; date unknown
British authors

**Sessue HAYAKAWA**
Kintaro HAYAKAWA
1889–1973
Japanese-born American film actor. He changed his name in 1913 when he entered show business

**Melissa HAYDEN**
Mildred HERMAN
1928–
American ballet dancer

**Russell HAYDEN**
Hayden LUCID
1912–
American cowboy actor

**Sterling HAYDEN**
John HAMILTON
1916–
American film actor

**Helen HAYE**
Helen HAY
1874–1957
British stage actress in occasional films

**Allison HAYES**
Mary Jane HAYES
1930–
American actress

**Helen HAYES**
Helen BROWN
1900–
American stage actress who made some film appearances

**Henry HAYES**
Ellen KIRK
1842–*c.* 1910
American novelist

**Peter Lind HAYES**
Joseph Conrad LIND
1915–
American actor and comedian, Hayes was his mother's maiden name

**HAYMAN**
Hazel PEEL
1930–
British author

**Dorothy K. HAYNES**
Dorothy GRAY

1918–
British author
**Michael HAYNES**
Ronald BIGGS
1930–
English criminal, one of the Great Train Robbers. Biggs used this pseudonym when on the run in Brazil
**Joan HAYTHORNE**
Joan HAYTHORNTHWAITE
1915–
British stage actress
**Louis HAYWARD**
Seafield GRANT
1909–
South African-born actor; in Hollywood from 1935
**Susan HAYWARD**
Edythe MARRINER
1918–1975
American film actress
**Rita HAYWORTH**
Margarita CANSINO
1918–
American actress and singer, daughter of Eduardo and Volga (Haworth) Cansino who were professional dancers. She made several films between 1935 and 1940 as Margarita Cansino and then changed her name to Rita Hayworth (adding 'y' to her mother's maiden name)
**Hy HAZELL**
Hyacinth Hazel O'HIGGINS
1920–1970
British singer and actress
**Horace HAZELTINE**
Charles WAYNE
1858–?
American author
**H. F. HEARD**
Gerald HEARD
1889–
Anglo-American author
**Veronica HEATH**
Veronica BLACKETT

1927–
British writer on show jumping
**Van HEFLIN**
Emmett Evan HEFLIN
1910–1971
American film actor
**Ernest HELFENSTEIN**
Elizabeth SMITH
1806–1893
American reformer and poet
**HELIOSTROPOLIS, Etc.**
Daniel FOE
1660–1731
English journalist and novelist; called Daniel Defoe
**Theodor HELL**
Karl WINKLER
1775–1856
German poet and composer
**Brigitte HELM**
Gisele Eve SCHITTENHELM
1906–
German film star of the silent era
**James HELVICK**
Claud COCKBURN
1904–
British journalist
**Elizabeth HELY**
Elizabeth YOUNGER
1913–
British author
**Margaux HEMINGWAY**
Margot HEMINGWAY
1954–
American actress. She changed the spelling of her first name when she discovered that she had been conceived after her parents had downed a bottle of Château Margaux
**Sylvia HENDERSON**
Sylvia ASHTON-WARNER
1908–
New Zealand novelist
**Paul HENREID**
Paul von HENREID
1907–
Austrian actor, in Hollywood from 1940

**O. HENRY**
William Sidney PORTER
1862–1910
American short story writer. He served three years in prison for embezzlement (1898–1900), where he began to write short stories and adopted his pseudonym. It is an abbreviation for the name of a French pharmacist, Étienne Ossian Henry, whose name appeared in the *U.S. Dispensatory*, a book Porter used when he worked as the prison pharmacist

**Uncle HENRY**
George Henry SMITH
1873–1931
American writer of children's stories

**Will HENRY**
Henry ALLEN
1912–
American author

**Gladys HENSON**
Gladys GUNN
1897–
Irish stage and screen character actress

**Audrey HEPBURN**
Audrey HEPBURN-RUSTON
1929–
British actress; in U.S.A. since 1951

**Mort HERBERT**
Mort PELOVITZ
1925–
American jazz musician

**HERBLOCK**
Herbert L. BLOCK
1909–
American cartoonist

**Eileen HERLIE**
Eileen HERLIHY
1919–
British stage actress, who made occasional films

**HERMAN**
Peter NOONE
1947–
British pop singer

**Stephen HERMLIN**
Rudolf LEDER
1915–
German poet

**Geilles HERRING**
Edith Oenome SOMERVILLE
1858–1949
Irish author. She and her cousin, Violet Martin, wrote *An Irish Cousin* (1889) under the pseudonyms Geilles Herring and Martin Ross. Miss Somerville's pen-name was borrowed from an ancestor and was discarded with the appearance of the second edition. Thereafter, the cousins wrote under the names, E. Œ. Somerville and Martin Ross

**Irene HERVEY**
Irene HERWICK
1916–
American film actress

**Dennis HESSING**
Harold DENNIS-JONES
1915–
British author

**Stefan HEYM**
Hellmuth FLIEGEL
1913–
German novelist and journalist

**Anne HEYWOOD**
Violet PRETTY
1931–
British film actress

**HIERRO**
Victor HUGO
1802–1885
French poet and author

**HILDEGARDE**
Hildegarde SELL
1906–
American café and radio singer of the thirties

**James HILL**
(Margaret) Storm JAMESON
1897–
British novelist. She wrote two

novels under this pseudonym: *Loving Memory* (1937), and *No Victory for the Soldier* (1938)

**Steven HILL**
Solomon BERG
1924–
American stage actor

**Jan HILLIARD**
Hilda KAY
1910–
Canadian author

**Joseph HILTON**
Joseph Hilton SMYTH
1901–
American publisher and author

**Thomas HINDE**
Sir Thomas Willes CHITTY
1926–
British novelist

**Jerome HINES**
Jerome HEINZ
1921–
American opera singer

**William Randolph HIRSCH**
Marvin KITMAN
1936–
American humorist. He wrote the *Red Chinese Air Force Exercise, Diet and Sex Book* under this pseudonym

**HISTORICUS**
Benjamin FRANKLIN
1706–1790
American philosopher, scientist and statesman

**Sir Adolf HITLER**
Jimmie ARTIS
1954–
American college student. He applied to change his name in 1974 'because there are too many Jimmies'

**Rose HOBART**
Rose KEEFER
1906–
American film actress, usually in character roles

**John Oliver HOBBS**
Pearl Mary CRAIGIE

1867–1906
American novelist and playwright

**HO CHI MINH**
Nguyen That THANH
1892–1969
Vietnamese political leader. Before adopting the name Ho Chi Minh (meaning 'most enlightened one') in the early 1940s, he had been known by various aliases, including Nguyen Ai Quoc, Ly Thuy, Song Man Tcho, Nguyen O Phap and Nguyen Sinh Chin

**Jakob van HODDIS**
Hans DAVIDSOHN
1884–1942
German poet. From 1914 he lived in mental homes until he was removed and murdered by the Nazis

**Dennis HOEY**
Samuel HYAMS
1893–1960
British character actor, acted mostly in Hollywood

**HOFF**
Syd HOFF
1912–
American author

**Harry Summerfield HOFF**
William COOPER
1910–
British novelist

**Hans HOFMEYER**
Anthony FLEISCHER
1928–
South African author

**Fay HOLDEN**
Fay HAMMERTON
1894–1973
British stage actress, who originally used the name of Dorothy Clyde. She went to Hollywood in 1935; played the mother in the Andy Hardy series

**William HOLDEN**
William BEEDLE, Jr.
1918–
American film actor. 'Beedle! It

sounds like an insect' said a Paramount executive in 1938, before naming him Holden after a newspaper friend

**Judy HOLLIDAY**
Judith TUVIM
1922–1965
American actress and comedienne. In Hebrew the name Tuvim means holiday

**Earl HOLLIMAN**
Anthony NUMKENA
1928–
American film actor

**Carol HOLLISTON**
James N. GIFFORD
1896–1957
American author

**Saxe HOLM**
Helen Hunt JACKSON
1830–1885
American novelist and poet

**Libby HOLMAN**
Elizabeth HOLZMAN
1908–
American actress and singer

**Herbert HOLMES**
Edward SANGER
1882–1956
British actor; in Hollywood from 1917

**Marty HOLMES**
Marty HAUSMAN
1925–
American jazz musician

**Patrick HOLT**
Patrick PARSONS
1912–
British actor

**Tim HOLT**
Charles HOLT
1918–1973
American film actor

**Leonard HOLTON**
Leonard P. O'Connor WIBBERLEY
1915–
British author

**Evelyn HOME**
Peggy ASKINS
c. 1907–
English journalist

**Henry HOMESPUN**
Solomon SOUTHWICK
1773–1839
American writer

**Brenda HONEYMAN**
Brenda CLARKE
1926–
British author

**Andrew HOPE**
Anthony HERN
1916–
British author

**Anthony HOPE**
Sir Anthony Hope HAWKINS
1863–1933
British novelist. He started writing novels when he was practising as a barrister and used a pseudonym to keep his two careers apart

**Bob HOPE**
Leslie Townes HOPE
1903–
American comedian. At school Les Hope soon became 'Hopeless', so when he entered show business in 1928 he changed his first name to Bob

**Hedda HOPPER**
Elda FURRY
1890–1966
American actress (of the silent era), journalist and Hollywood gossip columnist. In 1913 she married De Wolf Hopper, a comedian. Her husband's four previous· wives had been called Ella, Ida, Edna and Nella, so she consulted a numerologist who suggested the name Hedda to distinguish her from her predecessors

**Trader HORN**
Alfred Aloysius SMITH
1861–1931
British writer and adventurer

**Howard HORNE**
Robert PAYNE
1911–
English author
**Horace HORNEM**
George Gordon BYRON
1788–1824
English poet. He wrote 'The Waltz: An Apostrophic Hymn' (1813), a satire against dancing, under this pen-name
**Rosemary HORSTMANN**
Rosemary WATERS
1920–
British author
**HOSPITA**
Charles LAMB
1775–1834
English essayist
**HOTSPUR**
Lt. Com. Bryan CURLING
1911–
British author
**Harry HOUDINI**
Erich WEISS
1874–1926
American magician and escapologist. The son of a Rabbi, he was born in Hungary and arrived in America in 1875. His stage name, which dates from 1891, derives from Harry Kellar, a popular American magician, and Jean Eugene Robert-Houdin, a famous French magician, whose life he investigated in *The Unmasking of Robert-Houdin* (1908)
**Elizabeth HOUGHTON**
Elizabeth GILZEAN
1913–
British author
**John HOUSEMAN**
Jacques HAUSSMANN
1902–
Rumanian-born American theatrical producer
**Renée HOUSTON**
Katherina Houston GRIBBIN

1902–
British TV personality
**Barbara HOWARD**
John Russell CORYELL
1852–1924
American dime novelist
**Joan HOWARD**
Patricia GORDON
1904–
American author
**John HOWARD**
John Cox
1913–
American film actor
**Johnnie HOWARD**
Jessie JAMES
1847–1882
American outlaw. He was using this alias when he was killed
**Leslie HOWARD**
Leslie STAINER
1893–1943
British actor of Hungarian origin. He changed his name in 1917
**Police Captain HOWARD**
Luis Philip SENARENS
1863–1939
American dime novelist
**Warren HOWARD**
James N. GIFFORD
1896–1957
American author
**James Wong HOWE**
Wong Tung JIM
1899–1976
American cinematographer; in Hollywood from 1916
**Frankie HOWERD**
Francis HOWARD
1922–
English comedian. He changed his name in 1946 so that it would at least be noticed as a misprint
**HOWLIN' WOLF**
Chester BURNETT
1910–1976
American blues singer
**George HOY**
George FORMBY

1905–1961
English music hall comedian. In order to avoid confusion with his famous comedian father, also George Formby, he used his mother's maiden name when he first went on the stage in 1921. He reverted to Formby in 1925

**John HOYT**
John HOYSRADT
1905–
American character actor

**Jeffrey HUDSON**
Michael CRICHTON
1942–
American author

**Rock HUDSON**
Roy SCHERER
1925–
American actor. He adopted the surname of his stepfather, Wallace Fitzgerald, whom his mother married in 1933. Henry Willson, a talent scout for Selznick Studios, discovered him in 1946. Willson named him Rock, after the Rock of Gibraltar, and Hudson after the Hudson River. Willson had considered the names Crash and Brick before deciding on Rock. Years later Hudson said 'I blushed when I was given that name. I still haven't got used to it. So much so that I still have occasional difficulty pronouncing it'

**Charles John HUFFAM**
Charles DICKENS
1812–1870
British novelist. John and Huffam are his second and third names

**Brenda HUGHES**
Brenda COLLOMS
1919–
British author

**Kathleen HUGHES**
Betty VON GERLEAN
1929–
American film actress

**Josephine HULL**
Josephine SHERWOOD
1884–1957
American stage actress

**Sir Henry HUMM**
George Alexander STEVENS
1731–1784
English writer and lecturer

**Engelbert HUMPERDINCK**
Arnold DORSEY
1936–
British pop singer

**Geoffrey HUMPHRYS**
Leslie George HUMPHRYS
1921–
British author

**Charlotte HUNT**
Doris HODGES
1915–
British author

**Kyle HUNT**
John CREASEY
1908–1973
English writer of detective and suspense stories

**Marsha HUNT**
Marcia HUNT
1917–
American actress

**Alison HUNTER**
Norma HUNTER-BLAIR
1932–
British author

**Clingham HUNTER, M.D.**
William Taylor ADAMS
1822–1897
American writer of travel books

**Evan HUNTER**
Evan LOMBINO
1926–
American novelist, who also writes under the pseudonym Ed McBain. The son of a New York Italian postman, he changed his name legally to Evan Hunter in 1952

**Jeffrey HUNTER**
Henry H. McKINNIES
1925–1969
American film actor

**Kim HUNTER**
Janet COLE
1922–
American actress. Her name was changed by David O. Selznick – 'he told me that Janet Cole could be anyone, but that Kim Hunter had individuality and would go far as an actress'

**Mollie HUNTER**
Maureen McILWRAITH
1922–
British author

**Ross HUNTER**
Martin FUSS
c. 1924–
American film producer. When he started in Hollywood as an actor in 1944, he was given the name Ross Hunter by Max Arnow, the casting director at Columbia Pictures

**Tab HUNTER**
Art GELIEN
1931–
American film actor

**Mary HUNTON**
Elizabeth GILZEAN
1913–
British author

**Bob HUSH**
Sir Robert WALPOLE
1676–1745
English statesman

**Leonard HUSSEY**
Brian PEARCE

1915–
British author

**Ruth HUSSEY**
Ruth O'ROURKE
1914–
American film actress

**Walter HUSTON**
Walter HOUGHSTON
1884–1950
American character actor, in Hollywood from 1928. Father of film director John Huston

**Betty HUTTON**
Betty THORNBURG
1921–
American actress and singer. Her name was changed by Vincent Lopez, a Detroit bandleader, in 1937 after consulting a numerologist

**Ina HUTTON**
Odessa COWAN
1916–
American jazz bandleader and singer

**Marion HUTTON**
Marion THORNBURG
1920–
American singer, sister of Betty Hutton

**Robert HUTTON**
Robert WINNE
1920–
American film actor

# I

**IAGO**
Sir Robert WALPOLE
1676–1745
English statesman

**IANTHE**
Emma EMBURY
1806–1863

American poet

**ICHABOD**
Walt WHITMAN
1819–1892
American poet

**ICONOCLAST**
Charles BRADLAUGH

1833–1891
British social reformer
**An IDLER**
George S. HILLARD
1808–1879
American writer
**Francis ILES**
Anthony Berkeley COX
1893–1971
English author who wrote *Malice Aforethought* (1932). Cox never admitted or denied being Francis Iles but it is generally accepted in London publishing circles that he was. He also used the pen-name Anthony Berkeley
**M. IMHOF**
François Marie AROUET
1694–1778
French philosopher and writer better known as Voltaire
**An IMPARTIAL HAND**
Dr. Samuel JOHNSON
1709–1784
English lexicographer, critic and poet
**Philip INCLEDON**
Philip WORNER
1910–
British author
**Robert INDIANA**
Robert CLARKE
1928–
American artist
**Rex INGRAM**
Reginald HITCHCOCK
1893–1950
Irish-American film director; in Hollywood during the twenties

**Michael INNES**
John STEWART
1906–
British literary historian who used this pseudonym for detective stories
**IRENE**
Irene LENTZ
1901–1962
American fashion designer, worked for MGM in the forties
**An IRISHMAN**
Thomas MOORE
1779–1852
Irish poet
**The IRISH WHISKEY DRINKER**
John SHEEHAN
1831–1896
Irish barrister and poet
**Ralph IRON**
Oliver SCHREINER
1855–1920
South African novelist. She wrote *The Story of an African Farm* (1883) under this pseudonym
**Henry IRVING**
John Henry BRODRIBB
1838–1905
British actor-manager. He changed his name to avoid embarrassing his parents who were ashamed of their son's chosen profession. He named himself Irving after Edward Irving, a popular religious writer, and Washington Irving, his favourite boyhood author. He first appeared on the stage on 11 August 1856 as Romeo at the Royal Soho Theatre

# J

**J...H.....**
John HORNIHOLD
1751–1792
English writer

**J.R.**
John RUSKIN
1819–1900
British art critic and author

**JABEZ**
Eric NICOL
1919–
British author

**Neville JACKSON**
Gerald M. GLASKIN
1923–
Australian author

**Preston JACKSON**
James Preston McDONALD
1904–
American jazz trombonist

**Dean JAGGER**
Dean JEFFRIES
1903–
American character actor

**Andrew JAMES**
James KIRKUP
1924–
British author

**Griffith JAMES**
James N. GIFFORD
1896–1957
American author

**Jimmy JAMES**
James CASEY
1892–1965
English music hall comedian. He changed his name when an agent, booking him work in Wales, told him the name Casey would not be popular there

**Joni JAMES**
Joan BABBO
1946–
American singer

**Eric JAMESON**
Eric TRIMMER
1923–
British author

**JAN**
John READ
1917–
British author

**Emil JANNINGS**
Theodor Emil JANENZ
1884–1950
German actor. He made a few films in Hollywood

**Hank JANSON**
Stephen D. FRANCIS
1912–
American writer of pulp fiction

**David JANSSEN**
David MEYER
1930–
American actor. He adopted the name of his mother's second husband

**W. M. JASON**
Milton R. MACHLIN
1924–
American author

**Clare JAYNES**
Jane MAYER and Clara SPIEGEL
1903– ; date unknown
American twentieth-century authors

**JEAMES OF BUCKLEY SQUARE**
William Makepeace THACKERAY
1811–1963
British author

**JEAN PAUL**
Johann RICHTER
1763–1825
German novelist and humorist

**Gloria JEAN**
Gloria Jean SCHOONOVER
1928–
American child actress

**Ursula JEANS**
Ursula McMINN
1906–1973
British stage actress

**Mahatma Kane JEEVES**
William Claude DUKINFIELD
1879–1946
American comedian, better known as W. C. Fields. This was one of the pseudonyms he used for writing screen plays

**Sarah JEFFERSON**
Eve FARJEON
1919–
British author

**Jeff JEFFRIES**
Jeff BOATFIELD
1924–
British author
**Alan JENKINS**
Alfred McGONEGAL
1900–1974
American comic actor; in Holly-
wood during the thirties
**Jacquetta Agneta Mariana JENKS,
of Belgrove Priory in Wales**
William BECKFORD
1760–1844
English author and eccentric
**Heather JENNER**
Heather POTTER
1914–
British author
**Richard JEREMY**
Charles FOX
1921–
British author
**Maria JERITZA**
Mitzi JEDLICKA
1887–
Austrian opera singer
**JETSAM**
Malcolm McEACHRAN
1885–1945
English singer; one half of the
comic song duo, Flotsam and
Jetsam, popular in the 1930s
**JILLANA**
Jillana ZIMMERMANN
1934–
American ballerina
**Joshua Jedediah JINKS**
William B. DICK
1828–1893
American writer
**A JOBBER**
Daniel FOE
1660–1731
English journalist and novelist;
called Daniel Defoe
**Archibald JOBBRY**
John GALT
1779–1839

Scottish writer and Canadian
pioneer
**Robert JOFFREY**
Abdullah Jaffa Bey KHAN
1930–
American choreographer and
ballet company director
**Elizabeth JOHANSON**
Johanna VERWER
1911–
Dutch author
**Dr. JOHN**
Malcolm REBERNACK
1940–
American pop singer
**Elton JOHN**
Reginald DWIGHT
1947–
British pop singer
**Rosamund JOHN**
Nora JONES
1913–
British actress
**St. JOHN OF THE CROSS**
Juan de YEPES Y ALVAREZ
1542–1591
Spanish mystic and poet
**Foster JOHNS**
Gilbert SELDES
1893–
American critic and playwright.
He wrote mystery novels under
this pen-name
**June JOHNS**
June Johns SMITH
1925–
British author
**A. E. JOHNSON**
Annabel JOHNSON
1921–
American author
**Benj. F. JOHNSON of Boone**
James Whitcomb RILEY
1849–1916
American poet. He wrote *Leven
More Poems* (1883) under this
pen-name
**Effie JOHNSON**
Euphemia RICHMOND

1825–c. 1910
American novelist

**Pete JOLLY**
Peter CERAGIOLI
1932–
American jazz musician

**Al JOLSON**
Asa YOELSON
c. 1886–1950
Jewish-American singer and entertainer, born in Srednik, Lithuania. When he was 10, his older brother told him that unless he changed his name he would not be able to hold his head up high. When he was 14 he changed his name to Al Joelson. Later when he was on the stage with his brother and Joe Palmer as Joelson, Palmer and Joelson he dropped the 'e' at the suggestion of a printer who wanted to fit the name on a card

**Buck JONES**
Charles JONES
1889–1942
American actor; in Hollywood during twenties and thirties, mainly in westerns

**Chuck JONES**
Charles M. JONES
1915–
American film cartoonist; directed Bugs Bunny and Sylvester cartoons

**Clara JONES**
Dorothy BALDWIN
1934–
British author

**Hal JONES**
Harry A. JONES
1912–
British author

**Jennifer JONES**
Phyllis ISLEY
1919–
American actress; discovered by David O. Selznick in 1941 who sent her to New York to study drama while his organisation spent nearly a year thinking up her new name. He introduced Jennifer Jones to the New York press in 1942 as his next star. A reporter asked her how she came by her name, 'My mother must have been reading an English novel', she replied, 'but I suppose they'll change it once I get to Hollywood'

**Joanna JONES**
John F. BURKE
1922–
British author

**John Paul JONES**
John PAUL
1747–1792
Scottish-born American naval hero. In 1772 he bought a ship in the West Indies and in the following year killed the leader of a mutinous crew. To avoid trial he changed his name to Jones and went into hiding for two years. During the American War of Independence he plundered British shipping

**Richard JONES**
Theodore Edward HOOK
1788–1841
English novelist and editor

**Spike JONES**
Lindley Armstrong JONES
1911–1965
American comedy bandleader

**Tom JONES**
Thomas Jones WOODWARD
1940–
Internationally famous pop singer, born in Pontypridd, Wales. He was originally known as 'Tommy Scott, The Twisting Vocalist'

**Flavius JOSEPHUS**
Joseph BEN MATTHIAS
A.D. 37–95
Jewish historian and soldier. He won the favour of Roman emperor Titus Flavius Vespasian, whose name he took

**Louis JOURDAN**
Louis GENDRE
1919–
French actor, long resident in Hollywood. In 1939 he took the name Pierre Jourdan and in 1941 changed Pierre to Louis

**Leatrice JOY**
Leatrice Joy ZEIDLER
1899–
American actress in silent films

**Brenda JOYCE**
Betty LEABO
1918–
American film actress

**Thomas JOYCE**
Joyce CARY
1888–1957
British novelist

**JUBA**
Benjamin ALLEN
1789–1829
American poet and clergyman

**Caroline Silver JUNE**
Laura Roundtree SMITH
1876–1924
American author

**Jennie JUNE**
Jane Cunningham CROLY
1829–1901
American journalist, the first newspaper woman

**JUNIOR RECTOR OF ST. MICHAEL**
Daniel FOE
1660–1731
English journalist and novelist; called Daniel Defoe

**JUNIUS**
(unknown)
date unknown
English journalist. The pseudonym was used for a series of letters to the *Public Advertiser* from 1769–1772. The letters strongly attacked the government, and revealed intimate knowledge of the scandals of the day. Nearly fifty people have been put forward as the possible author, Sir Philip Francis (1740–1818) being one of the most likely suggestions

**JUSTICIAR**
Vincent POWELL-SMITH
1939–
British author

**JUSTINOPHILUS**
Rev. Samuel BADCOCK
1747–1788
English clergyman and author

# K

**Ish KABIBBLE**
Mervin BOGUE
1908–
American entertainer

**Saul KAIN**
Siegfried SASSOON
1886–1967
British poet and novelist. He wrote *The Daffodil Murderer* under this pseudonym

**Le Major KAISERLING**
François Marie AROUET
1694–1778
French philosopher and writer better known as Voltaire

**Lev Borisovich KAMENEV**
Lev Borisovich ROSENFELD
1883–1936
Russian revolutionary and government official; executed by Stalin in the Great Purge

**Michael KARAGEORGE**
Poul ANDERSON
*c.* 1924–
American science fiction writer

**Anna KARINA**
Hanne Karin BEYER
1940–
Danish actress in French films

**Miriam KARLIN**
Miriam SAMUELS
1925–
British actress and comedienne

**Boris KARLOFF**
William PRATT
1887–1969
British actor; in the U.S.A. from
1911. He took the name Karloff
from ancestors of his mother

**Phil KARLSON**
Philip KARLSTEIN
1908–
American film director

**Fred KARNO**
Fred WESTCOTT
1866–1941
English music hall artist

**Kurt KATCH**
Isser KAC
1896–1958
Polish film actor; in Hollywood
from 1942

**Barbara KAY**
Ethel KELLER
1878–
American novelist

**Connie KAY**
Conrad KIRNON
1927–
American jazz drummer

**Barbara KAYE**
Barbara GOWLING
c. 1905–
British novelist

**Danny KAYE**
David Daniel KAMINSKY
1913–
American entertainer of stage,
film and TV

**Elia KAZAN**
Elia KAZANJOGLOUS
1909–
American film and stage director
of Greek/Turkish descent. He
went to America in 1913 where his
parents shortened their name to
Kazan. Acted in New York, then,
in the late 1930s, he went to
Hollywood where the studio tried,
unsuccessfully, to change his name
to Cezanne

**Constance KEANE**
Constance OCKLEMAN
1919–1973
Blonde American film actress,
better known as Veronica Lake.
She used this pseudonym for a
few bit parts before she was
renamed

**Buster KEATON**
Joseph Francis KEATON
1895–1966
Great comedian of the silent film
era. He went on the stage at the
age of three as part of his parents
knockabout comedy act. Harry
Houdini, who was in the same
travelling show, nicknamed him
Buster in 1898

**Myron KEATS**
Charles STRONG
1906–
American novelist

**Howard KEEL**
Harold KEEL
1917–
American singer and film actor

**Bob KEENE**
Robert KUHN
1922–
American jazz clarinettist

**Faraday KEENE**
Cora JARRETT
1877–
American novelist

**James KEENE**
Will COOK
1921–
American novelist

**Brian KEITH**
Robert KEITH
1921–
American film actor

94

**David KEITH**
Francis STEEGMULLER
1906–
American author
**Ian KEITH**
Keith ROSS
1899–1960
American film actor
**Joseph KELL**
John Burgess WILSON
1917–
British novelist. Wrote *One Hand Clapping* (1961) and *Inside Mr. Enderby* (1963) under this pen-name
**Pamela KELLINO**
Pamela OSTRER
1916–
British actress and TV personality. Kellino is the name of her first husband. She later married James Mason
**Will P. KELLINO**
William P. GISLINGHAM
1873–1958
British circus clown and acrobat
**Glenn KELLY**
Mildred McNEILLY
1910–
American writer of mystery stories
**Jeremy KEMP**
Edmund WALKER
1934–
British actor
**Kay KENDALL**
Justine McCARTHY
1926–1959
British actress
**Suzy KENDALL**
Frieda HARRISON
1944–
British actress
**Rose KENNEDY**
Metta Victoria VICTOR
1831–1886
American dime novelist
**Jean KENT**
Joan SUMMERFIELD
1921–

British film actress
**Simon KENT**
Max CATTO
1909–
British author
**Maxwell KENTON**
Terry SOTHERN
1924–
American novelist. He wrote the novel *Candy* (1955) under this pseudonym
**Deborah KERR**
Deborah KERR-TRIMMER
1921–
British film star; in Hollywood since the early 1950s
**Frederick KERR**
Frederick KEEN
1858–1933
British character actor; in Hollywood from 1927
**Orpheus C. KERR**
Robert Henry NEWELL
1836–1901
American editor and humorist
**Norman KERRY**
Arnold KAISER
1889–1956
American actor in silent films
**Johnny KIDD**
Frederick HEATH
1929–1966
British pop singer
**Alan KING**
Irwin KNIBERG
1924–
American nightclub and TV comedian
**Andrea KING**
Georgetta BARRY
1915–
French-American stage and screen actress
**B.B. KING**
Riley B. KING
1925–
American blues singer; started in show business as 'Riley King, the Blues Boy from Beale Street', later

95

he shortened this to 'Blues Boy
King', then to B.B.

**Carole KING**
Carole KLEIN
1938–
American folksinger and composer

**Dennis KING** ·
Dennis PRATT
1900–1966
British opera singer

**Nosmo KING**
Vernon WATSON
1885–
British music hall comedian. He
got the idea for his pseudonym
from a 'No Smoking' sign

**Sampson KING**
Arnold BENNETT
1867–1931
British writer

**Sidney KINGSLEY**
Sidney KIESCHNER
1906–
American playwright

**Phyllis KIRK**
Phyllis KIRKEGAARD
1926–
American film actress of the 1950s

**Henry KISSINGER**
Heinz KISSINGER
1923–
American Secretary of State 1973–
1977. Born in Furth, Germany,
Kissinger changed his first name
after arriving in America in 1938

**Dick KITKAT**
Richard DOYLE
1824–1883
British caricaturist, book illustrator and watercolour painter. He
contributed to *Punch*

**Sir Godfrey KNELLER**
Gottfried KNILLER
1646–1723
English portrait painter, born in
Germany. Court painter in the
reign of Charles II

**Cholly KNICKERBOCKER**
Igor LOIEWSKI
1915–
Russian-born American gossip
columnist, generally known as
Igor Cassini.

**Diedrich KNICKERBOCKER**
Washington IRVING
1783–1859
American short story writer and
historian. Wrote *A History of New
York* (1809) under this pseudonym.
Knickerbockers was the name
given to descendants of the original
Dutch settlers in New York.

**The KNIGHT**
Sir Robert WALPOLE
1676–1745
English statesman

**David KNIGHT**
David MINTZ
1927–
American actor

**Fuzzy KNIGHT**
J. Forrest KNIGHT
1901–1976
American comic film actor. In
many westerns

**Anne KNISH**
Arthur Davison FICKE
1883–1945
American poet and critic who, in
collaboration with Witter Bynner
(pseud. Emanuel Morgan) concocted the Spectrist literary hoax

**Patric KNOWLES**
Reginald KNOWLES
1911–
British actor. In Hollywood from
1936

**KOBA**
Iosif Vissarionovich
DZHUGASHVILI
1879–1953
Russian political leader, better
known as Stalin. Dzhugashvili
used the pseudonym Koba –
which is Turkish for 'Fearless' –

between 1905 and 1910, he then began calling himself Stalin

**Fritz KORTNER**
Fritz KOHN
1892–1970
Austrian actor; in international films

**Charles KORVIN**
Geza KAISER
1907–
Czech-born American actor

**Martin KOSLECK**
Nicolai YOSHKIN
1907–
Russian actor; in Hollywood from 1936

**Henry KOSTER**
Hermann KOSTERLITZ
1905–
German film director; in Hollywood from 1936

**Michael KRAWBRIDGE**
John BOYLE
(Earl of Cork and of Orrery)
1707–1762
Irish writer

**Dr. Carl KUON SUO**
Cyril Henry HOSKINS
1910–
British author and eccentric. He adopted this pseudonym in 1948, and was later known as Tuesday Lobsang Rampa

# L

**Barbara LAAGE**
Claire COLOMBAT
1925–
French film actress

**A LADY**
George Alexander STEVENS
1731–1784
English writer and lecturer

**A LADY OF BOSTON**
Miss Susan D. NICKERSON
c. 1840–c. 1890
American writer

**A LADY OF QUALITY**
Lady JONES
1889–
British novelist and playwright; this pen-name was used for the novel *Serena Blandish* (1925). Better known as Enid Bagnold

**Rene LAFAYETTE**
Lafayette Ronald HUBBARD
1911–
American writer and founder of Scientology. He used this pen-name for writing science fiction

**Suzette LA FLESCHE**
INSHATATHEANBA
1854–1903
American Indian author. Her Indian name means 'Bright Eyes'

**Bert LAHR**
Irving LAHRHEIM
1895–1968
American vaudeville comedian

**Cleo LAINE**
Clementina CAMPBELL
1928–
British singer

**Denny LAINE**
Brian HINES
1941–
British pop singer

**Frankie LAINE**
Frank LO VECCHIO
1913–
American popular singer. When he started in show business he adopted the name Frankie Lane but later, when he discovered a girl singer named Frances Lane, he added the 'i' to avoid confusion

**Arthur LAKE**
Arthur SILVERLAKE
1905–
American comedy actor. His name was changed by the Hollywood producer, Carl Lammle, Jr

**Veronica LAKE**
Constance OCKLEMAN
1919–1973
Blonde American film actress, popular during the 1940s. After the death of her father, her mother married Anthony Keane and Constance adopted this name. She got a few bit parts in films as Constance Keane then she was renamed by Arthur Hornblow, Jr., a producer at Paramount. He told her that her classical features brought to mind the name Veronica and her deep blue eyes the word Lake

**Ashton LAMAR**
Harry Lincoln SAYLER
1863–1913
American writer of boys' books

**Barbara LA MARR**
Reatha WATSON
1896–1926
American actress in silent films

**Hedy LAMARR**
Hedwig KIESLER
1913–
Austrian actress; in Hollywood from 1937

**William LAMB**
(Margaret) Storm JAMESON
1897–
British novelist. She wrote one novel, *The World Ends* (1937), under this pen-name

**Dorothy LAMOUR**
Dorothy KAUMEYER
1914–
American actress who played with Bing Crosby and Bob Hope in the 'Road' series

**Elsa LANCHESTER**
Elizabeth SULLIVAN
1902–
British actress; in Hollywood from 1940. Married Charles Laughton. Lanchester is her mother's maiden name which Elsa first used in 1921

**Ann LANDERS**
Esther FRIEDMAN
1918–
American columnist. Ann Landers was the name of Ruth Crowley, a columnist with the Chicago *Sun Times* until 1955 when it and the job were taken over by Esther Friedman

**Lew LANDERS**
Lewis FRIEDLANDER
1901–1962
American film director

**Carole LANDIS**
Frances RIDSTE
1919–1948
American film actress of the 1940s

**Michael LANDON**
Michael OROWITZ
1937–
American actor

**Allen LANE**
Allen WILLIAMS
1902–1973
British publisher, founded Penguin Books in 1935. He changed his name by deed poll in 1919 before joining the publishing firm of John Lane, The Bodley Head

**Angel LANE**
Reginald LANE
1954–
British male striptease artist

**Burton LANE**
Burton LEVY
1912–
American composer of popular music

**Lupino LANE**
Henry LUPINO
1892–1959
British comedian

**Rocky LANE**
Harry ALBERSHART

1904–
American actor. A Western star of the thirties

**Eddie LANG**
Salvatore MASSARO
1904–1933
American jazz guitarist

**Pearl LANG**
Pearl LACK
1922–
American choreographer and dancer. She changed her name in 1943, when a member of the Martha Graham Dance Company

**Ronny LANG**
Ronald LANGINGER
1927–
American jazz musician

**Launcelot LANGSTAFF**
James Kirke PAULDING
1778–1860
American author

**Leo LANIA**
Lazar HERRMANN
1896–1961
Russian-born American author

**Mario LANZA**
Alfredo COCOZZA
1921–1959
American singer

**Rod LA ROCQUE**
Roderick La Rocque DE LA ROUR
1896–1969
American actor in silent films

**Lida LARRIMORE**
Lida L. TURNER
1897–
American novelist

**Danny LA RUE**
Daniel CARROLL
1928–
British female impersonator

**Jack LA RUE**
Gaspare BIONDOLILLO
1903–
American film actor

**LASSIE**
PAL
1940–1949
American Collie (a dog not a bitch). He made several movies in the early forties as Lassie, starting with *Lassie Come Home* (1942)

**The LATE BEN SMITH**
Cornelius MATHEWS
1817–1889
American lawyer and poet

**Yusef LATEEF**
William EVANS
1921–
American jazz musician

**Frank LATIMORE**
Frank KLINE
1925–
American actor

**Tomline LA TOUR**
William Schwenck GILBERT
1836–1911
British librettist of the 'Gilbert and Sullivan' light operas. He used this pseudonym for a *Happy Land*, a burlesque (1873)

**Anne LATTIN**
Lois Dwight COLE
c. 1910–
American author

**Stan LAUREL**
Arthur Stanley JEFFERSON
1890–1965
British-born comedian; in Hollywood from 1916. Billed as Stan Jefferson without great success, until 1916, when he noted that his name had thirteen letters. He then changed it to Stan Laurel

**Piper LAURIE**
Rosetta JACOBS
1932–
American film actress

**Charles LA VERE**
Charles La Vere JOHNSON
1910–
American jazz musician

**Albertus LAVINGENSIS**
Albertus MAGNUS
c. 1206–1280
Dominican teacher

**Jody LAWRANCE**
Josephine Lawrence GODDARD
1930–
American actress

**Carol LAWRENCE**
Carol LARAIA
1932–
American dancer and singer. She changed her name in 1952 because television announcers stumbled over the name Laraia

**Elliot LAWRENCE**
Elliot Lawrence BROZA
1925–
American bandleader of the forties and fifties

**Gertrude LAWRENCE**
Alexandre LAWRENCE-KLASEN
1898–1952
British actress and singer. Starred in several Noël Coward plays

**Steve LAWRENCE**
Sidney LEIBOWITZ
1935–
American singer and actor. He adopted the first names of his two nephews in 1951

**W. B. LAWSON**
George C. JENKS
1850–1929
English-born American novelist, the creator of the character Diamond Dick

**Wilfrid LAWSON**
Wilfrid WORSNOP
1900–1966
British stage and film actor

**Yank LAWSON**
John LAUSEN
1911–
American jazz trumpet player

**A LAYMAN**
Thomas HUGHES
1822–1896
British reformer and writer

**A LAYMAN**
Sir Walter SCOTT
1771–1832

Scottish poet and novelist

**Joe LAYTON**
Joe LICHTMAN
1931–
American choreographer

**LEADBELLY**
Huddie LEDBETTER
1888–1949
American blues singer

**Rufus LEARSI**
Israel GOLDBERG
1887–
American author

**Jean-Paul LE CHANOIS**
Jean-Paul DREYFUS
1909–
French film director

**Andrew LEE**
Louis AUCHINCLOSS
1917–
American novelist

**Anna LEE**
Joanna WINNIFRITH
1914–
British actress; in U.S.A. since late thirties

**Anna S. LEE**
Mabel MURPHY
1870–
American author

**Brenda LEE**
Brenda Lee TARPLEY
1944–
American pop singer

**Canada LEE**
Leonard CANEGATA
1907–1952
American actor. Started as a professional boxer. He acquired his pseudonym when an announcer had difficulty in pronouncing Lee Canegata

**Carolina LEE**
Peggy DERN
1896–
American novelist

**Carolyn LEE**
Carolyn COPP
1935–

American child actress of the early forties

**Gypsy Rose LEE**
Rose Louise HOVICK
1914–1970
American burlesque artiste

**Lila LEE**
Augusta APPLE
1902–
American actress in silent films

**Michele LEE**
Michele DUSIAK
1942–
American actress and singer

**Peggy LEE**
Norma EGSTROM
1920–
American singer. In 1938, when working as a singer on radio station WDAY, the manager, Ken Kennedy, christened her Peggy Lee

**Pinky LEE**
Pinkus LEFF
1916–
American television comedian

**William LEE**
William BURROUGHS
1914–
American novelist. His first book *Junkie* (1953), an account of his addiction to morphine, was published under this pen-name. It was reprinted under his own name in 1964

**Andrea LEEDS**
Antoinette LEES
1914–
American actress; in Hollywood during the thirties

**Herbert I. LEEDS**
Herbert I. LEVY
1901–
American film director

**The LEFT HAND**
Benjamin FRANKLIN
1706–1790
American philosopher, scientist and statesman

**Janet LEIGH**
Janette MORRISON
1927–
American film actress

**Vivien LEIGH**
Vivian HARTLEY
1913–1967
British actress. She married Herbert Leigh Holman in 1932, and in the same year adopted his middle name as her stage name, and changed the 'a' in her first name to 'e'

**Murray LEINSTER**
Will F. JENKINS
1896–
American writer of mystery and science fiction stories

**Sir Peter LELY**
Pieter VAN DER FAES
1618–1680
Portrait painter of Dutch origin, born in Soest, Westphalia. He settled in London in 1641

**Vladimir Ilyich LENIN**
Vladimir Ilyich ULYANOV
1870–1924
Russian revolutionary and political leader. Ulyanov assumed the name N. Lenin in 1902 – sometimes arbitrarily interpreted as meaning Nikolai Lenin. He later varied the initials, V. I. Lenin and V. I. Ulyanov Lenin coming into use. The pseudonym was chosen in connection with political disturbances on the River Lena in Siberia

**Lotte LENYA**
Karoline BLAMAUER
1900–
Austrian singer and actress. Married German composer Kurt Weill and starred in his operas

**Jack E. LEONARD**
Leonard LEBITSKY
1911–1973
American nightclub comedian

**Sheldon LEONARD**
Sheldon BERSHAD
1907–
American character actor. He played gangsters in films during thirties and forties, and is now a TV producer

**Baby LE ROY**
Ronald Le Roy OVERACKER
1932–
American child actor of the thirties. Paramount signed him up on a seven year contract when he was eight months old but he retired from the screen at the age of three

**Mrs. Madeline LESLIE**
Harriette BAKER
1815–1893
American author

**Corinne L'ESTRANGE**
Henry HARTSHORNE
1823–1897
American novelist

**Melinto LEUTRONIO**
St. Thomas AQUINAS
1225–1274
Italian theologian

**George LEWIS**
George L. ZENON
1900–1968
American jazz musician, played clarinet and alto sax

**Jerry LEWIS**
Joseph LEVITCH
1926–
American comedian. He used the same pseudonym as his parents, who were also in show business. 'How could anyone called Levitch get laughs?'

**Mel LEWIS**
Melvin SOKOLOFF
1929–
American jazz drummer

**Ted LEWIS**
Theodore FRIEDMAN
1889–1971
American band leader of the thirties

**Edward LEXY**
Edward LITTLE
1897–
British actor

**LIBERACE**
Wladziu Valentino LIBERACE
1919–
American pianist and TV personality

**Winnie LIGHTNER**
Wilifred HANSON
1901–1971
American comedienne

**Beatrice LILLIE**
Constance MUNSTON
1898–
British actress and comedienne

**Frank LIN**
Gertrude ATHERTON
1857–1948
American novelist. She occasionally used this pseudonym

**Abbey LINCOLN**
Anna WOOLDRIDGE
1930–
American pop singer

**Elmo LINCOLN**
Otto Elmo LINKENHELTER
1889–1952
American actor, the first to play Tarzan on the screen

**Max LINDER**
Gabriel LEVIELLE
1883–1925
French comedian, in films from 1904

**Margaret LINDSAY**
Margaret KIES
1910–
American actress

**Art LINKLETTER**
Arthur Gordon KELLEY
1912–
American TV personality, born in Canada. At the age of one month he was adopted by Fulton and Mary Linkletter. Family moved to

California in 1915. Started his radio and TV show, *People are Funny* in 1942

**Carolus LINNAEUS**
Carl LINNÉ
1707–1778
Swedish botanist who established a classification system for plants

**LIN PIAO**
LIN YU-YUNG
1908–1972
Chinese soldier and political leader. When at military academy in Canton he changed his name from Yu-Yung which means 'fostering demeanour' to Piao which means 'tiger cat'

**Jacques LIPCHITZ**
Jacques LIPSCHITZ
1891–
Lithuanian-born sculptor, lived in Paris from 1909 to 1941 and in the United States from 1941. He owes his change in name to a French police official who issued him with an identification card in 1909

**Virna LISI**
Virna PIERLISI
1937–
Italian actress; in international films

**Frances LITTLE**
Fannie MACAULEY
1863–1941
American author

**Thomas LITTLE Esq.**
Thomas MOORE
1779–1852
Irish poet

**LITTLE ANTHONY**
Anthony GOURDINE
1941–
American pop singer

**LITTLE BROTHER**
Eurreal MONTGOMERY
1907–
American blues pianist

**Cornelius LITTLEPAGE**
James Fenimore COOPER
1789–1851
American novelist

**LITTLE RICHARD**
Richard PENNIMAN
1935–
American pop singer

**Maxim LITVINOV**
Meir WALACH
1876–1951
Soviet politician

**Margaret LIVINGSTONE**
Mary M. FLYNN
1915–
Australian author

**Mary LIVINGSTONE**
Sadye MARKS
*c.* 1898–
American actress. Married to Jack Benny

**Weston LLEWMYS**
Ezra POUND
1885–1972
American poet. He used this pen-name for a magazine article in 1908. It is derived from his full name Ezra Weston Loomis Pound

**Jerome LLOYD**
Jerome HURWITZ
1920–
American jazz musician

**Marie LLOYD**
Matilda WOOD
1870–1922
English music hall entertainer She used Bella Delamare as her stage name at first, but changed it on 17 August 1885 to Marie Lloyd, when she appeared at the Star Palace of Varieties, Bermondsey. She named herself after *Lloyd's Weekly Newspaper*

**Tuesday LOBSANG RAMPA**
Cyril Henry HOSKINS
1910–
British eccentric, author of books on Tibet

103

**Joseph LOCKE**
Joseph McLAUGHLIN
1922–
Irish tenor, popular during the fifties

**Gary LOCKWOOD**
John Gary YUSOLFSKY
1937–
American actor

**Margaret LOCKWOOD**
Margaret DAY
1916–
British actress

**Joe LOCO**
Jose ESTEVES, Jr.
1921–
American jazz musician

**John LODER**
John LOWE
1898–
British actor

**Ford LOGAN**
D. B. NEWTON
1916–
American writer of cowboy stories

**Jimmy LOGAN**
James SHORT
1928–
British actor

**Bliss LOMAX**
Harry Sinclair DRAGO
1888–
American writer of cowboy stories

**Carole LOMBARD**
Jane Alice PETERS
1908–1942
American actress-comedienne

**Julie LONDON**
Julie PECK
1926–
American singer and actress

**A LONDONER**
Charles LAMB
1775–1834
English essayist

**Gerry LONG**
William F. LARKINS
1931–
Australian author

**Harry LONGBAUGH**
William GOLDMAN
1931–
American novelist and playwright. He wrote the novel *No Way to Treat a Lady* under this pen-name, and the screenplay for *Butch Cassidy and the Sundance Kid* (1969). Harry Longbaugh was the name of the original Sundance Kid

**Professor LONGHAIR**
Reg BYRD
1918–
American singer

**Irwin LONGMAN**
Ingersoll LOCKWOOD
1841–1918
American author

**Jack LORD**
John Joseph RYAN
1922–
American actor

**Jeremy LORD**
Ben Ray REDMAN
1896–1961
American author. He wrote detective stories under this pen-name

**Sophia LOREN**
Sophia SCICOLONI
1934–
Italian actress

**Peter LORING**
Samuel SHELLABARGER
1888–1954
American educator and novelist

**Marion LORNE**
Marion Lorne MacDOUGAL
1886–1968
American actress

**Anne LORRAINE**
Lilian Mary CHISHOLM
1906–
British writer of romantic fiction

**Peter LORRE**
Lazzlo LOEWENSTEIN
1904–1964
Hungarian actor; in Hollywood from mid-thirties

104

**Joan LORRING**
Magdalen ELLIS
1926–
British actress; in Hollywood from
1940

**Pierre LOTI**
Louis Marie Julien VIAUD
1850–1923
French writer. He joined the navy
in 1867, and adopted this pen-
name in 1872. Loti means 'rose' in
Tahitian

**Joe LOUIS**
Joseph Louis BARROW
1914–
American boxer

**Morris LOUIS**
Morris BERNSTEIN
1912–1962
American abstract painter

**Anita LOUISE**
Anita Louise FREMAULT
1915–1970
American actress; in films from
1924

**Helen LOURIE**
Catherine STORR
1913–
British author

**Bessie LOVE**
Juanita HORTON
1898–
American actress. She has lived in
London since the mid-thirties

**A LOVER OF PEACE AND
TRUTH**
Joseph PRIESTLEY
1733–1804
English Presbyterian minister and
chemist

**A LOVER OF THE GOSPEL**
Joseph PRIESTLEY
1733–1804
English Presbyterian minister and
chemist

**Robert LOWERY**
Robert Lowery HANKS
1916–1971
American actor

**Anne LOWING**
Christine GEACH
1930–
British author

**Myrna LOY**
Myrna WILLIAMS
1905–
American actress. She took the
pseudonym in 1923 because 'the
plain old Welsh name of Williams
just didn't seem flossy enough'

**Sibrandus LUBERTUS**
Hugh GROTIUS
1583–1645
Dutch jurist and statesman

**Arthur LUCAN**
Arthur TOWLE
1887–1954
British music hall comedian, well-
known from 1937 for his imper-
sonation of Old Mother Riley.
His name is derived from the
Lucan Dairy in Dublin, where he
was on tour in 1913

**LUCANIUS**
John CALVIN
1509–1564
French theologian and religious
reformer

**Victoria LUCAS**
Sylvia PLATH
1932–1963
American poet and author

**LUCAS VAN LEYDEN**
Lucas JACOBSZ
1494–1533
Dutch painter and engraver

**LUCEBERT**
Lubertus Jacobus SWAANSWIJK
1924–
Dutch poet and artist

**Lucky LUCIANO**
Charles Salvatore LUCANIA
1897–1962
Sicilian-born American narcotics
smuggler

**Park LUDLOW**
Theron BROWN
1832–1914

American Baptist clergyman and writer

**Bela LUGOSI**
Bela Lugosi BLASKO
1882–1956
Hungarian actor. Star of many Hollywood horror films

**LUIMARDEL**
Luis MARTÍNEZ-DELGADO
1896–
Colombian writer

**Paul LUKAS**
Pal LUKACS
1891–1971
Hungarian actor; in Hollywood from 1928

**LULU**
Marie LAWRIE
1948–
British pop singer

**Peter LUM**
Lady Bettina CROWE
1911–
British author

**LUMINUS**
Leonard MELLING
1913–
British author

**Roger LUNCHBASKET**
Alan REEVES-JONES
1914–
British author

**Sidney LUSKA**
Henry HARLAND
1861–1905
American novelist

**Viola LYEL**
Violet WATSON

1900–1972
British stage actress

**M. R. LYN**
Sir Robert WALPOLE
1676–1745
English statesman

**Barre LYNDON**
Alfred EDGAR
1896–
British dramatist; worked in Hollywood as a scriptwriter

**Diana LYNN**
Dolores LOEHR
1926–1971
American film actress

**Jeffery LYNN**
Ragnar LIND
1909–
American actor

**Margaret LYNN**
Gladys BATTYE
1915–
British writer

**Ann LYNTON**
Claire RAYNER
1931–
British author

**Elinor LYON**
Elinor WRIGHT
1921–
British author

**Jessica LYON**
Cateau DE LEEUW
1903–
American author

**Jimmy LYTELL**
James SARRAPEDE
1904–
American jazz clarinettist

# M

**M.B.**
Frederick FAUST
1892–1944
American writer of adventure stories

**M.E.W.S.**
Mary Elizabeth Wilson SHERWOOD
1826–1903
American writer

**Jan MABUSE**
Jan GOSSAERT
*c.* 1478–*c.* 1533
Flemish painter

**Frank A. McALISTER**
Frank HALSEY
1890–1941
American author

**Ed McBAIN**
Evan LOMBINO
1926–
American detective story writer. He also writes under his now legalised name, Evan Hunter

**Sidney McCALL**
Mary McNeil FENOLLOSA
1879–1954
American novelist and poet

**Lawrence McCANN**
Jerome BEATTY
1886–
American author

**Shaun McCARTHY**
Cormac SWAN
1916–
British author

**William McCLELLAN**
Charles STRONG
1906–
American novelist

**Greg McCLURE**
Dale EASTON
1918–
American actor

**F. J. McCORMICK**
Peter JUDGE
1891–1947
Irish actor

**Hugh MacDIARMID**
Christopher Murray GRIEVE
1892–
Scottish poet. Pioneer of the Scottish literary renaissance, he chose a Gaelic pseudonym when he began writing Scots poetry

**John Ross MACDONALD**
Kenneth MILLAR
1915–
American detective story writer.

He has also used the pseudonyms Ross Macdonald and John Macdonald

**Marcia MACDONALD**
Grace HILL
1865–1947
American novelist

**Marie McDONALD**
Marie FRYE
1923–1965
American actress

**Spanky McFARLAND**
George Emmett McFARLAND
1928–
American child actor of the thirties

**Fibber McGEE**
James Edward JORDAN
1897–
American radio comedian

**Molly McGEE**
Marion DRISCOLL
1898–1961
American radio comedienne

**John MACGROM**
Guy McMASTER
1829–1887
American poet

**Brian McGUINNESS**
Bernard F. McGUINNESS
1927–
British author

**Mickey McGUIRE**
Joe YULE
1920–
American actor. Later he changed his name to Mickey Rooney

**Hugh McHUGH**
George HOBART
1867–1926
American journalist and playwright

**Connie MACK**
Cornelius McGILLICUDDY
1862–1956
American baseball club manager. He shortened his name in 1884 to fit on the scoreboards

**Kelvin McKAY**
Charles STRONG
1906–
American novelist

**Shirley MACLAINE**
Shirley BEATY
1934–
American film actress. Her pseudonym is an adaptation of her mother's maiden name – Maclean. She is Warren Beatty's sister

**Herschel McLANDRESS**
John Kenneth GALBRAITH
1908–
American economist. He used this pseudonym to review a pseudonymous work

**Christina MACLEAN**
Christina CASEMENT
1933–
British author

**Sally Platt McLEAN**
Sarah GREENE
1856–1935
American author

**Fiona MACLEOD**
William SHARP
1855–1905
Scottish novelist. He wrote a series of romantic novels under this pseudonym. The secret of Fiona's real name was carefully kept; Sharp even entered her in *Who's Who* and listed her interests as 'boating, hill-climbing and listening'

**Michael MacLIAMMOIR**
Alfred WILLMORE
1899–
Irish actor

**Clark McMEEKIN**
Dorothy CLARK and Isabella McMEEKIN
1899– ; 1895–
American novelist

**Stephen McNALLY**
Horace McNALLY
1913–
American actor

**Gus McNAUGHTON**
Augustus HOWARD
1884–1969
British comic actor

**Janet McNEIL**
Janet ALEXANDER
1907–
British author

**Maggi McNELLIS**
Margaret ROCHE
1917–
American radio and television commentator. Assumed her stage name in 1939 upon the suggestion of Gertrude Lawrence

**Butterfly McQUEEN**
Thelma McQUEEN
1911–
American actress. In 1935, she danced in the *Butterfly Ballet* in a New York show and afterwards her friends nicknamed her Butterfly

**Thursty McQUILL**
Wallace BRUCE
1844–1914
American poet who wrote guide-books on the Hudson River under this pen-name

**Theresa MacWHORTER**
William Makepeace THACKERAY
1811–1863
British author

**Jean MADEIRA**
Mrs. John BROWNING
1924–
American opera singer

**MADELEINE**
Noor Inayat KHAN
1914–1944
British agent who worked with the Resistance in France during the Second World War. She was captured and executed by the Germans

**Guy MADISON**
Robert MOSELEY

1922–
American actor
**Noel MADISON**
Nathaniel MOSCOVITCH
1904–
American actor
**MAHARISHI MAHESH YOGI**
Mahesh Prasad VARMA
1918–
Indian guru
**Jock MAHONEY**
Jacques O'MAHONEY
1919–
American actor
**Marjorie MAIN**
Mary TOMLINSON
1890–1975
American character actress
**MAKARIOS III**
Michail Christodoulou
MOUSKOS
1913–
Cypriot politician; Archbishop
and Primate of the Orthodox
Church of Cyprus
**MAKSIM THE GREEK**
Michael TRIVOLIS
*c.* 1470–1556
Greek religious writer
**Malachi MALAGROWTHER**
Sir Walter SCOTT
1771–1832
Scottish poet and novelist
**MALCOLM X**
Malcolm LITTLE
1925–1965
American black Nationalist leader.
Received his Muslim 'X' from
Elijah Muhammad, the Black
Muslim leader, in 1952 – 'the
Muslim's "X" symbolised the
true African family name that he
never could know. For me, my
"X" replaced the white slave-
master name of "Little" which
some blue-eyed devil named Little
had imposed upon my paternal
forebears. . . . Mr. Muhammad
taught that we would keep this

"X" until God Himself returned
and gave us a Holy Name from
His own mouth'
**Karl MALDEN**
Mladen SEKULOVICH
1914–
American stage and film actor.
Born in Chicago to Yugoslav-born
parents. He changed his name 'to
fit theater marquees'
**Abdul MALIK**
Michael DE FREITAS
1933–1975
West Indian Black Power leader.
Executed for murder in Trinidad.
He was known as Michael X
when living in Britain
**Gina MALO**
Janet FLYNN
1909–1963
American film actress of the
thirties
**Dorothy MALONE**
Dorothy MALONEY
1925–
American film actress
**A MAN**
Horace WALPOLE
1717–1797
English writer
**THE MAN IN THE MOON**
Daniel FOE
1660–1731
English journalist and novelist;
called Daniel Defoe
**A MANCHESTER
MANUFACTURER**
Richard COBDEN
1804–1865
English politician and economist
**Miles MANDER**
Lionel MANDER
1888–1946
British actor; in Hollywood from
the mid-thirties
**Marline MANLY**
St. George Henry RATHBONE
1854–1928

American writer of dime novels and boys' books

**Herbie MANN**
Herbert SOLOMON
1930–
American jazz musician

**David MANNERS**
Rauff de Ryther Duan ACKLOM
1901–
Canadian actor in Hollywood in the thirties

**Mrs. Horace MANNERS**
Algernon Charles SWINBURNE
1837–1909
English poet and critic

**Irene MANNING**
Inez HARVUOT
1917–
American film actress

**MANOLETE**
Manuel RODRIGUEZ Y SANCHEZ
1917–1947
Spanish matador

**Jayne MANSFIELD**
Vera Jane PALMER
1932–1967
American film actress

**Katherine MANSFIELD**
Kathleen Middleton MURRY
1888–1923
English short story writer, born in New Zealand

**Peter MANTON**
John CREASEY
1908–1973
British writer. This is one of his earlier pseudonyms under which he composed thirteen crime novels between 1937 and 1954

**Giacomo MANZU**
Giacomo MANZONI
1908–
Italian sculptor, born in Bergamo. Manzu is the Bergamask form of his name which he later adopted

**Adele MARA**
Adelaida DELGADO
1923–
Spanish-American dancer

**Jean MARAIS**
Jean MARAIS-VILLAIN
1913–
French actor. He dropped Villain when he started playing heroes

**Dolores MARBOURG**
Mary BACON
1870–1934
American author

**Fredric MARCH**
Frederick McIntyre BICKEL
1897–1975
American actor. He changed his name at the suggestion of John Cromwell, the director, who said that Bickel sounded like pickle. The name March derives from his mother's maiden name Marcher. Years later March said 'I wish I'd left it as it was – after all Theodore Bickel did all right'

**Hilary MARCH**
Lalage PULVERTAFT
1925–
British author

**MARCUS AURELIUS ANTONINUS**
MARCUS ANNIUS VERUS
121–180
Roman emperor and philosopher

**David MARGERSON**
David M. DAVIES
1923–
British author

**MARGO**
Maria BOLDAO Y CASTILLA
1918–
Spanish dancer and actress

**MARIA**
Clemens BRENTANO
1778–1842
German novelist, dramatist and poet

**Mona MARIS**
Maria CAPDEVIELLE
1903–
Franco-Argentinian film actress

**MARISOL**
Marisol ESCOBAR
1930–
American artist
**Robert MARKHAM**
Kingsley AMIS
1922–
British poet and novelist. He wrote
James Bond type adventure stories
under this pseudonym
**Alicia MARKOVA**
Lilian MARKS
1910–
British prima ballerina
**Roy MARLIN**
Basil N. ASHMORE
1915–
British author and journalist
**MARLINSKY THE COSSACK**
Alexandre BESTOUJEFF
1793–1837
Russian novelist
**The Right Hon. Lady Harriet
MARLOW**
William BECKFORD
1760–1844
English author and eccentric
**Hugh MARLOWE**
Hugh HIPPLE
1914–
American film actor
**Florence MARLY**
Hana SMEKALOVA
1918–
France-Czech actress
**J. J. MARRIC**
John CREASEY
1908–1973
British writer. Creasey began
using this pseudonym in 1955 to
write novels about Inspector
Gideon of Scotland Yard
**Moore MARRIOTT**
George MOORE-MARRIOTT
1885–1949
British actor-comedian
**Carol MARSH**
Norma SIMPSON

1926–
British actress
**Garry MARSH**
Leslie March GERAGHTY
1902–
British character actor
**Marion MARSH**
Violet KRAUTH
1913–
American film actress in the
thirties
**Brenda MARSHALL**
Ardis ANKERSON
1915–
American film actress
**Henry MARSHALL**
Nella HENNEY
1894–
American author
**Tully MARSHALL**
Tully Marshall PHILLIPS
1864–1943
American actor in silent films
**William MARSHALL, Gent.**
Horace WALPOLE
1717–1797
English writer. In 1764 wrote his
best known book *The Castle of
Otranto. A Story Translated by
William Marshall, Gent. From the
Original Italian of Onuphrio
Muratto*
**Richard MARSTEN**
Evan LOMBINO
1926–
American novelist, better known
as Ed McBain and Evan Hunter
**Chink MARTIN**
Martin ABRAHAM
1886–
American jazz musician, played
bass, tuba, and guitar
**Dean MARTIN**
Dino CROCETTI
1917–
American singer and actor. He
started singing in his home town
Steubenville, Ohio, and was billed
at first as 'Dino Martini – Nino

111

Martini's cousin'. (Nino Martini was a popular singer of the time.) Soon after (1939) he changed to Dean Martin

**Edward Winslow MARTIN**
James D. McCABE
1842–1883
American author

**Peter MARTIN**
Christine CHAUNDLER
1887–
British author

**Richard MARTIN**
John CREASEY
1908–1973
British writer of detective stories

**Ross MARTIN**
Martin ROSENBLATT
1920–
Polish-American character actor

**Tony MARTIN**
Alvin MORRIS
1913–
American singer

**Hawser MARTINGALE**
John SLEEPER
1794–1878
American mariner and journalist

**Peter MARTYR**
Pietro Martire VERMIGLI
1500–1562
Italian preacher and scholar

**Ik MARVEL**
Donald Grant MITCHELL
1822–1908
American author

**Chico MARX**
Leonard MARX
1886–1961
American comedian

**Groucho MARX**
Julius MARX
1890–
American comedian

**Harpo MARX**
Adolph MARX
1888–1964
American comedian. Later called Arthur

**MASACCIO**
Tomasso GUIDI
1401–1429
Italian painter

**MASOLINO DA PANICALE**
Tamasso di Christoforo FINÌ
1383–c. 1447
Italian painter

**Edith MASON**
Edith BARNES
1893–1973
American opera singer

**Shirley MASON**
Leona FLUGRATH
1900–
American actress in silent movies, sister of Viola Dana

**MASSACHUSETTENSIS**
Daniel LEONARD
1740–1829
British writer. He used this pen-name for a series of letters (1774–1775) to the inhabitants of Massachusetts Bay

**Ilona MASSEY**
Ilona HAJMASSY
1912–1974
Hungarian actress in Hollywood from 1936

**Léonide MASSINE**
Leonid MIASSINE
1896–
Russo-American dancer and choreographer

**Georgina MASSON**
Marion JOHNSON
1912–
British author

**MATA HARI**
Margareta Gertruda ZELLE
1876–1917
Dutch dancer, courtesan and spy. Shot by the French on charges of spying for the Germans. She married a Dutch army officer of Scottish extraction named Campbell in 1895 and lived in Java from 1896–1902. Began dancing in Paris in 1905 under the name Mata

Hari which is a Malay phrase meaning 'the sun'

**Walter MATTHAU**
Walter
MATUSCHANSKAYASKY
1920–
American actor. His father had been a Catholic (Eastern Rite) priest in Czarist Russia, but ran afoul of Orthodox authorities by his preaching of papal supremacy. He left Russia and lived for a time in Lithuania where he met his wife, who is Jewish. Walter was born in New York

**André MAUROIS**
Emile HERZOG
1885–1967
French writer

**MAX**
Sir Max BEERBOHM
1872–1956
British essayist and caricaturist

**Lois MAXWELL**
Lois HOOKER
1927–
Canadian actress; in Britain since 1949

**Marilyn MAXWELL**
Marvel MAXWELL
1921–1972
American actress

**Elaine MAY**
Elaine BERLIN
1932–
American comedienne. May is the name of her ex-husband, Marvin May, whom she married in her teens

**Joe MAY**
Joseph MANDEL
1880–1954
German film director; in Hollywood since 1933

**Sophie MAY**
Rebecca CLARKE
1833–1906
American writer of children's stories

**Millie MAYFIELD**
Mary HOMES
1830–c. 1880
American poet and novelist

**Leger D. MAYNE**
William B. DICK
1828–1893
American writer

**Virginia MAYO**
Virginia JONES
1920–
American actress

**Jules MAZARIN**
Giulio MAZARINI
1602–1661
French statesman and cardinal. Born in Italy, he became a naturalised Frenchman in 1639

**Mike MAZURKI**
Mikhail MAZURWSKI
1909–
American actor of Ukrainian descent. Former wrestler

**Audrey MEADOWS**
Audrey COTTER
1922–
American television comedienne

**Jayne MEADOWS**
Jane COTTER
1920–
American television actress. She added the 'y' in school – 'I was fed up with being plain Jane'

**MEDIUS**
Benjamin FRANKLIN
1706–1790
American philosopher, scientist and statesman

**MEDVECZKY**
Gyozo HATAR
1914–
Hungarian author

**MEHBOOB**
Ramjankhan MEHBOOBKHAN
1907–
Indian film director

**Golda MEIR**
Golda MABOVITZ
1898–

Israeli politician, born Golda Mabovitz in Kiev, Russia; daughter of Moshe Mabovitz, a carpenter. She emigrated to the United States in 1906 and settled in Milwaukee, and married Morris Meyerson, a sign painter from Denver, in 1917. In 1921 she sailed for Palestine, and was Prime Minister of Israel from 1969 to 1974. When she was first made a minister in 1956, Ben-Gurion insisted that she choose a Hebrew name. In doing so she went as near to Meyerson as she could, calling herself Meir, meaning 'illuminate'

**MELANCHTHON**
Phillip SCHWARZERD
1497–1560
German scholar and follower of Luther. The pseudonym is Greek for Schwarzerd, i.e. 'black earth'

**MELANIE**
Melanie SAFKA
1947–
American singer

**Nellie MELBA**
Helen MITCHELL
1859–1931
Australian opera singer

**My-Heele MENDSOALE**
John TAYLOR
1580–1653
English pamphleteer and poet

**Gerhardus MERCATOR**
Gerhard KREMER
1512–1594
Flemish cartographer and mathematician. Gerhadus Mercator is the latinized form of his original name

**Vivien MERCHANT**
Ada THOMPSON
1929–
British actress

**Leon MERIAN**
Leon MEGERDICHIAN
1923–
American jazz musician

**MERLIN**
Alfred TENNYSON
1809–1892
English poet

**Ethel MERMAN**
Ethel ZIMMERMANN
1908–
American musical comedy star

**Mary MERRALL**
Mary LLOYD
1890–1973
British character actress

**David MERRICK**
David MARGULOIS
1912–
American theatrical producer. He practised as a lawyer in St. Louis, Missouri, and changed his name when he went to New York to act, so that if he failed in the theatre, he would be able to return to his law practice

**Dina MERRILL**
Nedenia Hutton RUMBOUGH
1928–
American actress

**E. B. MERRIT**
Miriam WADDINGTON
1917–
Canadian author

**Tristram MERTON**
Thomas Babington MACAULAY
1800–1859
British historian

**MERULAN**
Robert Dwyer JOYCE
1836–1883
Irish poet and physician

**Curé MESLIER**
François Marie AROUET
1694–1778
French philosopher and writer better known as Voltaire

**George METCALF**
George M. JOHNSON
1885–
American writer of cowboy stories

**Mezz MEZZROW**
Milton MESIROW
1899–
American jazz clarinettist
**MICHAEL X**
Michael DE FREITAS
1933–1975
West Indian Black Power leader,
executed for murder in Trinidad.
Known also as Abdul Malik
**Ralph MICHAEL**
Ralph Champion SHOTTER
1907–
British character actor
**Barbara MICHAELS**
Barbara MERTZ
1927–
American author
**MICHELANGELO**
Michelagniolo di Ludovico
BUONARROTI
1475–1564
Italian sculptor, painter and poet
**Giles MIDDLESTITCH**
William MAGINN
1794–1842
Irish journalist
**Robert MIDDLETON**
Samuel G. MESSER
1911–
American character actor
**Mrs. Mary MIDNIGHT**
John NEWBERY
1713–1767
English publisher and author
**Ozias MIDWINTER**
Lafcadio HEARN
1850–1904
American writer
**Stan MIKITA**
Stanislav GVOTH
1904–
American hockey player
**Lizzie MILES**
Elizabeth PAJAUD
1895–1963
American jazz singer
**Peter MILES**
Gerald PERREAU-SAUSSINE

1938–
American child actor of the forties
**Vera MILES**
Vera RALSTON
1929–
American actress
**Ray MILLAND**
Reginald TRUSCOTT-JONES
1907–
Welsh actor; in Hollywood since
the thirties. After his mother's
second marriage, he adopted his
stepfather's surname of Mullane.
When he first went on stage he
took the name Jack Milland; Ray
was a later development
**Ann MILLER**
Lucy Ann COLLIER
1919–
American dancer
**Joaquin MILLER**
Cincinnatus MILLER
1839–1913
American poet
**Margaret J. MILLER**
Margaret DALE
1911–
British author
**Martin MILLER**
Rudolph MULLER
1899–
Czechoslovakian actor in Britain
since the thirties
**Marvin MILLER**
Marvin MUELLER
1913–
American actor
**Max MILLER**
Thomas SARGENT
1895–1963
English music hall comedian
**Martin MILLS**
Martin BOYD
1893–
Australian author
**Osmington MILLS**
Vivian BROOKS
1922–
British author

**Harry Dubois MILMAN**
John Russell CORYELL
1852–1924
American dime novelist

**Johnny MINCE**
John Henry
MUENZENBERGER
1912–
American jazz clarinettist

**Jozsef MINDSZENTY**
Jozsef PEHM
1892–1975
Roman Catholic primate of Hungary. He changed his German-sounding name in protest against Hungary's pro-Hitler stand during the thirties

**Nelson MINIER**
Laura N. BAKER
1911–
American author

**A MINISTER OF THE GOSPEL**
Nathaniel CLAP
1668–1745
American clergyman and author

**MINSTREL OF THE BORDER**
Sir Walter SCOTT
1771–1832
Scottish poet and novelist

**Mary Miles MINTER**
Juliet REILLY
1902–
American actress; in silent films

**Mr. MINUS**
Thomas MOORE
1779–1852
Irish poet

**Carmen MIRANDA**
Maria de Carmo Miranda DE CUNHA
1914–1955
American actress and singer

**Isa MIRANDA**
Ines Isabella SANPIETRO
1909–
Italian actress

**MIROSLAVA**
Miroslava STERN
1926–1955
American actress

**Gregory MISO-SARUM**
Jonathan SWIFT
1667–1745
Irish writer and satirist

**MISTINGUETT**
Jeanne Marie BOURGEOIS
1874–1956
French actress and dancer

**Gabriela MISTRAL**
Lucila GODOY DE ALCAYAGA
1889–1957
Chilean educationalist, diplomatist and poet, who won the Nobel Prize for Literature (1945). She used her pseudonym for the first time in 1915 when she entered for a poetry competition in Santiago. It is a composite taken from two European poets whom she admired: Gabriele D'Annunzio and Frédéric Mistral

**Guy MITCHELL**
Al CERNICK
1925–
American popular singer. In 1948 he was discovered by Mitch Miller who asked him to change his name. Cernick couldn't think of anything so Miller said 'Look, you're a nice *guy* and my name is *Mitchell* so how about Guy Mitchell?' Cernick accepted the name reluctantly – 'You wouldn't like to end up being someone else, would you?'

**Jean-Pierre MOCKY**
Jean MOKIEJESWKI
1929–
French film director

**Paul MOER**
Paul MOERSCHBACHER
1916–
American jazz musician

**Leonide MOGUY**
Leonide MAGUILEVSKY
1899–
Russian film director

**MOKO**
Sidney MEAD
1927–
New Zealand author

**MOLIÈRE**
Jean Baptiste POQUELIN
1622–1673
French dramatist. Molière was his stage name

**Vyacheslav Mikhailovich MOLOTOV**
Vyacheslav Mikhailovich SKRIABIN
1890–
Russian politician. Foreign minister (1939–1949) and (1953–1957). He used many pseudonyms between 1906 and 1917, one of which, Molotov (hammer), he came in time to adopt permanently

**La MOME MOINEAU**
Lucienne GARCIA
1905–1968
French popular singer of the thirties. Her pseudonym means 'Kid Sparrow'

**Pierre MONDY**
Pierre CUQ
1925–
French actor

**Peter MONNOW**
Glynn CROUDACE
1917–
British author

**Marilyn MONROE**
Norma Jean BAKER
1926–1962
American film actress

**Bull MONTANA**
Luigi MONTAGNA
1887–1950
American actor in silent films

**Yves MONTAND**
Ivo LEVI
1921–
French actor and singer

**Lola MONTEZ**
Maria GILBERT
1818–1861
Irish adventuress and dancer, who became the mistress of Ludwig I of Bavaria

**Maria MONTEZ**
Maria DE SANTO SILAS
1918–1951
American film actress

**Douglass MONTGOMERY**
Robert D. MONTGOMERY
1908–
American actor

**George MONTGOMERY**
George Montgomery LETZ
1916–
American film actor

**Robert MONTGOMERY**
Henry MONTGOMERY
1904–
American film actor

**David MONTROSS**
Jean BACKUS
1914–
American writer of mystery stories

**Ron MOODY**
Ron MOODNICK
1924–
British actor-comedian

**MOONDOG**
Louis HARDIN
1916–
American composer

**Anacreon MOORE**
Thomas MOORE
1779–1852
Irish poet

**Coleen MOORE**
Kathleen MORRISON
1900–
American actress of the silent screen

**Debby MOORE**
Emmaline MAULTSBY
1928–
American singer

**Edward MOORE**
Edwin MUIR
1887–1959
British writer

**Garry MOORE**
Thomas MORFIT
1915–
American TV comedian. In 1940, after two years as a radio comedian, he decided to change his name since he found that Morfit was frequently mispronounced. A contest was held to select a new name, and a Pittsburgh woman won $50 and a trip to Chicago for suggesting Garry Moore

**Kieron MOORE**
Kieron O'HANRAHAN
1925–
Irish actor

**Terry MOORE**
Helen KOFORD
1929–
American actress

**Pat MORAN**
Helen MUDGETT
1934–
American jazz musician

**Alberto MORAVIA**
Alberto PINCHERLE
1907–
Italian novelist

**Eric MORECAMBE**
Eric BARTHOLOMEW
1926–
English comedian, formed a comedy team with Ernie Wise in 1943. He took his pseudonym from his birthplace – Morecambe in Lancashire

**Jean MORÉAS**
Iannis PAPADIAMANTOPOULOS
1856–1910
Greek-born French poet

**André MORELL**
André MESRITZ
1909–
British character actor

**Rita MORENO**
Rosita ALVERIO
1931–
Puerto-Rican actress and dancer

**Clara MORETON**
Clara MOORE
1824–1899
American author

**Charlie MORGAN**
Charles FEATHERS
1932–
American singer

**Dennis MORGAN**
Stanley MORNER
1910–
American actor

**Emanuel MORGAN**
Witter BYNNER
1881–
American poet. With Arthur Davison Ficke, he perpetrated one of the most amusing of literary hoaxes. Irritated by the pretentiousness of poetic groups calling themselves Vorticist and Imagist, they decided to form the Spectrist school and published *Spectra: A Book of Poetic Experiments* (1916), using the pseudonyms Emanuel Morgan and Anne Knish. The alleged school was taken seriously for nearly two years, Bynner actually writing a rave review of their book in *The New Republic*

**Frank Morgan**
Francis WUPPERMAN
1890–1949
American actor

**Harry MORGAN**
Harry BRATSBURG
1915–
American actor

**Michèle MORGAN**
Simone ROUSSEL
1920–
French film actress

**Patricia MORISON**
Eileen MORISON
1915–
American stage and film actress

**MORITURUS**
Charles LAMB
1775–1834
English essayist

**Gaby MORLAY**
Blanche FUMOLEAU
1897–1964
French actress

**Karen MORLEY**
Mildred LINTON
1905–
American actress of the thirties

**Skip MORR**
Charles W. COOLIDGE
1912–
American jazz trombonist

**Ruth MORRIS**
Ruth WEBB
1926–
Australian author

**Wayne MORRIS**
Bert DE WAYNE MORRIS
1914–1959
American stage and screen actor

**Buddy MORROW**
Muni ZUDEKOFF
1919–
American jazz trombonist

**Anthony MORTON**
John CREASEY
1908–1973
Creasey originally used this pseudonym to write a series of thrillers about the Baron, a gentleman burglar and private sleuth. The hero of the 1963 Morton books is John Mannering an art dealer who solves cases as an unofficial investigator

**Hugh MORTON**
C. M. S. McLELLAN
1865–1916
American playwright

**Jelly Roll MORTON**
Ferdinand Joseph LA MENTHE
1885–1941
American jazz musician. Morton was the name of a porter who married Jelly Roll's mother after Mr. La Menthe left her. His nickname proclaims sexual prowess

**Snub MOSLEY**
Lawrence MOSELY
1909–
American jazz musician

**Mickie MOST**
Michael HAYES
1940–
British pop song producer

**The MOST ARTFUL MAN ALIVE**
Richard Brinsley SHERIDAN
1751–1816
Irish-born English dramatist and parliamentary orator

**Zero MOSTEL**
Samuel MOSTEL
1915–
American actor. He acquired the nickname in school because of his low grades

**Mary MOTLEY**
Comtesse de RENEVILLE
1912–
British author

**Louis MOUNTBATTEN, Earl Mountbatten of Burma**
Louis BATTENBERG
1900–
British sea lord. The Battenbergs changed their surname in 1917

**Leonard MUDIE**
Leonard Mudie CHEETHAM
1884–1965
British character actor; in Hollywood from the thirties

**William MUGGINS**
Charles SELBY
1801–1863
English comedian

**Elijah MUHAMMAD**
Elijah POOLE
1897–1975
American Black Muslim Leader. In 1930 he met Allah in the person of one W. D. Fard, a peddler of

silks from Mecca who was spreading the news of the 'Lost-Found Nation of Islam in the Wilderness of North America'. When Fard mysteriously disappeared in 1934, Poole changed his name to Muhammad and announced that the Master had designated him his Messenger

**MUHAMMAD ALI**
Cassius Marcellus CLAY
1942–
American boxer. World Heavyweight champion (1964–1967) and (1974–)

**Jean MUIR**
Jean Muir FULLERTON
1911–
American actress

**Omar MULDOON**
Harvey MATUSOW
1926–
British author

**Gerhardt MULLER**
Richard BICKERS
1917–
British author

**MULLIGAN OF KILBALLYMULLIGAN**
William Makepeace THACKERAY
1811–1863
British author

**Morty Macnamara MULLIGAN**
William MAGINN
1794–1842
Irish journalist

**MULTATULI**
Eduard Douwes DEKKER
1820–1887
Dutch author. His pen-name means 'I have suffered much'

**Max MUNDY**
Sylvia MATHESON
1923–
British author

**Paul MUNI**
Muni WEISENFREUND

1896–1967
American stage and film actor

**R. MUNROE**
Sir Joseph Lister CHEYNE
1914–
British author

**Patrice MUNSEL**
Patrice MUNSIL
1925–
American opera singer. Changed her name in 1943 to simplify the pronunciation

**Ona MUNSON**
Ona WOLCOTT
1906–1955
American actress

**Frances MUNTHE**
Frances COWEN
1915–
British author

**Onuphrio MURALTO**
Horace WALPOLE
1717–1797
English writer

**MURGATROYD**
James A. JONES
1791–1854
American author

**F. W. MURNAU**
F. W. PLUMPE
1889–1931
German film director; in Hollywood from 1927

**Princess Tulip MURPHY**
Virginia FAULKNER
1913–
American author

**Arthur MURRAY**
Arthur Murray TEICHMAN
1895–
American dancing teacher. Dropped the name Teichman 'for business reasons' in 1920

**Cromwell MURRAY**
Murray MORGAN
1916–
American author

**Ken MURRAY**
Don COURT

1903–
American comic actor and entertainer

**Lieut. MURRAY**
Maturin M. BALLOU
1820–1895
American novelist

**Mae MURRAY**
Marie Adrienne KOENIG
1889–1965
American actress of the silent screen

**Edward R. MURROW**
Egbert Roscoe MURROW
1908–1965
American radio and television commentator

**Kartikeya MUSHAFIR**
Shripad TIKEKAR
1901–
Indian writer

**P. MUSTAPAA**
Martti HAAVIO
1899–
Finnish poet

**Eadweard MUYBRIDGE**
Edward MUGGERIDGE
1830–1904
English-born American photographer. He was the first photographer to record animals and humans in motion. After being acquitted of murdering his wife, he changed his name to its Anglo-Saxon equivalent and emigrated to America

**MY AUNT MARGARET NICHOLSON**
Percy Bysshe SHELLEY
1792–1822
English poet

**MYLES NA GOPALEEN**
Brian O'NOLAN
1911–1968
Irish novelist and journalist

# N

**Laurence NAISMITH**
Lawrence JOHNSON
1908–
British character actor

**Nita NALDI**
Anita DOOLEY
1899–1961
American actress of the silent screen

**NANA SAHIB**
Dandhu PANTH
c. 1821–c. 1859
Indian military leader

**Alan NAPIER**
Alan NAPIER-CLAVERING
1903–
British character actor; in Hollywood since 1939

**Diana NAPIER**
Molly ELLIS
1908–
British actress of the 1930s

**Phil NAPOLEON**
Filippo NAPOLI
1901–
American jazz trumpet player

**Owen NARES**
Owen Nares RAMSAY
1888–1943
British actor of the silent screen

**Petroleum Vesuvius NASBY**
David Ross LOCKE
1833–1888
American journalist

**Simon NASH**
Raymond CHAPMAN

1924–
British author
**Anna NEAGLE**
Marjorie ROBERTSON
1904–
British actress. Neagle is her mother's maiden name
**NECHUY**
Ivan LEVYTSKY
1838–1918
Ukrainian novelist
**Hildegarde NEFF**
Hildegarde KNEF
1925–
German actress
**Pola NEGRI**
Appolonia CHALUPEK
1897–
Polish-born American film actress
**Roy William NEILL**
Roland DE GOSTRIE
1890–1946
Irish-born American film director
**Gene NELSON**
Gene BERG
1920–
American actor, dancer and film director
**Rick NELSON**
Eric NELSON
1940–
American pop singer and light actor, also known as Ricky Nelson
**Nadia NERINA**
Nadine JUDD
1927–
South African ballet dancer. Nadia is a diminutive of Nadezda, her Russian mother's name, and Nerina is the name of a red lily which grows around Cape Town, the dancer's home. She first used the name Nadia Moore
**NERO**
Claudius Daesar Drusus GERMANICUS
A.D. 37–68
Roman emperor

**Pablo NERUDA**
Neftalí Ricardo REYES
1904–
Chilean poet
**Gérard NERVAL**
Gérard LABRUNIE
1808–1855
French writer
**Louis NEUVILLE**
Albert CAMUS
1913–1960
French writer. He used this name during the Second World War
**Mary NEWLAND**
Lilian OLDLAND
1905–
British actress of the silent film era
**Margaret NEWMAN**
Margaret POTTER
1926–
British author
**Julie NEWMAR**
Julia NEWMEYER
1930–
Swedish actress
**Fred NIBLO**
Federico NOBILE
1874–1948
American director of silent films
**F. R. E. NICHOLAS**
Nicolas FREELING
1927–
British crime novelist. He used this pen-name for the novel *Valparaiso* (1963)
**Mike NICHOLS**
Michael Igor PESCHKOWSKY
1931–
German-born American cabaret entertainer turned film director
**Kitty NOBLE**
Kitty KILLINGSWORTH
1928–
American singer
**NOEL-NOEL**
Lucien NOEL
1897–
French actor

**John NOEL**
Dennis Leslie BIRD
1930–
British writer on skating
**NONAME**
Luis Philip SENARENS
1863–1939
American dime novelist
**Sir Gregory NONSENCE**
John TAYLOR
1580–1653
English pamphleteer and poet
**T. R. NOON**
Olive NORTON
1913–
British author
**Tommy NOONAN**
Thomas NOON
1921–1968
American comedian
**Charles NORDEN**
Lawrence DURRELL
1912–
British writer. He used this pseudonym for his second novel *Panic Spring* (1937). The publishers, Faber and Faber, suggested that he should use a pseudonym because of the failure of his first book *Pied Pipers of Lovers* (1935)
**Mabel NORMAND**
Mabel FORTESCUE
1894–1930
American actress. A star of silent movies
**NORMYX**
Norman DOUGLAS
1868–1952
British novelist and essayist. His first book, *Unprofessional Tales* (1901), was written in collaboration with his wife under this pseudonym
**Gil NORTH**
Geoffrey HORNE
1916–
British author
**Leigh NORTH**
Elizabeth PHELPS

*c.* 1860–1920
American author
**Mark NORTH**
Wright W. MILLER
1903–
British author
**Sheree NORTH**
Dawn BETHEL
1933–
American film actress
**Red NORVO**
Kenneth NORVILLE
1908–
American jazz musician. Played vibes and piano
**Max NOSSECK**
Alexander NORRIS
1902–
Polish film director. In Hollywood from 1939
**NOSTALGIA**
James W. BENTLEY
1914–
British author
**NOSTRADAMUS**
Michel de NOTREDAME
1503–1566
French astrologer. Nostradamus is the latinized form of his name
**Nicolaus NOTABENE**
Sören KIERKEGAARD
1813–1855
Danish philosopher and theologian
**Joseph NOVAK**
Jerzy KOSINSKI
1933–
American writer
**Kim NOVAK**
Marilyn NOVAK
1933–
American actress. Her name was changed by Columbia Pictures who at one time thought of grooming her as a possible rival to Marilyn Monroe
**NOVALIS**
Friedrich Leopold von
HARDENBERG

1772–1801
GermanRomantic poet

**Ramon NOVARRO**
Ramon SAMANIEGOS
1899–1968
Mexican romantic actor in silent films

**Ivor NOVELLO**
Ivor DAVIES
1893–1951
Welsh actor, playwright and composer. Son of David Davies and Clara Novello Davies, a singing teacher

**Mrs. NUSSBAUM**
Minerva PIOUS
1909–
American radio comedienne. Named by Fred Allen on whose show she appeared from 1933 to 1949

**Columbus NYE**
James Russell LOWELL
1819–1891
American poet and diplomat

# O

**O.K.**
Olga de Kireef NOVIKOFF
1842–c. 1900
Russian author

**Jack OAKIE**
Lewis Delaney OFFIELD
1903–1975
American comedian. The name 'Oakie' derives from Oklahoma where he spent his childhood

**Vivian OAKLAND**
Vivian ANDERSON
1895–1958
American actress

**Annie OAKLEY**
Phoebe Annie Oakley MOZEE
1859–1926
American sharpshooter. She starred in Buffalo Bill's Wild West show

**Merle OBERON**
Estelle O'Brien Merle THOMPSON
1911–
British film actress. Started acting under the name Queenie Thompson. In 1932, after landing the part of Anne Boleyn in *The Private Life of Henry VIII* she chose the name Merle O'Brien. Korda, the director, felt that O'Brien was too common and changed it to Merle Auberon. This became Oberon only after his original choice had aroused the vehement protest of a prominent Bond Street hairdresser of the same name

**Hugh O'BRIAN**
Hugh KRAMPKE
1925–
American actor. He used the pseudonym Jaffer Gray for a short time before becoming Hugh O'Brian in 1946

**Dave O'BRIEN**
David BARCLAY
1912–1969
American actor; starred in the Pete Smith comedy shorts of the forties

**Edward Stevenson O'BRIEN**
Isaac BUTT
1813–1879
Irish politician. He contributed to the *Dublin University Magazine* under this pen-name

**Flann O'BRIEN**
Brian O'NOLAN

1911–1968
Irish novelist and journalist

**Margaret O'BRIEN**
Angela O'BRIEN
1937–
American child actress. She changed her name to that of the heroine in her first film *Journey for Margaret* in 1942

**Dermot O'BYRNE**
Sir Arnold BAX
1883–1953
British composer. Influenced by the Celtic revival, he wrote Irish short stories under this pseudonym (1912)

**Sean O'CASEY**
John CASEY
1880–1964
Irish playwright. He wrote under the name Sean O'Cathasaigh from 1918, then anglicised this to O'Casey when his first play, *The Shadow of a Gunman* (1923) was produced

**John O'CATARACT**
John NEAL
1793–1876
American editor, novelist and poet

**Frank O'CONNOR**
Michael O'DONOVAN
1903–1966
Irish writer. He assumed this pseudonym for political reasons. O'Connor was his mother's maiden name

**Dawn O'DAY**
Dawn PARIS
1918–
American child actress of the twenties. She was later known as Anne Shirley

**ODETTA**
Odetta GORDON
1930–
American folk singer

**ODETTE**
Odette BRAILLY
1912–
French spy

**Mary ODETTE**
Odette GOIMBAULT
1901–
French actress in British silent films

**Cathy O'DONNELL**
Ann STEELY
1923–1970
American film actress

**Donat O'DONNELL**
Conor CRUISE O'BRIEN
1917–
Irish writer and politician

**An OFFICER OF RANK**
William GLASCOCK
1790–1841
British naval officer and author

**Gavin OGILVY**
J. M. BARRIE
1860–1937
British playwright and novelist. He used this pen-name for articles in the *British Weekly* in the 1880s

**George O'HANLON**
George RICE
1917–
American comic actor

**Maureen O'HARA**
Maureen FITZSIMMONS
1920–
Irish actress; in Hollywood from 1938

**Hideki OKADA**
John GLASSCO
1909–
Canadian writer

**Dennis O'KEEFE**
Edward FLANAGAN
1908–1968
American actor

**Corry O'LANUS**
John STANTON
1826–1871
American journalist

**Ivan OLBRACHT**
Kamil ZEMAN
1882–1952
Czech writer

**Sidney OLCOTT**
John Sidney ALCOTT
1873–1949
Irish-Canadian film director
**The OLD BLOCK**
Alonzo DELANO
1806–1874
American writer
**An OLD BOY**
Thomas HUGHES
1822–1896
British reformer and writer
**OLD COLONY**
Rev. F. N. ZABRISKIE
1810–1881
American theologian
**OLD EBONY**
William BLACKWOOD
1776–1834
Scottish publisher and bookseller
**Zoë OLDENBOURG**
Zoë IDALIE
1916–
French writer
**Polywarp OLDFELLOW, M.D.**
Charles SMART, M.D.
c. 1830–1891
American physician and novelist
**Barney OLDFIELD**
Berna Eli OLDFIELD
1878–1946
American racing driver
**OLD STAGER**
William Taylor ADAMS
1822–1897
American writer of travel books
**Jonathan OLDSTYLE, Gent.**
Washington IRVING
1783–1859
American short story writer and historian. His first work was *The Letters of Jonathan Oldstyle, Gent.* (1802–3)
**The OLD WHIG**
Joseph ADDISON
1672–1719
English essayist
**Pat O'LEARY**
Albert GUERISSE

1911–
Belgian secret agent. He formed an escape organisation in France in 1941 known as 'Operation Pat' which helped hundreds of Allied Servicemen to return to Britain. He received his code name from the British Secret Service
**Oleksander OLES**
Oleksander KANDYBA
1878–1944
Ukrainian poet
**Edna May OLIVER**
Edna May COX-OLIVER
1883–1942
American character actress
**George OLIVER**
Oliver ONIONS
1872–1961
British novelist. He changed his name to George Oliver, but always wrote under his original one
**Vic OLIVER**
Victor von SAMEK
1898–1964
Austrian-born British comedian
**Anny ONDRA**
Anny ONDRAKOVA
1903–
German-Czech actress in British silent movies
**Philothée O'NEDDY**
Théophile DONDEY
1811–1875
French writer. His pen-name is an anagram of his real name
**Sally O'NEIL**
Virginia NOONAN
1913–1968
American actress of the silent screen
**Egan O'NEILL**
Elizabeth LININGTON
1921–
American author
**Marie O'NEILL**
Marie ALGOOD
1885–1952

Irish actress. Sister of Sarah Algood

**ONE OF THE FANCY**
Thomas MOORE
1779–1852
Irish poet

**ONE OF THE FIRM**
Anthony TROLLOPE
1815–1882
British novelist

**ONE OF THEMSELVES**
William Makepeace
THACKERAY
1811–1863
British writer. He wrote an article for *Punch* called 'The Snobs of England' (1846) under this pseudonym

**ONE OF THE PEOPLE CALLED QUAKERS**
Daniel FOE
1660–1731
English journalist and novelist; called Daniel Defoe

**ONE WHO KEEPS HIS EYES AND EARS OPEN**
Henry Ward BEECHER
1813–1887
American Congregationalist preacher and author

**Max OPHULS**
Max OPPENHEIMER
1902–1957
German film director

**An OPIUM EATER**
Thomas QUINCY
1785–1859
English writer

**Oliver OPTIC**
William Taylor ADAMS
1822–1897
American author. He wrote books for boys under this pen-name

**Andrea ORCAGNA**
Andrea di CIONE
*c.* 1308–1368
Italian painter, sculptor and architect. Orcagna is a nickname derived from *Arcagnuolo* (Archangel)

**David ORMSBEE**
Stephen LONGSTREET
1907–
American author

**Moses ORTHODOX**
John Boyle
(Earl of Cork and of Orrery)
1707–1762
Irish writer

**George ORWELL**
Eric Arthur BLAIR
1903–1950
British writer. He used this pseudonym for his first book *Down and Out in Paris and London* (1933). He had considered four names: P. S. Burton, Kenneth Miles, H. Lewis Allways, and George Orwell, and the final choice was made by Victor Gollancz, his publisher. The reason he gave for using a pseudonym, was that the book might cause embarrassment to his parents, but his friends felt that the real reason was that he was trying to escape from his genteel middle-class background by creating a second self: Orwell, the Author

**OSANDER**
Benjamin ALLEN
1789–1829
American poet and clergyman

**Henry OSCAR**
Henry WALE
1891–1970
British character actor

**OSCEOLA**
Baroness Karen
BLIXEN-FINECKE
1885–1962
Danish novelist and story-teller. Better known as Isak Dinesen

**OSNOVYANENKO**
Hryhoriy KVITKA
1778–1843
Ukrainian writer

**M. Flor O'SQUARR**
Jonathan SWIFT
1667–1745
Irish writer and satirist

**Gilbert O'SULLIVAN**
Raymond SULLIVAN
1945–
Irish pop singer

**Richard OSWALD**
Richard ORNSTEIN
1880–1963
German film director

**OUIDA**
Louise DE LA RAMÉE
1839–1908
British popular novelist. Her pseudonym is a pet form of Louise

**Gérard OURY**
Max-Gérard TANNENBAUM
1919–
French actor and film director

**Claire May OVERY**
Clara May BASS
1910–
British poet

**Bill OWEN**
Bill ROWBOTHAM
1914–
British actor-comedian

**Seena OWEN**
Signe AUEN
1894–1966
American actress of the silent film era

# P

**P.T. Esq.**
Philip THICKNESSE
1719–1792
English writer

**PACIFICUS**
Alexander HAMILTON
1757–1804
American lawyer and statesman

**Mrs. Clarissa PACKARD**
Caroline GILMAN
1794–1888
American poet. She wrote *Recollections of a Housekeeper* (1834) under this pen-name

**The PAGAN**
George MOORE
1852–1933
Irish writer

**Gale PAGE**
Sally RUTTER
1913–
American film actress

**Patti PAGE**
Clara Ann FOWLER
1927–
American pop singer, named by the Page Company, a dairy in Tulsa, Oklahoma, when she appeared in their radio commercials

**Debra PAGET**
Debralee GRIFFIN
1933–
American film actress

**Janis PAIGE**
Donna Mae JADEN
1923–
American actress and singer. She took her first name from the popular First World War personality, Elsie Janis, and adopted the name Paige from a grandparent

**Robert PAIGE**
John Arthur PAGE
1910–
American actor

**W. Harassing PAINSWORTH**
William Harrison AINSWORTH
1805–1882
British novelist

128

**Jack PALANCE**
Walter PALANUIK
1920–
American actor

**Aldo PALAZZESCHI**
Aldo GIURLANI
1885–
Italian poet and novelist

**PALINURUS**
Cyril CONNOLLY
1903–1974
English writer and critic. He wrote *The Unquiet Grave* (1944), under the pseudonym of Palinurus, the name of the ill-fated Trojan steersman who fell overboard and was later killed

**Betsy PALMER**
Patricia BRUMECK
1929–
American actress

**Gregg PALMER**
Palmer LEE
1927–
American actor

**Lilli PALMER**
Maria Lilli PEISER
1914–
German-born British actress, in Britain from 1935. She took the name Palmer from an English actress whom she admired

**PANDORA**
Edith HYDE
1895–
American clairvoyant

**PANSY**
Isabella ALDEN
1841–1930
American novelist

**PARACELSUS**
Theophrastus Bombast von HOHENHEIM
1493–1541
German writer

**Cecil PARKER**
Cecil SCHWABE
1897–1971
British actor

**Jean PARKER**
Mae GREEN
1915–
American actress

**Seth PARKER**
Phillips LORD
1902–
American playwright

**Suzy PARKER**
Cecilia PARKER
1932–
American actress

**Willard PARKER**
Worster VAN EPS
1912–
American actor

**Larry PARKS**
Samuel KLAUSMAN
1914–1975
American actor

**PARKYAKARKUS**
Harry EINSTEIN
1904–1958
American radio comedian

**Dita PARLO**
Gerthe KORNSTADT
1906–1972
German actress

**PARMIGIANO or PARMIGIANINO**
Girolamo Francesco Maria MAZZOLA
1503–1540
Italian painter

**Louella PARSONS**
Louella OETTINGER
1880–1972
Hollywood gossip columnist. Parsons was the name of her first husband whom she married in 1910

**Mohammed PASHA**
William HOWE
1833–1909
American lawyer and author. He wrote *The Pasha Papers* (1859)

**La PASIONARIA**
Dolores IBÁRRURI
1896–

Spanish communist famed for her impassioned speeches before and during the Spanish Civil War

**PASQUINO**
J. Fairfax McLAUGHLIN
1839–1903
American lawyer and author

**Tony PASTOR**
Antonio PESTRITTO
1907–1967
American jazz musician

**Wally PATCH**
Walter VINICOMBE
1888–1971
British cockney character actor

**Gail PATRICK**
Margaret FITZPATRICK
1911–
American actress

**Keats PATRICK**
Walter KARIG
1898–1956
American author

**Peter PATTIESON**
Sir Walter SCOTT
1771–1832
Scottish poet and novelist

**PAUL**
Sir Walter SCOTT
1771–1832
Scottish poet and novelist

**Ernest PAUL**
Ernest FOCKE
1896–
British author

**Les PAUL**
Lester POLFUS
1916–
American guitarist

**Lyn PAUL**
Lynda BELCHER
1949–
British pop singer

**Marisa PAVAN**
Marisa PIERANGELI
1932–
Italian actress; in Hollywood from 1951. Sister of Pier Angeli

**Mrs. Mark PEABODY**
Metta Victoria VICTOR
1831–1886
American dime novelist

**Cora PEARL**
Eliza Emma CROUCH
1835–1888
British-born French courtesan

**Irene PEARL**
Irene GUYONVARCH
1915–
British author

**Dave PEARSON**
Dave BARRACLOUGH
1928–
American jazz musician

**Andrei PECHERSKY**
Pavel MEL'NIKOV
1819–1883
Russian novelist

**Santo J. PECORA**
Santo J. PECORARO
1902–
American jazz trombonist

**John PEEL**
John RAVENSCROFT
1938–
British disc jockey

**Jan PEERCE**
Jacob PERELMUTH
1904–
American opera singer

**PELE**
Edson Arantes DO NASCIMENTO
1940–
Brazilian soccer player. The name Pele is meaningless and he does not remember how, or when, he received it

**Thomas PEMBROKE**
Tom HOPKINSON
1905–
British writer

**Arthur PENDENNIS**
William Makepeace THACKERAY
1811–1863
British author

**Anser PEN-DRAGON, Esq.**
William Henry IRELAND
1777–1835
English literary forger
**Amabel PENFEATHER**
James Fenimore COOPER
1789–1851
American novelist
**E. M. PENNANCE**
George FINKIL
1909–
British author
**Joe PENNER**
Joe PINTER
1904–1941
Hungarian-American radio comedian
**Hugh PENTECOST**
Judson Pentecost PHILIPS
1912–
American author. His great-uncle, Hugh Pentecost, was a well-known lawyer in New York at the end of the nineteenth century
**Joan PEPPER**
Joan ALEXANDER
1920–
British author
**Peter PEPPERCORN**
Thomas Love PEACOCK
1785–1866
English novelist and poet
**Pip PEPPERPOD**
Charles W. STODDARD
1843–1909
American poet
**Florence PERCY**
Elizabeth AKERS
1832–1911
American novelist and poet
**Cleofas PEREZ**
Carlos LLERAS RESTREPO
1910–
Columbian politician and journalist
**François PERIER**
François PILU
1919–
French film actor

**Tribulation PERIWINKLE**
Louisa May ALCOTT
1832–1888
American writer of children's books
**Eli PERKINS**
Melville de Lancey LANDON
1839–1910
American humorous writer
**Gigi PERREAU**
Ghislaine PERREAU-SAUSSINE
1941–
American child actress; in Hollywood in the forties
**Clyde PERRIN**
Howard Vincent O'BRIEN
1888–1947
American writer of adventure stories
**Capt. William B. PERRY**
William P. BROWN
1847–1923
American writer of boys' stories
**PERSONNE**
Felix DE FONTAINE
1834–1896
American journalist
**A PERSON OF HONOUR**
Jonathan SWIFT
1667–1745
Irish writer and satirist
**PERUGINO**
Pietro VANNUCCI
c. 1445–1523
Italian painter. *Perugino* means 'the Perugian'
**Roberta PETERS**
Roberta PETERMAN
1930–
American opera singer
**Susan PETERS**
Suzanne CARNAHAN
1921–1952
American film actress
**Pascale PETIT**
Anne-Marie PETIT
1938–
French actress

**Olga PETROVA**
Muriel HARDING
1886–
British-born actress; in Hollywood during the twenties

**PHANTASTES**
William HAZLITT
1778–1830
English essayist

**Frederick PHELPS**
Johnston McCULLEY
1883–
Canadian playwright and author

**Uncle PHILIP**
Francis Lister HAWKS
1798–1866
American clergyman. He used this pen-name for the children's books he wrote

**Flip PHILLIPS**
Joseph FILIPELLI
1915–
American jazz musician

**PHILOMATH**
Benjamin FRANKLIN
1706–1790
American philosopher, scientist and statesman

**T. N. PHILOMATH**
Jonathan SWIFT
1667–1745
Irish writer and satirist

**Margaret PHIPPS**
Laura TATHAM
1919–
British author

**PHIZ**
Hablot Knight BROWNE
1815–1882
British artist. He illustrated some of Charles Dickens's novels

**Terenlius PHLOGOBOMBOS**
Samuel JUDAH
1799–1876
American author

**John PHOENIX**
George Horatio DERBY
1823–1861
American humorous writer

**Kata PHUSIN**
John RUSKIN
1819–1900
English art critic, and author

**Edith PIAF**
Edith GASSION
1915–1963
French singer. Piaf is Parisian slang for sparrow

**Pablo PICASSO**
Pablo RUIZ Y PICASSO
1881–1973
Spanish painter. He started to use his mother's family name only in 1901, because it sounded musical

**Mary PICKFORD**
Gladys Marie SMITH
1893–
Canadian-born film star, on stage from the age of five. She was discovered in 1907 by the producer, David Belasco, who changed her name to Pickford which is a family name

**Slim PICKINS**
Louis Bert LINDLEY
1919–
American cowboy film actor

**Peregrine PICKLE**
George Putnam UPTON
1834–1919
American journalist and author

**Le PICKLEUR**
Robert Louis STEVENSON
1850–1894
British writer

**PICTOR IGNOTUS**
William BLAKE
1757–1827
English painter, poet and mystic

**PIERROT**
George ARNOLD
1834–1865
American journalist and poet

**Robert L. PIKE**
Robert L. FISH
1912–
American author

**Boris PILNYAK**
Boris Andreyevich VOGAU
1894–?1938
Russian novelist

**Ezio PINZA**
Fortunio PINZA
1892–1957
Italian opera singer. Born in Rome, his parents wanted to call him Ezio but a priest objected to using the name of a pagan Roman general for a Christian child, so he was named Fortunio. As a child only his family called him Ezio but later the name came to be generally used

**Evelyn PIPER**
Mrs. Merrian MODELL
1908–
American novelist

**Andrea PISANO**
Andrea DA PONTEDERA
*c.* 1270–1348
Italian sculptor and architect

**Frank PITCAIRN**
Claud COCKBURN
1904–
British journalist

**Archie PITT**
Archibald SELINGER
*c.* 1840–
British music hall comedian. Once married to Gracie Fields

**Josephine PLAIN**
Isabel MITCHELL
1893–
Australian author

**PLATO**
ARISTOCLES
*c.* 427–*c.* 347 B.C.
Greek philosopher. According to Diogenes he was called Plato (meaning broad shouldered) because of his powerful build

**King PLEASURE**
Clarence BEEKS
1922–
American jazz singer

**Jean PLOKOF**

**François Marie AROUET**
1694–1778
French philosopher and writer better known as Voltaire

**Edgar Allan POE**
Edgar POE
1809–1849
American poet and short-story writer. He was left an orphan in early child-hood and was adopted by John Allan, a merchant of Richmond, Virginia, from whom he took his middle name

**The POET AT THE BREAKFAST TABLE**
Oliver Wendell HOLMES
1809–1894
American writer and physician

**The POET OF POETS**
Percy Bysshe SHELLEY
1792–1822
English poet

**Nikolay POGODIN**
Nikolay STUKALOV
1900–1962
Russian dramatist

**POLITIAN**
Angelo AMBROGINI
1454–1494
Italian poet. Named after the Latin name of his birthplace, Mons Politianus

**Michael J. POLLARD**
Michael J. POLLACK
1939–
American character film actor

**Snub POLLARD**
Harold FRASER
1886–1962
Australian comedian who acted in American silent films

**Rosa PONSELLE**
Rosa PONZILLO
1897–
American opera singer

**Lorenzo da PONTE**
Emanuele CONEGLIANO
1749–1838
Italian poet

**Jacopo da PONTORMO**
Jacopo CARUCCI
1494–1556
Italian painter

**Vivian POOLE**
Gabriel JAFFE
1923–
British author

**POPSKI**
Vladimir PENIAKOFF
1897–1951
A Belgian, of Russian parentage, he founded and commanded Popski's Private Army, a British raiding force which operated in North Africa and Italy during the Second World War

**Peter PORCUPINE**
William COBBETT
1763–1835
English political journalist

**Paul POSITIVE**
James MONTGOMERY
1771–1854
Scottish poet

**Adrienne POSTA**
Adrienne POSTER
1948–
British actress; in films since 1958

**Pipsissiway POTTS**
Rosella RICE
1827–c. 1900
American author

**Jane POWELL**
Suzanne BURCE
1929–
American singer and actress

**Richard Stillman POWELL**
R. H. BARBOUR and L. H. BICKFORD
1870–1944; 1878–1936
American novelists

**Teddy POWELL**
Alfred PAOLELLA
1905–
American jazz musician

**Mala POWERS**
Mary Ellen POWERS

1931–
American film actress

**Ollie POWERS**
Ollie POWELL
1890–1928
American jazz drummer

**Richard POWERS**
Tom KEENE
1896–
American actor

**Stefanie POWERS**
Stefania FEDERKIEWICZ
1942–
American film actress

**Walter E. PRAPROCK**
George S. CHAPPELL
1878–1946
American author and architect

**George R. PREEDY**
Margaret CAMPBELL
1888–1952
British novelist, she also used the names Marjorie Bowan and Joseph Shearing

**Karl PRENTISS**
Ken PURDY
1913–
British author

**Paula PRENTISS**
Paula RAGUSA
1939–
American film actress

**John PRESLAND**
Gladys BENDIT
1889–
British author

**Micheline PRESLE**
Micheline CHASSAGNE
1922–
French actress

**PRESTO**
Jonathan SWIFT
1667–1745
Irish writer and satirist

**Paul PRESTON**
Thomas PICTON
1822–1891

American author and soldier of fortune

**Richard PRESTON**
Jack LINDSAY
1900–
Australian writer

**Robert PRESTON**
Robert Preston MESSERVEY
1918–
American actor

**Marie PRÉVOST**
Marie Bickford DUNN
1898–1937
Anglo-French actress in American silent films

**Dennis PRICE**
Dennistoun ROSE-PRICE
1915–1973
British actor

**Vito PRICE**
Vita PIZZO
1929–
American jazz musician

**Peter PRIGGINS**
Rev. Joseph T. HEWLETT
1800–1847
British clergyman and writer

**A. PRIMCOCK**
James RALPH
1724–1762
American writer

**Aileen PRINGLE**
Aileen BISBEE
1895–
American actress in silent films

**PROBUS**
Thomas CHATTERTON
1752–1780
English poet

**PROBUS BRITANNICUS**
Dr. Samuel JOHNSON
1709–1784
English lexicographer, critic and poet

**P. J. PROBY**
James SMITH
1943–
American pop singer

**The PROFESSOR AT THE BREAKFAST TABLE**
Oliver Wendell HOLMES
1809–1894
American writer and physician

**Peregrine PROLIX**
Philip H. NICKLIN
1786–1842
American lawyer and writer

**Marjorie PROOPS**
Rebecca Marjorie PROOPS
1923–
British newspaper columnist. Originally Rebecca Marjorie Rayle. Stopped using the name Rebecca at the age of five when children at her school started calling her 'Becky the Jewgirl'. Proops, her husband's name, is of Dutch origin

**Boleslaw PRUS**
Alexsander GLOWACKI
1847–1912
Polish novelist

**PUBLIUS**
Alexander HAMILTON
1757–1804
American lawyer and statesman

**PUNCH**
Sir Robert WALPOLE
1676–1745
English statesman

**Reginald PURDELL**
Reginald GRASDORF
1896–1953
British light character actor, mostly on stage

**Eleanor PUTNAM**
Harriet BATES
1856–1886
American author

**J. Wesley PUTNAM**
Harry Sinclair DRAGO
1888–
American novelist

**Peter PUZZLE**
Joseph ADDISON
1672–1719
English essayist

# Q

**Q**
Sir Arthur QUILLER-COUCH
1863–1944
British writer
**Un QUAKER**
François Marie AROUET
1694–1778
French philosopher and writer
better known as Voltaire
**John QUALEN**
John OLESON
1899–
Canadian-born Norwegian character actor in Hollywood from the thirties
**Milton QUARTERLY**
John Russell CORYELL
1852–1924
American dime novelist
**Ellery QUEEN**
Manfred B. LEE and Frederic DANNAY
1905– ; 1905–1971
American writers of detective novels. Ellery was the first name of a boyhood friend of the authors and Queen was chosen because it sounded right. The authors had also considered the names James Griffen and Wilbur See

**QUIET GEORGE**
George Frederick PARDON
1825–1844
British author

**QUIZ**
Sir Max BEERBOHM
1872–1956
British essayist and caricaturist. He used this pen-name for notes to a catalogue of an exhibition of caricatures

**Richard QUONGTI**
Thomas Babington MACAULAY
1800–1859
British historian

# R

**Sir R–T W–PL–LE**
Sir Robert Walpole
1676–1745
English statesman
**Johnny RAE**
John POMPEO
1934–
American jazz musician
**Chips RAFFERTY**
John GOFFAGE
1909–1971
Australian actor
**George RAFT**
George RANFT
1895–
American actor

**RAIMU**
Jules MURAIRE
1883–1946
French actor and comedian
**Ella RAINES**
Ella RAUBES
1921–
American actress
**Ma RAINEY**
Gertrude Malissa PRIDGETT
1886–1939
American blues singer
**Rowena RALEY**
Johnston McCULLEY
1883–
Canadian author and playwright

**Jessie RALPH**
Jessie Ralph CHAMBERS
1864–1944
American actress
**Immanuel RAM**
Immanuel VELIKOVSKY
1895–
American author
**Walter RAMAL**
Walter DE LA MARE
1873–1956
British poet and novelist. He used this pen-name for his first book *Songs of Childhood* (1902)
**Marie RAMBERT**
Myriam RAMBERG
1888–
Polish-born British ballerina
**Natasha RAMBOVA**
Winnifred Shaughnessy De Wolfe HUDNUT
*c.* 1895–
American film designer and actress. Second wife of Rudolf Valentino. After her divorce she starred in her only film *When Love Grows Cold* (1925)
**Mrs. RAMSBOTTOM**
Theodore Edward HOOK
1788–1841
English novelist and editor
**Sally RAND**
Helen Gould BECK
*c.* 1904–
American entertainer
**Beverley RANDLE**
Beverley PRICE
1931–
New Zealand author
**Frank RANDLE**
Arthur McEVOY
1901–1957
British music hall comedian. He changed his name in 1917
**Ken RANGER**
John CREASEY
1908–1973
British writer. Creasey used this pseudonym to write Westerns as

well as those of Tex Riley and William K. Reilly
**Stephen RANSOME**
Frederick Clyde DAVIS
1902–
American author
**RAPHAEL**
Raffaello SANZIO or SANTI
1483–1520
Italian painter
**RATIONALIS**
William HAZLITT
1778–1830
English essayist
**Paul RAVEN**
Paul GADD
1933–
British pop singer, now called Gary Glitter
**Aldo RAY**
Aldo DA RE
1926–
American actor
**Man RAY**
(unknown)
*c.* 1890–1976
American artist, son of Russian-Jewish immigrants. He changed his name when at art school in Manhattan in order to avoid the jeers of his fellow students, and never revealed what his original name was
**Nicholas RAY**
Raymond Nicholas KIENZLE
1911–
American film director
**Rene RAY**
Irene CREESE
1912–
British actress
**Ted RAY**
Charles ALDEN
1909–
British radio comedian. When he was a boy his parents changed their name to Olden. He first performed as Hugh Neek, a comic violinist, then became 'Nedlo

(Olden backwards) the Gypsy Violinist', and finally changed to Ted Ray in honour of the British golfer of the same name who won the U.S. Open Championship in 1920

**Carol RAYE**
Kathleen CORKREY
1923–
British actress

**Martha RAYE**
Maggie O'REED
1916–
American actress and comedienne, the daughter of Irish immigrants. In 1932 she took the stage name Martha Raye from a telephone book

**Gene RAYMOND**
Raymond GUION
1908–
American actor

**John T. RAYMOND**
John O'BRIEN
1836–1887
American actor

**Paula RAYMOND**
Paula WRIGHT
1923–
American actress

**Miss READ**
Dora Jesse SAINT
1913–
British author

**Boswell REDIVIVUS**
William HAZLITT
1778–1830
English essayist

**Donna REED**
Donna MULLENGER
1921–
American actress

**Eliot REED**
Eric AMBLER and Charles RODDA
1909– ; 1891–
British writers of mystery stories

**Della REESE**
Deloreese EARLY
1932–
American blues singer. In 1952 she changed her name to Pat Ferro (her current husband's name was Taliaferro) but soon after changed to Della Reese

**George REEVES**
George BESSELO
1914–1959
American actor

**Seeley REGESTER**
Metta Victoria VICTOR
1831–1886
American dime novelist

**Christian REID**
Frances TIERNAN
1846–1920
American novelist

**William K. REILLY**
John CREASEY
1908–1973
British writer. In 1938, ten years before he first visited the United States, Creasey began to produce Westerns. Inspired by Zane Grey and the movies he wrote 29 novels of the American West. Creasey was the only British member of the Western Writers of America. He used three different pseudonyms for his Westerns – Tex Riley, Ken Ranger and the above

**Max REINHARDT**
Max GOLDMANN
1873–1943
Austrian theatre manager

**Erich Maria REMARQUE**
Erich P. REMARK
1897–1970
German novelist

**Duncan RENALDO**
Renault Renaldo DUNCAN
1904–
American actor

**Mary RENAULT**
Mary CHALLANS
1905–
South African writer

**Ludwig RENN**
Arnold von GOLSSENAU
1889–
German novelist

**Dick RETORT**
William COBBETT
1763–1835
English political journalist

**Paul Julius REUTER**
Israel BEER
1816–1899
German news agency owner. He founded Reuters Agency (1849)

**Reginald REVERIE**
Grenville MELLEN
1799–1841
American poet

**Fernando REY**
Fernando ARAMBILLET
1915–
Spanish actor, in international films

**Monte REY**
James FYFE
1901–
British singer

**Debbie REYNOLDS**
Marie Frances REYNOLDS
1932–
American actress. She dislikes the name Debbie which was given to her by Jack Warner of Warner Bros

**Vaclav REZAK**
Vaclav VONAVKA
1901–1956
Czech novelist

**Lord RHOONE**
Honoré de BALZAC
1799–1850
French novelist. He used this pen-name for early pornography

**Elmer RICE**
Elmer REIZENSTEIN
1892–
American playwright. He wrote *The Adding Machine* (1923). In 1914 he changed his name because it was so often misunderstood over the telephone

**Irene RICH**
Irene LUTHER
1891–
American actress of the silent film era

**Cliff RICHARD**
Harry WEBB
1940–
British pop singer. He changed name in 1958 in honour of Little Richard

**David RICHARDS**
Richard BICKERS
1917–
British author

**Emil RICHARDS**
Emilio RADOCCHIA
1932–
American jazz musician

**Harvey D. RICHARDS**
Noel SAINSBURY
1884–
American writer of children's books

**Johnny RICHARDS**
John CASCALES
1911–
American jazz musician

**Stephen RICHARDS**
Mark STEVENS
1916–
American actor. He also acts under his real name

**Henry Handel RICHARDSON**
Ethel Henrietta RICHARDSON
1870–1946
Australian novelist

**John Peter RICHMOND**
Richmond CARRADINE
1906–
American actor. He used this pseudonym from 1930 to 1935 then changed it to John Carradine, under which name he had great success in Hollywood during the thirties and forties

**Kane RICHMOND**
Frederick W. BOWDITCH
1906–1973
American actor

**John RIDDELL**
Corey FORD
1902–
American humorous writer

**John RIDGELEY**
John REA
1909–1968
American actor

**Ernest RIFFE**
Ingmar BERGMAN
1918–
Swedish film director. He used this pen-name for a magazine article on Charlie Chaplin

**RIGHT CROSS**
Paul ARMSTRONG
1869–1915
American journalist and playwright

**Tex RILEY**
John CREASEY
1908–1973
British writer. Creasey used this pseudonym to write Westerns as well as those of Ken Ranger and William K. Reilly

**Captain RINGBOLT**
John CODMAN
1814–1900
American writer of adventure stories

**Clay RINGOLD**
Ray HOGAN
1918–
American author

**Rita RIO**
Rita NOVELLA
1920–
Mexican singer

**RIQ**
Richard Tupper ATWATER
1892–
American author

**Elizabeth RISDON**
Elizabeth EVANS
1887–1958
British actress; in Hollywood from the thirties

**Ian RISK**

**Irving ROSE**
1938–
Scottish bridge player. He adopted this pseudonym so that his parents, who wanted him to be a doctor, would not discover that he was playing in tournaments

**Tex RITTER**
Woodward RITTER
1907–
American cowboy actor and singer

**Joan RIVERS**
Joan MOLINSKY
1935–
American comedienne

**Larry RIVERS**
Yitzroch Loiza GROSSBERG
1923–
American painter. He started as a jazz musician and formed his own group, 'Loiza Grossberg and his Combo', which, at the suggestion of a nightclub comedian, later became 'Larry Rivers and his Mudcats'

**Pearl RIVERS**
Eliza NICHOLSON
1849–1896
American writer

**Annie RIXON**
Annie STUDDERT
1885–
Australian author

**Harold ROBBINS**
Harold RUBIN
1912–
American novelist

**Jerome ROBBINS**
Jerome RABINOWITZ
1918–
American choreographer of many films

**Ben ROBERTS**
Ben EISENBERG
1916–
American writer

**Lynne ROBERTS**
Mary HART
1922–
American actress

**Ignatius Loyola ROBERTSON**
Samuel KNAPP
1783–1838
American author

**George ROBEY**
George WADE
1869–1954
British music hall comedian

**ROBIN**
Sir Robert WALPOLE
1676–1745
English statesman

**Edward G. ROBINSON**
Emanuel GOLDENBERG
1893–1973
American actor. Born in Bucharest, Rumania, he arrived in the United States in 1902. In 1911 he won a scholarship to the American Academy of Dramatic Arts where he was told to get an Anglo-Saxon name. He retained the initials E.G. to which he added the most Anglo-Saxon name he could think of. He later regretted his choice, as it took too long to write when signing autographs

**Madeleine ROBINSON**
Madeleine SVOBODA
1916–
French actress

**Mr. and Master ROBINSON**
Henry Hawley CRIPPEN and Ethel LE NEVE
1868–1910 ; 1893–1967
British murderer and his mistress. Crippen, after poisoning his wife, fled to America with Le Neve on the trans-Atlantic liner *Montrose*. Captain Henry Kendall, the master of the vessel, noticed that the only thing boyish about Master Robinson was his suit and sent a cable to London stating that he suspected that Crippen and his accomplice were on board. It was the first time that radio was used in a criminal inquiry

**Sugar Ray ROBINSON**
Walker SMITH
*c.* 1920–
American pugilist

**Patricia ROC**
Felicia RIESE
1918–
British actress of the forties

**Red RODNEY**
Robert CHUDNICK
1927–
American jazz trumpeter

**Chi Chi RODRIGUEZ**
Juan RODRIGUEZ
1935–
Puerto Rican professional golfer, named after Chi Chi Flores, a baseball idol of his childhood

**Floyd ROGERS**
William SPENCE
1923–
British author

**Ginger ROGERS**
Virginia McMATH
1911–
American actress. She acquired the nickname Ginger early in childhood. Her parents separated when she was a child and her mother married John Rogers in 1920, whose name Ginger adopted

**Roy ROGERS**
Leonard SLYE
1912–
American singing cowboy star. He changed his name to Dick Weston in 1930 and with Bob Nolan formed 'The Sons of the Pioneers', a cowboy singing group. Later, he adopted the name Roy Rogers

**Timmie ROGERS**
Timothy AIVERUM
1915–
American singer

**Eric ROHMER**
Jean Maurice SCHERER
1920–
French film director

**Sax ROHMER**
Arthur WARD or WADE
1886–
British author, creator of Dr. Fu
Manchu. In Anglo-Saxon the
word *sax* means blade and *rohmer*
means wandering, i.e. wandering
blade or freelance

**Gilbert ROLAND**
Luis DE ALONSO
1905–
Mexican actor in Hollywood from
1925

**Harry ROLLICKER**
William Makepeace
THACKERAY
1811–1863
British author

**C. H. ROLPH**
Cecil Rolph HEWITT
1901–
British journalist

**Jules ROMAINS**
Louis FARIGOULE
1885–1972
French writer

**Mike ROMANOFF**
Harry GERGUSON
1890–1972
American restaurant owner, born
in New York. He passed himself
off as a Russian prince, hence the
pseudonym. He had previously
used the names William
Wellington, Arthur Wellesley and
Count Gladstone. Once when
someone spoke Russian to him
at a party he turned away and
said to a friend, 'How vulgar, we
only spoke French at Court'

**Stewart ROME**
Septimus RYOTT
1887–1965
British actor

**Edana ROMNEY**
Edana RUBENSTEIN
1919–
South African actress, in British
films

**E. B. RONALD**
Ronald E. BARKER
1920–
British author

**Mickey ROONEY**
Joe YULE
1920–
American actor who entered films
in 1926 as Mickey McGuire. He
changed this to Mickey Rooney in
1933

**Abel ROPER**
Jonathan SWIFT
1667–1745
Irish writer and satirist

**ROSICRUX**
W. B. YEATS
1865–1939
Irish poet and dramatist. He used
this pen-name for 'High Crosses of
Ireland' in the *Dublin Daily
Express* (1899)

**Emperor ROSKO**
Mike PASTERNAK
1936–
British disc-jockey

**Milton ROSMER**
Arthur Milton LUNT
1881–
British actor and film director

**Annie ROSS**
Annabelle SHORT
1930–
British jazz singer

**Barnaby ROSS**
Frederic DANNAY and Manfred
B. LEE
1905–1971; 1905–
American writers of detective
stories, better known under the
pen-name Ellery Queen. They
used the pseudonym Barnaby
Ross to write about the detective,
Drury Lane. The pseudonym
comes from an Ellery Queen book
*The Roman Hat Mystery* in which
there is a reference to 'the now-
ancient Barnaby Ross murder
case'

**John Hume ROSS**
T. E. LAWRENCE
1888–1935
British author and soldier (commonly known as Lawrence of Arabia). He used this alias when he entered the Royal Air Force in 1922 as an aircraft hand

**Leonard ROSS**
Leo ROSTEN
1908–
American writer. He also used the pen-name Leonard Q. Ross

**Martin ROSS**
Violet MARTIN
1862–1915
Irish writer. She wrote novels in collaboration with her cousin Edith Oenone Somerville. She was born at Ross House, Co. Galway, from which she took her pen-name

**Shirley ROSS**
Bernice GAUNT
1909–
American singer and pianist

**Sutherland ROSS**
Thomas Henry CALLARD
1912–
British author

**Elenora ROSSI-DRAGO**
Palmina OMICCIOLI
1925–
Italian actress

**Primrose ROSTRON**
Joan HULBERT
1911–
British author

**Lillian ROTH**
Lillian RUTSTEIN
1910–
American actress

**Paul ROTHA**
Paul THOMPSON
1907–
British film producer, director and author

**Mark ROTHKO**
Mark ROTHKOVICH
1903–
Russian-born American painter

**ROTTERDAMENSIS**
Desiderius ERASMUS
c. 1466–1536
Dutch philosopher and scholar

**Roger ROUNDELAY**
William BIGLOW
1773–1844
American writer

**Ralph ROVER**
R. M. BALLANTYNE
1825–1894
Scottish author of boys' books

**Virginia ROWANS**
Edward Everett TANNER, III
1921–
American author

**T. ROWLEY**
Thomas CHATTERTON
1752–1780
English poet

**Rob ROY**
Robert MACGREGOR
1671–1734
Scottish outlaw

**Alma RUBENS**
Alma SMITH
1897–1931
American actress

**Anna RUSSELL**
Claudia RUSSELL-BROWN
1913–
Canadian comedienne and singer

**Lilian RUSSELL**
Helen LEONARD
1861–1922
American entertainer

**Lucy May RUSSELL**
John Russell CORYELL
1852–1924
American dime novelist

**Pee Wee RUSSELL**
Charles Ellsworth RUSSELL
1906–

American jazz clarinettist. Nick-
named thus by fellow musicians
because of his small size
**Raymond RUSSELL**
William BALFOUR
1923–
British author
**Trismagistur RUSTIFUSTIUS**
Thomas MOORE
1779–1852
Irish poet
**Mark RUTHERFORD**
William Hale WHITE

1831–1913
British novelist. He used a pen-
name to keep apart his twin
careers of novelist and civil
servant
**Maurice RUTLEDGE**
Marie HALE
1886–
American novelist
**Irene RYAN**
Irene RIORDAN
1903–1973
American comedienne

# S

S
Percy Bysshe SHELLEY
1792–1822
English poet
**S.J.**
Dr. Samuel JOHNSON
1709–1784
English lexicographer, critic and
poet
**S.P.A.M.**
Jonathan SWIFT
1667–1745
Irish writer and satirist
**S.S.**
H. G. WELLS
1866–1946
British writer. He used these
initials for 'A vision of the past' in
*Science Schools Journal* (1887).
They stood for: Sosthenes Smith
**SABU**
Sabu DASTAGIR
1924–1963
Indian actor. He appeared in
*Elephant Boy* (1937) and later
went to Hollywood
**SADI, SAADI, or SA'ADI**
Moslih ADDIN
*c.* 1184–1291

Persian poet
**Françoise SAGAN**
Françoise QUOIREZ
1935–
French novelist. She appropriated
the name of Princesse de Sagan, a
character in Proust's *A la recherche
du temps perdu*
**Victor ST. CLAIR**
George W. BROWNE
1851–1930
American writer of books for boys
**Harry ST. GEORGE**
St. George Henry RATHBONE
1854–1928
American writer of dime novels
and boys' books
**Raymond ST. JACQUES**
James JOHNSON
1930–
American actor
**Susan SAINT JAMES**
Susan MILLER
1946–
American actress
**Betta ST. JOHN**
Betty STREIDLER
1930–
American actress

**David ST. JOHN**
E. Howard HUNT
1923–
American author. Ex-C.I.A. agent who was involved in the Watergate affair
**Jill ST. JOHN**
Jill OPPENHEIM
1940–
American actress
**ST. JOHN PERSE**
Aléxis Saint-Léger LÉGER
1887–
French poet; awarded Nobel prize for Literature (1960)
**S. Z. SAKALL**
Eugene Gero SZAKALL
1884–1955
Hungarian comic actor; in Hollywood from 1939. Nicknamed Cuddles
**SAKI**
Hector Hugh MUNRO
1870–1916
British novelist and short story writer. Killed in the First World War. Saki is the female cup-bearer in the last stanza of the 'Ruba'iyat of Omar Khayyam'
**Masuccio SALERNITANO**
Tomasso GUARDATI
1415–1476
Italian short story writer
**Soupy SALES**
Milton HINES
c. 1926–
American comedian. In childhood he was called Soupy because Hines and Heinz sounded alike. He changed the name to Sales in 1952
**George SAND**
Aurore DUDEVANT, née DUPIN
1804–1876
French novelist. In 1831, with Jules Sandeau, she wrote articles for *Le Figaro* under the pseudonym Jules Sand and then in 1832 she wrote her first novel, *Indiana,* using the name George Sand
**Dominique SANDA**
Dominique VARAIGNE
1948–
French actress
**Cora SANDEL**
Sara FABRICIUS
1880–
Norwegian novelist
**Abel SANDERS**
Ezra POUND
1885–1972
American poet. He used this pen-name for a magazine article (1922)
**Winston P. SANDERS**
Poul ANDERSON
c. 1924–
American science fiction writer
**Ann SANGSTER**
Victoria SHENNAN
1917–
British author
**SAPPER**
H. C. McNEILE
1888–1937
British soldier and writer of adventure stories. Created the character Bulldog Drummond – a patriotic Englishman and modern Robin Hood—in 1920
**Kaarlo SARKIA**
Kaarlo SULIN
1902–1945
Finnish poet
**Leon SASH**
Leon SHASH
1922–
American jazz musician
**Richard SAUNDERS**
Benjamin FRANKLIN
1706–1790
American philosopher, scientist and statesman
**Richard SAVAGE**
Ivan ROE
1917–
British author

**Joseph SAWYER**
Joseph SAUER
1901–
American actor
**John SAXON**
James N. GIFFORD
1896–1957
American author
**John SAXON**
Carmen ORRICO
1935–
American actor
**Joe SAYE**
Joe SHULMAN
1923–
British jazz pianist
**SCAASI**
Arnold ISAACS
c. 1900–
American dress designer
**Gia SCALA**
Giovanna SCOGLIO
1934–1972
Italian actress
**SCARMENTADO**
François Marie AROUET
1694–1778
French philosopher and writer
better known as Voltaire
**B. V. H. SCHNEIDER**
Betty HUMPHREYS
1927–
American author
**Romy SCHNEIDER**
Rosemarie ALBACH-RETTY
1938–
Austrian born actress
**Dutch SCHULTZ**
Arthur FLEGENHEIMER
1902–1935
New York racketeer, gangleader
in the Prohibition era. Although
of German origin, Flegenheimer
was dubbed Dutch Schultz by the
Bergen gang in 1918
**SCIPIO**
Alexander HAMILTON
1757–1804
American lawyer and statesman

**Paul SCOFIELD**
David SCOFIELD
1922–
British actor
**A SCOTS GENTLEMAN IN THE
SWEDISH SERVICE**
Daniel FOE
1660–1731
English journalist and novelist;
called Daniel Defoe
**Gordon SCOTT**
Gordon M. WERSCHKUL
1927–
American actor. He was eleventh
in the line of screen Tarzans (1954)
**Lizabeth SCOTT**
Emma MATZO
1922–
American actress
**O. R. SCOTT**
Ralph GOTTLIEBSEN
1910–
Australian author
**Raymond SCOTT**
Harold WARNOW
1910–
American jazz bandleader
**Tony SCOTT**
Tony SCIACCA
1921–
American jazz musician
**Martinus SCRIBLERUS**
Alexander POPE
1688–1744
English poet
**Martinus SCRIBLERUS**
Jonathan SWIFT
1667–1745
Irish writer and satirist
**Satiricus SCULPTOR, Esq.**
William Henry IRELAND
1777–1835
English literary forger
**SEA-LION**
Geoffrey M. BENNETT
1909–
British naval officer and author
**Edward SEARCH**
William HAZLITT

1778–1830
English essayist
**January SEARLE**
John M. PHILLIPS
1816–1889
American author
**SECOND CHILDHOOD**
Edmund BURKE
1729–1797
English statesman and philosopher
**Solomon SECONDTHOUGHTS**
John P. KENNEDY
1795–1870
American politician and author
**John SEDGES**
Pearl BUCK
1892–1973
American novelist, won the Nobel
Prize for Literature in 1938. She
wrote *The Townsman* under this
pseudonym. Mrs. Buck's maiden
name was Sydenstricker
**Anna SEGHERS**
Netty RADVANYI
1900–
German novelist
**Steve SEKELY**
Istvan SZEKELY
1899–
Hungarian film director; in Holly-
wood from 1936
**Jane SELKIRK**
John and Mary CHAPMAN
1891– ; 1865–
British-born American novelists
**Morton SELTEN**
Morton STUBBS
1860–1940
British actor
**Mack SENNETT**
Michael SINNOTT
1880–1960
American film producer. Creator
of the Keystone Kops
**Aleksandr SERAFIMOVICH**
Aleksandr Serafimovich POPOV
1863–1949
Russian novelist

**Dr. SERENUS**
Dr. Wilhelm STEKEL
1868–1940
Austrian psychiatrist. Serenus is
Latin for calm
**Ernest Thompson SETON**
Ernest Seton THOMPSON
1860–1946
British writer, best known for his
books about animals
**Will SHADE**
Son BRIMMER
1898–
American blues singer
**Tristram SHANDY**
Jonathan SWIFT
1667–1745
Irish writer and satirist
**John SHANE**
Paul DURST
1921–
American author
**Del SHANNON**
Charles WESTOVER
1939–
American pop singer
**Omar SHARIF**
Michel SHALHOUZ
1932–
Egyptian actor. Started in films as
Omar El Sharif in 1953
**Lal Bahadour SHASTRI**
Lal BAHADOUR
1904–1966
Indian politician, Prime Minister
1964–66. He acquired the name
Shastri, meaning 'Graduate Brave
Jewel', as a result of academic
achievement
**Montague SHATT**
Latham C. STRONG
1847–1917
American poet and journalist
**Artie SHAW**
Arthur Jacob ARSHAWSKY
1910–
American bandleader
**Hank SHAW**
Henry SHALOFSKY

1926–
American jazz trumpeter

**Joan SHAW**
Joan DA COSTA
1930–
American pop singer

**Sandie SHAW**
Sandra GOODRICH
1948–
British pop singer

**Susan SHAW**
Patsy SLOOTS
1929–
British actress

**T. E. SHAW**
T. E. LAWRENCE
1888–1935
British author and soldier (commonly known as Lawrence of Arabia). He took this name when he entered the Royal Tank Corps in 1923, choosing it out of respect for George Bernard Shaw. It was legalised in 1927

**Victoria SHAW**
Jeanette ELPHICK
1935–
Australian actress; in Hollywood since 1956

**Dick SHAWN**
Richard SCHULEFAND
1929–
American comedian

**Robert SHAYNE**
Robert Shaen DAWE
1910–
American actor

**Schenor Zalman SHAZAR**
Schenor Zalman RUBASHEV
1889–
Israeli statesman. Hebraized his name by combining his former initials

**Al SHEAN**
Alfred SHOENBERG
1868–1949
German-born American vaudeville artist

**Moira SHEARER**
Moira KING
1926–
Scottish ballet dancer and actress

**Joseph SHEARING**
Gabrielle Margaret-Vere CAMPBELL
1886–1952
British novelist. She also used the names George R. Preedy and Marjorie Bowen

**Mickey SHEEN**
Milton SCHEINBLUM
1927–
American jazz drummer

**Michael SHEPLEY**
Michael SHEPLEY-SMITH
1907–1961
British actor

**Ann SHERIDAN**
Clara Lou SHERIDAN
1915–1967
American actress, known as the 'oomph girl' in the late thirties

**Paul SHERIFF**
Paul SHOUVALOV
1903–1962
Russian-born art director in British films

**Allan SHERMAN**
Allan COPELON
1924–
American comedian. After his parents' divorce in 1930, he took his mother's maiden name

**Joan SHERMAN**
Peggy DERN
1896–
American novelist

**Shorty SHEROCK**
Clarence CHEROCK
1915–
American jazz trumpeter

**Ann SHIRLEY**
Dawn PARIS
1918–
American actress

**Dame SHIRLEY**
Louise CLAPPE
1819–1906
American author

**A SHOEBOY**
Jonathan SWIFT
1667–1745
Irish writer and satirist

**Patric SHONE**
James HANLEY
1901–
British novelist. He used this pen-name for *The House in the Valley* (1951)

**Dinah SHORE**
Frances Rose SHORE
1917–
American popular singer. 'I started by changing my name from Frances Rose Shore to "Dinah" Shore. Everybody down in Nashville changed the Frances to "Fanny". They'd say, "Fanny sat on a tack. Fanny Rose. Fanny Rose sat on a tack. Did Fanny rise?" I had to do something.' The Dinah came from the song of that name

**Bob SHORT**
Alexander POPE
1688–1744
English poet

**Sampson SHORT-AND-FAT**
Samuel KETTELL
1800–1855
American author

**Harry Wandsworth SHORTFELLOW**
Mrs. Mary CLARKE
1809–1898
British writer

**Kid SHOTS**
Louis MADISON
1899–
American jazz musician

**A SHROPSHIRE GENTLEMAN**
Daniel FOE
1660–1731

English journalist and novelist; called Daniel Defoe

**Eddie SHU**
Edward SHULMAN
1918–
American jazz musician

**Nevil SHUTE**
Nevil Shute NORWAY
1899–1960
British novelist who emigrated to Australia

**George SIDNEY**
Sammy GREENFIELD
1878–1945
American vaudeville comedian

**Sylvia SIDNEY**
Sophia KOSOW
1910–
American actress of the thirties

**Simone SIGNORET**
Simone KAMINKER
1921–
French actress. Signoret is her mother's maiden name

**Beverly SILLS**
Belle SILVERMAN
1929–
American opera singer

**Ignazio SILONE**
Secondo TRANQUILLI
1900–
Italian writer and politician

**Phil SILVERS**
Philip SILVERSMITH
1912–
American actor and comedian

**Gabriel SILVERTONGUE, Gent.**
James MONTGOMERY
1771–1854
Scottish poet

**Georges SIM**
Georges SIMENON
1903–
Belgian crime novelist. One of the 16 different pen-names used for about 200 novels which were written between 1923 and 1933. Thereafter he used his own name

**Ginny SIMMS**
Virginia SIMS
1916–
American singer of the late thirties
**SIMON**
Yvonne SIMMS
1928–
British author
**Charlie May SIMON**
Charlie May HOGUE
1897–
American author
**Michel SIMON**
François SIMON
1895–
French actor
**Nina SIMONE**
Eunice WAYMON
1935–
American singer. First worked as a singer at the Midtown Bar, Atlantic City, New Jersey, and changed her name to avoid embarrassing her parents. She chose her first name because as a child she had been called Nina and Simone because it seemed to go well with it
**SINCERUS**
Samuel ADAMS
1722–1803
American statesman
**Emil SINCLAIR**
Hermann HESSE
1877–1962
Swiss writer. Wrote the novel *Demian* (1919) under this pseudonym. It won the Fontane Prize, a competition for first novels, which Hesse returned when his real identity was discovered
**Grant SINCLAIR**
Harry Sinclair DRAGO
1888–
American novelist
**Jo SINCLAIR**
Ruth SEID
1913–
American novelist

**SINGING SIBYL**
Metta Victoria VICTOR
1831–1886
American dime novelist
**Cilia SINGLE**
Benjamin FRANKLIN
1706–1790
American philosopher, scientist and statesman
**Ann SINGLETON**
Ruth BENEDICT
1887–1948
American anthropologist. She wrote poems under this pen-name
**Penny SINGLETON**
Dorothy McNULTY
1908–
American actress
**A SINGULAR MAN**
Samuel Ward FRANCIS
1835–1898
American writer
**John SINJOHN**
John GALSWORTHY
1867–1933
British novelist. He wrote his first four books under this penname
**Audrey Donatovich SINYAVSKY**
Abram TERTZ
1925–
Russian novelist and critic
**Paul SIOGVOLK**
Albert MATHEWS
1820–1903
American lawyer and poet
**SIR BOB**
Sir Robert WALPOLE
1676–1745
English statesman
**SIRIN**
Vladimir V. NABOKOV
1899–
Russian-born American novelist He uses this pseudonym when he writes in Russian. Sirin is the name of a legendary bird of paradise in Russian folklore

**Douglas SIRK**
Detlef SIERCK
1900–
Danish film director; in Hollywood from 1942

**Red SKELTON**
Richard SKELTON
1910–
American comedian

**Alison SKIPWORTH**
Alison GROOM
1875–1952
British actress; in Hollywood during the thirties

**Tod SLAUGHTER**
N. Carter SLAUGHTER
1885–1956
British actor

**Mia SLAVENSKA**
Mia CORAK
1917–
Yugoslav ballet dancer

**Robert SLENDER**
Philip FRENEAU
1752–1832
American sailor and poet

**Jonathan SLICK**
Ann S. STEPHENS
1813–1886
American novelist

**Sam SLICK of Slickville**
Thomas Chandler HALIBURTON
1796–1865
British judge and humorist

**Quicksilver SMALLTALK**
Rev. William G. SWETT
1781–1843
American clergyman and writer

**Parmenus SMARTWEED**
Homer D. L. SWEET
1826–1881
American author

**Frances SMEED**
Jesse Louis LASKY
1910–
American author

**Jim SMILEY**
Raymond SPEARS

1876–1950
American author

**Betty SMITH**
Elizabeth WEHNER
1904–
American novelist

**Carmichael SMITH**
Paul LINEBARGER
1913–
American author

**Farmer SMITH**
George H. SMITH
1873–1931
American writer of children's stories

**Gamaliel SMITH**
Jeremy BENTHAM
1748–1832
English philosopher and legal reformer

**John SMITH**
Henry S. McKEAN
1810–1857
American author

**John SMITH**
Robert VAN ORDEN
1931–
American actor

**Johnston SMITH**
Stephen CRANE
1871–1900
American writer. The youngest son of a Methodist minister in New Jersey, his first novel *Maggie: A Girl of the Streets* (1893) had to be published on borrowed money and under a pseudonym

**Keely SMITH**
Dorothy PRIMA
1932–
American singer

**Mr. SMITH**
Ralph Ingersoll LOCKWOOD
1798–1855
American lawyer and novelist

**SMITH and DALE**
Joseph SELTZER and Charles MARKS

1884– ; 1882–
American vaudeville comedians
**William SMITHIES**
Daniel FOE
1660–1713
English journalist and novelist;
called Daniel Defoe
**Montmorency Sneerlip SNAGS,
Esq.**
Thomas D. ENGLISH
1819–1902
American writer
**SNARLEY CHARLEY**
Charles CLARK
1821–1878
English poet
**Polexenes Digit SNIFT**
Benson E. HILL
1795–1845
British comic author
**SOCINUS**
Lelio Francesco SOZZINI
1525–1562
Italian theologian
**SODA WATER
MANUFACTURER**
William MAGINN
1794–1842
Irish journalist
**Fyodor SOLOGUB**
Fyodor Kuz'mich
TETERNIKOV
1863–1927
Russian poet, novelist and drama-
tist
**Ikey SOLOMONS, Jr.**
William Makepeace
THACKERAY
1811–1863
British writer
**SOMEBODY, M.D.C.**
John NEAL
1793–1876
American editor, novelist and poet
**Elke SOMMER**
Elke SCHLETZ
1940–
German actress
**SOMNABULUS**

Sir Walter SCOTT
1771–1832
Scottish poet and novelist
**SONNY**
Salvatore BONO
1935–
American pop singer
**Ensign SOPHT**
R. M. BALLANTYNE
1825–1894
Scottish author of boys' books
**SORANUS**
François Marie AROUET
1694–1778
French philosopher and writer
better known as Voltaire
**Jean SOREL**
Jean de ROCHBRUNE
1934–
French actor; in international films
**Ann SOTHERN**
Harriette LAKE
1909–
American actress. Her name was
changed by Columbia Pictures in
1935
**Gérard SOUZAY**
Gérard TISSERAND
1920–
French singer
**Mark SPADE**
Nigel BALCHIN
1908–
British author
**Tony SPARGO**
Antonio SBARBARO
1897–1969
American jazz drummer
**Ned SPARKES**
Edward SPARKMAN
1883–1957
Canadian comic actor; in Holly-
wood during the thirties
**Timothy SPARKES**
Charles DICKENS
1812–1870
British novelist
**Ned SPARLING**
Luis Philip SENARENS

1863–1939
American dime novelist
**SPECKLED RED**
Rufus PERRYMAN
1891–
American blues pianist
**Mickey SPILLANE**
Frank MORRISON
1918–
American crime novelist
**Dusty SPRINGFIELD**
Mary O'BRIEN
1940–
British pop singer
**Ziba SPROULE**
Lucius Manlius SARGENT
1786–1867
American author
**Simon SPUNKEY**
Thomas G. FESSENDEN
1771–1837
American writer
**John P. SQUIBOB**
George Horatio DERBY
1823–1861
American humorous writer
**Ronald SQUIRE**
Ronald SQUIRL
1886–1958
British character actor
**Robert STACK**
Robert MODINI
1919–
American actor
**Peter STAFFORD**
Paul TABORI
1908–
British author
**STAINLESS STEPHEN**
Clifford BAYNES
1891–
British music-hall comedian, born in Sheffield, of stainless steel fame, which was the origin of his stage name
**Joseph STALIN**
Iosif Vissarionovich DZHUGASHVILI
1879–1953

Soviet political leader. He began using the name Stalin, which means 'Man of Steel', in 1910. He had been using the pseudonym Koba from 1905 and there was an overlapping period when he used both. The name Stalin first appeared in print in *sotsial demokrat* in 1913
**Theodoros STAMOS**
Theodoros STAMATELOS
1922–
American abstract painter
**Silas STANDFAST**
George S. HILLARD
1808–1879
American writer
**Burt L. STANDISH**
William Gilbert PATTEN
1866–1945
American author
**Konstantin STANISLAVSKI**
Konstantin Sergeyevich ALEKSEEV
1865–1938
Russian actor, director and teacher
**Chuck STANLEY**
Charles STRONG
1906–
American novelist
**Kim STANLEY**
Patricia REID
1921–
American actress
**Paul STANTON**
David BEATY
1919–
British writer of novels about aviation
**Barbara STANWICK**
Ruby STEVENS
1907–
American film star
**Alvin STARDUST**
Bernard JEWRY
1943–
British pop singer, previously known as Shane Fenton. Alvin is derived from his favourite singers

Elvis Presley and Gene Vincent, and Stardust was chosen because it sounded more '1974'

**Richard STARK**
Donald E. WESTLAKE
1933–
American author

**Kay STARR**
Kathryn STARKS
1922–
American pop singer

**Ringo STARR**
Richard STARKEY
1940–
British pop star. He changed his name in 1961 when appearing with Rory Storm. Later he went to Hamburg where he joined the Beatles as drummer. His nickname was given to him by his mother, because of his passion for wearing rings

**Schuyler STAUNTON**
L. Frank BAUM
1856–1919
American author and playwright

**Byron STEEL**
Francis STEEGMULLER
1906–
American author

**Kurt STEEL**
Rudolph KAGEY
1904–1946
American philosopher. He wrote detective stories under this pen-name

**Bob STEELE**
Robert BRADBURY
1907–
American cowboy actor of the twenties and thirties

**Tommy STEELE**
Thomas HICKS
1936–
British pop singer and entertainer

**Frances STELOFF**
Ida Frances STOLOV
1887–
American bookseller. He founded

Gotham Book Mart, New York City

**Anna STEN**
Anjuschka STENSKI SUJAKEVITCH
1908–
Russian actress; in Hollywood from 1932

**STENDHAL**
Marie Henri BEYLE
1783–1842
French author

**Casey STENGEL**
Charles STENGEL
1891–
American baseball club manager. He was named after his home town Kansas City, i.e. K.C.

**Henry STEPHENSON**
Henry GARROWAY
1871–1956
British actor; in Hollywood from 1931

**STEPNIAK**
Sergei Mikhailovich KRAVCHINSKY
1852–1895
Russian writer, exiled for revolutionary activities

**Ford STERLING**
George Ford STITCH
1883–1939
American comic actor

**Jan STERLING**
Jane Sterling ADRIANCE
1923–
American actress

**Robert STERLING**
William Sterling HART
1917–
American film actor of the forties

**Stuart STERNE**
Gertrude BLOEDE
1845–1905
American poet

**Cat STEVENS**
Steve GEORGIOU
1947–
British pop singer

**Christopher STEVENS**
Paul TABORI
1908–
British author

**Connie STEVENS**
Concetta INGOLIA
1938–
American actress

**Craig STEVENS**
Gail SHEKLES
1918–
American actor

**Dan J. STEVENS**
Wayne D. OVERHOUSE
1906–
British author

**Inger STEVENS**
Inger STENSLAND
1935–1970
Swedish-born American actress

**K. T. STEVENS**
Gloria WOOD
1919–
American actress

**Onslow STEVENS**
Onslow Ford STEVENSON
1902–
American actor

**S. P. STEVENS**
Simon S. PALESTRANT
1907–
American author

**Anita STEWART**
Anna May STEWART
1895–1961
American actress, a star of silent films

**Ed STEWART**
Edward MAINWARING
1941–
British disc-jockey

**Elaine STEWART**
Elsy STEINBERG
1929–
American actress

**Max STIRNER**
Kaspar SCHMIDT
1806–1856
German teacher and anarchistic writer

**Georg STJERNHJELM**
Goran LILJA
1598–1672
Swedish poet and scholar

**Charles STODDARD**
Charles STRONG
1906–
American novelist

**George E. STONE**
George STEIN
1903–1967
Polish-born actor; in Hollywood from 1930

**Irving STONE**
Irving TENNENBAUM
1903–
American author

**Colonel STOOPNAGLE**
F. Chase TAYLOR
1897–
American radio comedian, popular during the thirties

**Gale STORM**
Josephine COTTLE
1922–
American actress

**Rory STORM**
Alan CALDWELL
1941–
British pop singer, popular in the early 1960s, and previously known as Jet Storme. Ringo Starr was drummer for his group in 1961 before joining the Beatles

**Les STRAND**
Leslie STRANDT
1924–
American jazz organist

**Paul E. STRAND**
Simon S. PALESTRANT
1907–
American author

**John STRATTEN**
John S. ALLDRIDGE
1914–
British author

155

**Harrington STRONG**
Johnston McCULLEY
1883–
Canadian author and playwright

**Gloria STUART**
Gloria Stuart FINCH
1909–
American actress; in films during the thirties

**Gordon STUART**
Harry Lincoln SAYLER
1863–1913
American writer of boys' books

**John STUART**
John CROALL
1898–
British actor

**STUDENT OF ASTROLOGY**
Jonathan SWIFT
1667–1745
Irish writer and satirist

**A STUDENT OF IRISH LITERATURE**
W. B. YEATS
1865–1939
Irish poet. He used this pen-name for letters to *United Ireland* (1894)

**STULTIFEX ACADEMICUS**
Edmond MALONE
1741–1812
Irish editor of Shakespeare. He used this pen-name in a pamphlet attacking the Provost of Trinity College, Dublin

**Carl STURDY**
Charles STRONG
1906–
American novelist

**Preston STURGES**
Edmond Preston BIDEN
1898–1959
American film director. He adopted the name of his mother's second husband, Solomon Sturges

**A SUBALTERN**
William COBBETT
1763–1835
English political journalist

**Kurt SUCKERT**
Curzio MALAPARTE
1898–1957
Italian political journalist

**Richard SUDBURY**
Charles GIBSON
1874–1954
American traveller and poet

**SUGARTAIL**
George Washington HARRIS
1814–1869
American humorous writer

**Barry SULLIVAN**
Patrick BARRY
1912–
American actor

**Maxine SULLIVAN**
Marietta WILLIAMS
1911–
American singer

**Yma SUMAC**
Emperatriz CHAVARRI
1927–
Peruvian singer; famous for her remarkable vocal range; popular during the fifties

**Charles SUMMERFIELD**
Alfred ARRINGTON
1810–1867
American lawyer and journalist

**Prudence SUMMERHAYES**
Violet Prudence Alan TURNER
1906–
British writer

**Rowland SUMMERSALES**
Robert GAINES
1912–
British author

**Edith SUMMERSKILL**
Mrs. E. J. SAMUEL
1901–
British Labour politician and physician. She retained her maiden name for feminist reasons. In 1961 she received a life peerage and adopted the name Baroness Summerskill of Ken Wood. Her children have also adopted the name Summerskill

**Slim SUMMERVILLE**
George SUMMERVILLE
1892–1946
American comic actor
**Charles SUMNER**
Howard HALL
c. 1875–1921
American author
**The SUNDANCE KID**
Harry LONGBAUGH
c. 1860–1909
American outlaw, member of the
Wild Bunch and companion of
Butch Cassidy. Acquired his nick-
name from the daring bank raid
he carried out in the town of
Sundance, Nevada. He was killed
by the Bolivian army
**Dick SUTTON**
Richard SCHWARTZ
1928–
American jazz trumpeter and
composer
**Henry SUTTON**
David SLAVITT
1935–
American author
**Han SUYIN**
Dr. Elizabeth CHOW
1917–
Chinese writer, born in Peking,
the daughter of a Chinese scholar
and engineer named Chow and a
Frenchwoman named Denis. In
1938 she married General Tang,
killed by the Communists in 1947.
In 1952 she married an English-
man, Leonard Comber
**Italo SVEVO**

**Ettore SCHMITZ**
1861–1928
Italian novelist. His pen-name
derives from his mixed German-
Italian parentage
**Gloria SWANSON**
Josephine SWENSON
1897–
American film star of the twenties
**Geoffrey SWAYNE**
Sidney CAMPION
1891–
British lawyer and author
**Emanuel SWEDENBORG**
Emanuel SVEDBERG
1688–1772
Swedish theologian and mystic
**Blanche SWEET**
Daphne WAYNE
1895–
American actress
**Alfalfa SWITZER**
Carl SWITZER
1926–1959
American actor
**SYLVANDER**
Robert BURNS
1756–1796
Scottish poet. This was the name
under which he corresponded with
a Mrs. Maclehose (Clarinda)
**Arthur SYLVESTER**
Arthur L. TUBBS
1867–1946
American drama and music critic
**Wladyslaw SYROKOMLA**
Ludwik KONDRATOWICZ
1835–1862
Polish poet

# T

**T**
Dr. Samuel JOHNSON
1709–1784
English lexicographer, critic and
poet

**T.B.**
Rev. Thomas BRADBURY
1677–1759
English Dissenting minister celebrated for his facetiousness

157

**T.J.V.**
Ezra POUND
1885–1972
American poet. He used these initials as theatre critic of the *Athenaeum* (1920)

**T\*\*\*Y M\*\*\*E**
Thomas MOORE
1779–1852
Irish poet

**TAFFRAIL**
Capt. Henry DORLING
1883–
British author

**Hugh TALBOT**
Argentine ALINGTON
1898–
British author

**Lyle TALBOT**
Lisle HENDERSON
1904–
American actor

**Richard TALMADGE**
Ricardo METZETTI
1896–
American film stunt man

**Malia TALVIO**
Maria MIKKOLA
1871–1951
Finnish novelist and dramatist

**TAMPA RED**
Hudson WHITTAKER
1900–
American blues singer

**TAN CHAU QUA OF QUANG CHEW FU, Gent.**
Sir William CHAMBERS
1726–1796
English architect. He used this pen-name for *A Dissertation on Oriental Gardening* (1774)

**Joe TARTO**
Joseph TORTORIELLO
1902–
American jazz musician

**Nahum TATE**
Nahum TEATE
1652–1715
Irish poet and dramatist. He was the son of a clergyman named Faithful Teate. He became Poet Laureate in 1692

**Jacques TATI**
Jacques TATISCHEFF
1908–
French comic actor and film director. Grandson of Count Dimitri Tatischeff, an attaché at the Russian Embassy in Paris who had married a Frenchwoman

**Estelle TAYLOR**
Estelle BOYLAN
1899–1958
American actress

**Kent TAYLOR**
Louis WEISS
1907–
American actor

**Laurette TAYLOR**
Laurette COONEY
1884–1946
American actress

**Robert TAYLOR**
Spangler Arlington BRUGH
1911–1969
American actor. His name was changed by Louis B. Mayer, head of MGM, in 1934

**Conway TEARLE**
Frederick LEVY
1878–1938
American actor

**TEKELI**
Theodore Edward HOOK
1788–1841
English novelist and editor

**Marie TEMPEST**
Marie ETHERINGTON
1864–1942
British actress

**Ann TEMPLE**
Penelope MORTIMER
1918–
British writer. She used this pseudonym for her agony column in the *Daily Mail* during the fifties

**Laurence TEMPLETON**
Sir Walter SCOTT
1771–1832
Scottish poet and novelist

**TERATHA JUN**
James KIRKUP
1924–
British author

**Alice TERRY**
Alice TAAFE
1899–
American actress

**Don TERRY**
Donald LOCHER
1902–
American actor

**Sonny TERRY**
Saunders TEDDELL
1911–
American blues singer and harmonica player

**TERRY-THOMAS**
Thomas Terry HOAR-STEVENS
1911–
British comedian. Started in show business in 1935 as Mot Snevets, then tried Thomas Terry. When people erroneously connected him with the theatrical Terry family, he reversed the name to Terry Thomas. He added the hyphen about 1947: 'The hyphen's the gap between my teeth'

**Timothy TESTY and Samuel SENSITIVE**
James BERESFORD
1764–1840
English clergyman

**Herr TEUFELSDRÖCKH**
Thomas CARLYLE
1795–1881
Scottish philosopher, critic and historian. Wrote *Sartor Resartus: The Life and Opinions of Herr Teufelsdröckh* (1836)

**Dame Maggie TEYTE**
Margaret TATE
1887–1976
British singer. Not wishing to be called Mlle. Tatt, she changed her name to Teyte. This provoked an American to write:
Tell us ere it be too late
Art thou known as Maggie Teyte?
Or, per contra, art thou hight
As we figure, Maggie Teyte?

**THEMISTOGENES OF SYRACUSE**
XENOPHON
*c.* 430–*c.* 355 B.C.
Greek historian, essayist and military commander

**Saint THERESA (or TERESA) OF AVILA**
Teresa de CEPEDA Y AHUMADA
1515–1582
Spanish nun, who re-established the Carmelite order

**John THINKINGMACHINE**
James Ferdinand MALLINCKRODT
*c.* 1840–*c.* 1890
American writer

**Donald THISTLE**
H. Clark BROWN
1898–
American writer

**Danny THOMAS**
Amos JACOBS
1914–
American TV comedian, born in Deerfield, Michigan to Lebanese immigrant parents. He changed his name in 1936 using the first names of two of his brothers

**Henry THOMAS**
Henry SCHNITTKIND
1888–
American author

**Jim THOMAS**
Thomas B. REAGAN
1916–
American author

**Carlos THOMPSON**
Juan Carlos MUNDANSCHAFFTER

1916–
Argentinian actor
**M. THOMSON**
François Marie AROUET
1694–1778
French philosopher and writer
better known as Voltaire
**Jesse THOOR**
Peter HOFLER
1905–1952
American poet
**Victor THORNE**
Frederick JACKSON
1886–1953
American novelist and playwright
**THORNY AILO**
John TAYLOR
1580–1653
English pamphleteer and poet
**Kamba THORPE**
Elizabeth BELLAMY
1837–1900
American author
**Richard THORPE**
Rollo THORPE
1896–
American film director
**Sylvia THORPE**
June Sylvia THIMBLETHORPE
1926–
British author
**Luke THRICE**
John RUSSELL
1885–1956
American author
**Tom THUMB**
Charles Sherwood STRATTON
1838–1883
American dwarf entertainer, 31
inches high
**A. R. THURMAN**
Arthur MANN
1901–
American sports writer
**Robert TIBBER**
Eve R. FRIEDMAN
1929–
British author
**Rosemary TIBBER**

Eve R. FRIEDMAN
1929–
British author
**TIBBS**
Charles DICKENS
1812–1870
British novelist
**Tabitha TICKLETOOTH**
Charles SELBY
1801–1863
English comedian
**TIGER LILY**
Lillie BLAKE
1835–1913
American novelist and reformer
**Robert TIMSOL**
Frederic M. BIRD
1838–1908
American author and clergyman
**T. TINKER**
Jonathan SWIFT
1667–1745
Irish writer and satirist
**TINTORETTO**
Jacopo ROBUSTI
1518–1594
Italian painter. His father was a
silk dyer (*tintore*), hence the
nickname
**TINY TIM**
Howard KHAURY
1929–
American pop singer. Early in his
career he used the names Larry
Love and Derry Dover
**TIRSO DE MOLINA**
Gabriel TÉLLEZ
*c.* 1571–1648
Spanish dramatist
**Timothy TITCOMB**
Josiah Gilbert HOLLAND
1819–1881
American poet, novelist and editor
**TITIAN**
Tiziano VECELLI
*c.* 1490–1576
Venetian painter
**Mr. Michael Angelo TITMARSH**
William Makepeace

**THACKERAY**
1811–1863
British author. He wrote *The Paris Sketch-Book* (1840) under this pseudonym

**Marshal TITO**
Josip BROZ
1892–
Yugoslavian political leader. He was jailed in 1928 for Communist activities. When released he changed his name to Tito (1934), a common personal name in his native Croatia

**Timo TITTERWELL**
Samuel KETTELL
1800–1855
American author

**Ann TODD**
Ann Todd MAYFIELD
1932–
American child actress of the thirties

**Mike TODD**
Avrom Hirsch GOLDBOGEN
1907–1958
American theatrical and film producer. When his father died in 1931, he took his son, Michael's, christian name and changed both their surnames to Todd derived from Avrom's nickname, Toat

**Alice B. TOKLAS**
Gertrude STEIN
1874–1946
American poet and critic. She wrote *The Autobiography of Alice B. Toklas* in 1933. Alice B. Toklas was her secretary and the book is really about Miss Stein

**TOKYO ROSE**
Iva Ikuko Toguri D'AQUINO
1916–
Japanese propaganda broadcaster during the Second World War. She was given the name Tokyo Rose by the American troops because of her seductive voice. An American citizen of Japanese parentage, she was found guilty of treason after the war and was sentenced to 10 years' imprisonment

**John TOLAND**
Janus Junius TOLAND
1670–1722
Irish deistical writer. His name was changed by his schoolteacher to stop the jeers of fellow students

**TOM and JERRY**
Art GARFUNKEL and Paul SIMON
1937– ; 1940–
American pop singers and composers. Started in show business as, Tom Graph and Jerry Landis, shortened to Tom and Jerry. They made many records between 1956 and 1959 then vanished from the musical scene until 1964, when they re-emerged as folk singers under their own names

**Jacob TONSON**
Arnold BENNETT
1867–1931
British novelist. He used this pseudonym when he reviewed for *The New Age*, and took great delight in attacking publishers under this name

**TOPOL**
Haym TOPOL
1935–
Israeli actor and singer

**Heller TOREN**
Mrs. Jess YATES
1939–
British novelist

**Miguel TORGA**
Alfredo ROCHA
1907–
Portuguese writer

**Rip TORN**
Elmore TORN
1931–
American actor

**Lee TORRANCE**
Sidney SADGROVE

1920–
British author
**Raquel TORRES**
Paula OSTERMAN
1908–
American film actress of the thirties
**A TORY**
Samuel ADAMS
1722–1803
American statesman
**TOTO**
Antonio Furst de CURTIS-GAGLIARDI
1897–1967
Italian comedian
**Maurice TOURNEUR**
Maurice THOMAS
1876–1961
French film director
**Stuart TOWNE**
Clayton RAWSON
1906–
American author
**Richard TOWNSEND**
Richard BICKERS
1917–
British author
**Arthur TRACY**
Harry ROSENBERG
1903–
American singer, popular in England during the thirties; known as 'The Street Singer'
**A TRADESMAN OF PHILADELPHIA**
Benjamin FRANKLIN
1706–1790
American philosopher, scientist and statesman
**A TRAVELLING BACHELOR**
James Fenimore COOPER
1789–1851
American novelist
**Ben TRAVEN**
(unknown)
*c.* 1886– ?
German novelist who lived in Mexico for many years, and wrote several novels during twenties and thirties, one of which, *Treasure of the Sierra Madre*, was made into a film (1956). His real identity and whereabouts are unknown
**Robert TRAVER**
John VOELKER
1903–
American writer. He wrote *Anatomy of a Murder* (1958)
**Henry TRAVERS**
Travers HEAGERTY
1874–1965
British character actor; in America from 1901
**Linden TRAVERS**
Florence LINDON-TRAVERS
1913–
British actress
**Nick TRAVIS**
Nicholas TRAVASCIO
1925–
American jazz trumpeter
**Richard TRAVIS**
William JUSTICE
1913–
American actor
**Arthur TREACHER**
Arthur Treacher VEARY
1894–1975
British actor in Hollywood from the mid-thirties
**Martha TRENT**
Dorothy SMITH
1893–
American author
**Austin TREVOR**
Austin SCHILSKY
1897–
British actor
**Claire TREVOR**
Claire WEMLINGER
1909–
American actress
**Stephen A. TRING**
Lawrence MEYNELL
1899–
British author

**Dr. Andrew TRIPE**
Jonathan SWIFT
1667–1745
Irish writer and satirist

**TRISTAN**
François L'HÉRMITE
1600–1655
French dramatist

**Leon TROTSKY**
Lev Davidovich BRONSTEIN
1879–1940
Russian revolutionary. He was arrested in 1898 for Marxist activities and exiled to Siberia. In 1902 he escaped and reached England by means of a forged passport in the name of Trotsky, a former jailer

**Kilgore TROUT**
Kurt VONNEGUT, Jr.
1922–
American novelist

**Ben TROVATO**
Samuel LOVER
1797–1868
Irish writer and painter

**TSUYUKI SHIGERU**
James KIRKUP
1924–
British author

**Richard TUCKER**
Reuben TICKER
1913–
American opera singer

**Sophie TUCKER**
Sophia ABUZA
1884–1966
American entertainer, known as 'The Last of the Red-hot Mamas'. She was born when her mother was travelling by wagon out of Russia on her way to join her husband in America. The family name was Kalish, but on his journey to America her father, who had a terror of the Russian authorities, took the name of an Italian friend named Charles Abuza, who died on the trip

**Antony TUDOR**
(unknown)
1909–
British choreographer; in America from 1938

**Sonny TUFTS**
Bowen Charleston TUFTS
1911–1970
American actor

**Timothy TUGMUTTON, Esq.**
Charles CHORLEY
1810–1874
British journalist

**Lana TURNER**
Julia TURNER
1920–
American actress. Her name was changed by the film director, Mervyn Le Roy, in 1935

**Mark TWAIN**
Samuel Langhorne CLEMENS
1835–1910
American novelist and travel writer. He worked as a journeyman printer before becoming a pilot on the Mississippi River boats (1857). In 1861, when he was city editor of the *Virginia City Enterprise*, he first used the pseudonym Mark Twain – the call of the pilots when taking soundings. It means 'two fathoms deep'

**Mark TWAIN**
Isaiah SELLERS
1802–1864
American author and Mississippi River pilot. He wrote articles for the *New Orleans Daily Picayune* under this pen-name which was later adopted by Samuel L. Clemens

**Helen TWELVETREES**
Helen JURGENS
1908–1958
American actress

**TWIGGY**
Leslie HORNBY
1949–
British fashion model. She was

called Sticks at school. In 1964 she met Justin de Villeneuve who named her Twiggy and managed her modelling career

**TWINKLE**
Lynne RIPLEY
1954–
British pop singer

**Conway TWITTY**
Harold JENKINS
1933–
American singer. He was renamed in 1957 by Don Seat, his manager

**Tom TYLER**

Vincent MARKOWSKY
1903–1954
American cowboy actor of the thirties

**Philip TYNAN**
Cormac SWAN
1916–
British author

**TYRO**
H. G. WELLS
1866–1946
British writer. He used this penname for an article 'The devotee of art' in *Science Schools Journal* (1888)

# U

**Paolo UCCELLO**
Paolo di DONO
1397–1475
Florentine painter

**Miles UNDERWOOD**
John GLASSCO
1909–
Canadian writer

**Lesya UKRAINKA**
Larysa KOSACH
1871–1913
Ukrainian poet

**Althea URN**
Consuelo FORD
*c.* 1925–
American writer

**URSUS**
Ambrose BIERCE

1842–1914
American writer

**Maurice UTRILLO**
Maurice VALADON
1883–1955
French painter. The son of Suzanne Valadon and an untalented amateur painter named Boissy. Maurice's surname was given to him by Miguel Utrillo, a Spanish art critic who formally adopted him when he was eight years old. When he started painting, he signed his paintings Maurice Valadon, he later changed this to Maurice Utrillo-Valadon and finally settled on Maurice Utrillo V

# V

**VACUUS VIATOR**
Thomas HUGHES
1822–1896
British reformer and writer

**Catherine VADE**
François Marie AROUET
1694–1778
French philosopher and writer

better known as **Voltaire**

**Roger VADIM**
Roger Vadim PLEMIANNIKOW
1927–
French film director

**Vera VAGUE**
Barbara Jo ALLEN
1904–1974
American radio comedienne

**Amanda VAIL**
Warren MILLER
*c*. 1930–
American author

**Suzanne VALADON**
Marie-Clementine VALADON
1865–1938
French painter. She modelled for
Renoir, Toulouse-Lautrec and
Degas. During the year of the
birth of her son (Maurice Utrillo,
the painter), she began to draw
and showed such talent that
Degas and Lautrec persuaded her
to change her career from that of a
model to artist, she then took the
name Suzanne

**Keith VALE**
W. Paul CLEGG
1936–
British author

**Richie VALENS**
Richard VALENZUELA
1941–1959
American pop singer

**VALENTINA**
Valentina SANINA
1904–
American dress designer

**Joseph VALENTINE**
Guiseppe VALENTINO
1903–1948
American cinematographer

**Rudolph VALENTINO**
Rudolpho GUGLIELMI
1895–1926
American film actor, born in Italy

**Rudy VALLEE**
Hubert Prior VALLEE
1901–

American actor and singer. He
adopted the name Rudy from
Rudy Wiedoeft, a saxophonist
popular in the twenties

**Alida VALLI**
Alida Maria ALTENBURGER
1921–
Italian actress

**Virginia VALLI**
Virginia McSWEENEY
1898–1968
American actress; in silent films

**Varick VANARDY**
Frederick DEY
1865–1922
American dime novelist

**Irene VANBRUGH**
Irene BARNES
1872–1949
British actress

**Violet VANBRUGH**
Violet BARNES
1876–1942
British actress

**Abigail VAN BUREN**
Pauline FRIEDMAN
1918–
American newspaper columnist.
She started her advice column
'Dear Abby' in the San Francisco
*Chronicle* in 1956. The pseudonym
is her own invention

**Clara VANCE**
Mary A. DENISON
1826–1911
American author

**Ethel VANCE**
Grace Zaring STONE
1896–
American novelist

**Margaret VANDEGRIFT**
Margaret JANVIER
1844–1913
American poet

**S.S. VAN DINE**
Willard Huntington WRIGHT
1888–1939
American writer of detective
stories and creator of Philco

Vance, the dilettante detective. Van Dine was taken from Van Dyne, an old family name and S.S. was derived from Steam Ship. He wrote literary criticism under his real name

**Mamie VAN DOREN**
Joan Lucille OLANDER
1933–
American actress

**Edith VAN DYNE**
L. Frank BAUM
1856–1919
American author. He wrote books for girls under this pen-name

**James VAN HEUSEN**
Edward BABCOCK
1913–
American composer

**David VAN KRIEDT**
David KRIEDT
1922–
American composer

**Turk VAN LAKE**
Vanig HOUSEPIAN
1918–
American jazz composer and guitarist

**Victor VARCONI**
Mihaly VARKONYI
1896–
Hungarian actor

**Frankie VAUGHAN**
Frank ABELSON
1928–
British pop singer

**Peter VAUGHAN**
Peter OHM
1923–
British actor

**Ilias VENEZIS**
MELLOS
1904–
Greek novelist

**A. VENISON**
Ezra POUND
1885–1972
American poet. He used this pen-name for a magazine article in 1935

**Charlie VENTURA**
Charles VENTURO
1916–
American jazz saxophonist and bandleader

**VERA-ELLEN**
Vera-Ellen ROHE
1926–
American dancer and actress. Her mother saw the name Vera-Ellen in a dream several nights before she was born

**Violette VERDY**
Nelly GUILLERM
1933–
French-born American ballerina. She changed her name in 1949 when she starred in a feature film called *Dream Ballerina*

**Karen VERNE**
Ingabor KLINCKERFUSS
1915–1967
German actress; in Hollywood from the late thirties

**Anne VERNON**
Edith VIGNAUD
1925–
French actress; in international films

**Max VERNON**
Vernon KELLOGG
1867–1937
American zoologist and author

**VERONESE**
Paolo CAGLIARI
1528–1588
Italian painter of the Venetian School. Born in Verona

**Andrea del VERROCCHIO**
Andrea CIONI
1435–1488
Florentine sculptor and painter

**Odile VERSOIS**
Militza de POLIAKOFF-BAIDAROV
1930–
French actress

166

**Dziga VERTOV**
Dennis KAUFMAN
1896–1954
Russian film director
**Victoria VETRI**
Angela DORIAN
1944–
Australian actress
**Martha VICKERS**
Martha MACVICAR
1925–1971
American actress
**VICTOR**
Percy Bysshe SHELLEY
1792–1822
English poet
**Florence VIDOR**
Florence ARTO
1895–
American actress
**Jean VIGO**
Jean ALMEREYDA
1905–1934
French film director
**Pancho VILLA**
Doroteo ARANGO
1877–1923
Mexican revolutionary
**Frank VILLARD**
François DROUINEAU
1917–
French actor
**François VILLON**
François DE MONTCORBIER
1431– ?
French poet. His father died when he was a child, and he took the name of his guardian Guillaume De Villon, a priest and relative 'who was more than a father to me'
**Gene VINCENT**
Vincent Eugene CRADDOCK
1935–1953
American rock and roll singer
**VINDICATOR**
Tom HOPKINSON
1905–
British writer

**Helen VINSON**
Helen RULFS
1907–
American actress
**The VISIONARY**
Sir Walter SCOTT
1771–1832
Scottish poet and novelist
**Monica VITTI**
Monica CECIARELLI
1933–
Italian actress
**VIVA**
Susan HOFFMAN
1943–
American actress
**Marina VLADY**
Marina de POLIAKOFF-BAIDAROFF
1938–
French actress, sister of Odile Versois
**The VOICE OF EXPERIENCE**
Marion Sayle TAYLOR
1889–1942
American radio lecturer
**A. VOLODIN**
A. LIFSHITS
1919–
Russian dramatist
**VOLTAIRE**
François Marie AROUET
1694–1778
French writer and philosopher. A prolific pamphleteer, he used over fifty pseudonyms to conceal his identity. In 1718 he assumed the name Voltaire, which is supposed to be an anagram of Arouet l(e) j(eune)
**Bastien VON HELMHOLTZ**
Ezra POUND
1885–1972
American poet. He used this name for contributions to periodicals (1914)
**Kurt VON RACHEN**
Lafayette Ronald HUBBARD

1911–
American writer and scientologist.
He used this pen-name for writing
science fiction
**Josef VON STERNBERG**
Josef STERN
1894–1969
Austrian film director; in Holly-
wood from the twenties
**Erich VON STROHEIM**

Hans Erich Maria Stroheim von
NORDENWALL
1885–1957
Austrian actor and film director,
in Hollywood from the twenties
**Arminius VON
THUNDERTENTRONCLE**
Matthew ARNOLD
1822–1888
British writer and poet

# W

**Lancelot WAGSTAFF**
William Makepeace
THACKERAY
1811–1863
British author
**Simon WAGSTAFF, Esq.**
Jonathan SWIFT
1667–1745
Irish writer and satirist
**Theophile WAGSTAFF**
William Makepeace
THACKERAY
1811–1863
British author. He used this
pseudonym for 'Flore et Zepher',
a collection of ballet-deriding
lithographs
**Anton WALBROOK**
Adolf WOHLBRUCK
1900–1968
German actor; in British films
from the mid-thirties
**Herwath WALDEN**
Georg LEWIN
1878– ?
German author and art critic, who
emigrated to Russia in 1930. He
disappeared in 1940
**Junior WALKER**
Autrey DE WALT
1943–
American saxophonist

**Nancy WALKER**
Anna Myrthle SWOYER
1922–
American actress and comedienne
**Max WALL**
Maxwell LORIMER
1908–
British comedian, born in Scot-
land. Wall derives from his step-
father's name, Wallace
**Jean WALLACE**
Jean WALLASEK
1923–
American actress
**Mike WALLACE**
Myron Leon WALLIK
1918–
American TV interviewer
**George WALLINGTON**
Giorgio FIGLIA
1924–
American jazz musician
**Bruno WALTER**
Bruno Walter SCHLESINGER
1876–
German conductor
**Walter WANGER**
Walter FEUCHTWANGER
1894–1968
American film producer
**Artemus WARD**
Charles Farrer BROWNE

1834–1867
American humorous writer

**Mrs. H. O. WARD**
Clara MOORE
1824–1899
American author

**Polly WARD**
Byno POLUSKI
1908–
British actress

**Andy WARHOL**
Andy WARHOLA
c. 1926–
American artist and film producer

**Jack WARNER**
Jack WATERS
1894–
British actor and comedian

**John WARWICK**
John McIntosh BEATTIE
1905–
Australian actor in British films

**Robert WARWICK**
Robert BIEN
1878–1965
American character actor

**Dionne WARWICKE**
Dionne WARWICK
1941–
American pop singer. She added the 'e' in 1974

**WASHBOARD SAM**
Robert BROWN
1910–
American blues singer

**Dinah WASHINGTON**
Ruth JONES
1924–
American singer

**The WATER POET**
John TAYLOR
1580–1653
English pamphleteer and poet

**Muddy WATERS**
McKinley MORGANFIELD
1915–
American blues singer

**Th. WATSON**
John SMITH

1580–1631
English adventurer

**Wylie WATSON**
John Wylie ROBERTSON
1889–1966
British actor

**Franz WAXMAN**
Franz WACHSMANN
1906–1967
German composer; worked in Hollywood from the mid-thirties

**Chuck WAYNE**
Charles JAGELKA
1923–
American jazz musician

**David WAYNE**
Wayne McKEEKAN
1914–
American actor

**Dorothy WAYNE**
Noel SAINSBURY
1884–
American author of children's books

**John WAYNE**
Marion MORRISON
1907–
Film actor. Winfield Sheehan, head of production at Fox Studios, gave Morrison the name John Wayne for his first starring role in *The Big Trail* (1930). His nickname, 'Duke', was given to him by local firemen in Glendale, California. Duke was the name of his Airedale dog and he eagerly accepted the nickname as he was teased about his name, Marion, at school. Studio handouts once explained the nickname by implying that he had a noble relative in England

**Joseph WAYNE**
Wayne D. OVERHOLSER
c. 1915–
American novelist

**Thomas WAYNE**
Thomas PERKINS

1940–
American pop singer
**Charley WEAVER**
Cliff ARQUETTE
1906–
American author
**Clifton WEBB**
Webb Parmalee HOLLENBECK
1893–1966
American actor
**John WELCOME**
John BRENNAN
1914–
Irish author
**Tuesday WELD**
Susan Ker WELD
1943–
American actress
**Oskar WERNER**
Josef SCHLIESSMAYER
1922–
Austrian actor; in international films
**Nathanael WEST**
Nathan WEINSTEIN
1904–1940
American novelist. He changed his name legally in 1926 – 'Horace Greeley said, "Go West, young man," so I did'
**Rebecca WEST**
Mrs. H. M. ANDREWS
née Cicily FAIRFIELD
1892–
British writer
**Ward WEST**
Hal BORLAND
1900–
American writer
**John WESTGATE**
Anthony BLOOMFIELD
1922–
British author
**Mary WESTMACOTT**
Lady MALLOWAN
1891–1975
Better known as Agatha Christie, the writer of detective stories; she used this pseudonym for straight fiction
**Dick WESTON**
Leonard SLYE
1912–
American singing cowboy star. In 1930 he took this pseudonym and with Bob Nolan formed the 'Sons of the Pioneers', a cowboy singing group. He later took the name Roy Rogers
**Helen WESTCOTT**
Myrthas Helen HICKMAN
1929–
American actress
**Harold WESTRIDGE**
Harold AVERY
1903–
British physician and writer on medicine
**J. G. WETCHEEK**
Lion FEUCHTWANGER
1889–1958
German novelist
**Michael WHALEN**
Joseph SHOVLIN
1899–1974
American actor
**H. G. WHEELS**
H. G. WELLS
1866–1946
British writer. He used this pen-name for 'Specimen day' an article on a cycling holiday in *Science Schools Journal* (1891)
**Wade WHIPPLE**
George Alexander STEVENS
1731–1784
English writer and lecturer
**Charles Erskine WHITE, D.D.**
Laughton OSBORN
c. 1800–1878
American poet and playwright
**Jesse WHITE**
Jesse WIEDENFELD
1918–
American comic actor
**The Late Captain Barabbas WHITEFEATHER**

Douglas William JERROLD
1803–1857
British writer. He used this pen-name for *The Handbook of Swindling* (1839)

**WHITEHOOK**
Edward KELLOGG
1790–1858
American economist and author

**WHITE RABBIT**
Forest Frederick YEO-THOMAS
1902–
British agent who operated in France during the Second World War, he also used the code name Shelley

**George WHITLEY**
Arthur CHANDLER
1912–
British author

**Elliott WHITNEY**
Harry Lincoln SAYLER
1863–1913
American writer of boys' books

**Lucia WHITNEY**
Ethel KELLER
1878–
American novelist

**Peter WHITNEY**
Peter King ENGLE
1916–1972
American actor

**Hernia WHITTLEBOT**
Nöel COWARD
1899–1973
British actor and playwright. He wrote *Chelsea Buns* under this pseudonym

**Felix WHYE**
Arthur DIXON
1921–
British author

**Ireene WICKER**
Irene WICKER
1909–
American radio entertainer, known as 'The Singing Lady'. Added the second 'e' in her first name on the advice of an astrologer who said that by so doing she would reap great rewards

**Mary WICKES**
Mary WICKENHAUSER
1916–
American comic actress

**Johnny WIGGS**
John HYMAN
1899–
American jazz cornet player

**Homer WILBUR**
James Russell LOWELL
1819–1891
American poet and diplomat

**Marty WILDE**
Reginald SMITH
1939–
British pop singer

**Patricia WILDE**
Patricia WHITE
1928–
Canadian ballerina. She changed her name in 1945 when a member of the Ballet Russe de Monte Carlo, to avoid confusion with her sister, Nora, who was also a member of the company

**Billy WILDER**
Samuel WILDER
1906–
Austrian film director and writer; in Hollywood from 1934

**WILLIAM**
William Ewart GLADSTONE
1809–1898
British statesman

**WILLIAM THE FOURTH**
William PITT
1708–1778
English statesman

**Warren WILLIAM**
Warren KRECH
1895–1948
American actor

**Bill WILLIAMS**
William KATT

1916–
American actor
**Cara WILLIAMS**
Bernice KAMIAT
1925–
American television comedienne
**Frederick Benton WILLIAMS**
Herbert HAMBLEN
1849–*c.* 1920
American author
**Joe WILLIAMS**
Joseph GOREED
1918–
American singer
**Mary Lou WILLIAMS**
Mary Elfrieda SCRUGGS
1910–
American jazz pianist and composer
**Rex WILLIAMS**
Rex WEI
1933–
British author
**Tennessee WILLIAMS**
Thomas Lanier WILLIAMS
1914–
American playwright. During the Depression he worked in a shoe factory while writing short stories which did not sell. Always very critical of his writing, he began to feel that his name had been 'compromised' and in 1939 he took the name 'Tennessee'. Among the many reasons given for his choice is that his father was of pioneer Tennessee stock
**Homer WILSON**
James Russell LOWELL
1819–1891
American poet, essayist, editor and diplomat. He used this pseudonym to write *The Biglow Papers* (1848)
**Marie WILSON**
Katherine WHITE
1916–1972
British actress
**Robb WILTON**
Robert Wilton SMITH

1881–1957
British music hall comedian, popular during the Second World War
**Barbara WINDSOR**
Barbara DEEKS
1937–
British actress
**Claire WINDSOR**
Olga CRONK
1902–
American actress in silent films
**Marie WINDSOR**
Emily Marie BERTELSON
1923–
American actress
**George WINSLOW**
George WENZLAFF
1946–
American child actor of the forties
**Shelley WINTERS**
Shirley SCHRIFT
1922–
American actress. She chose the stage name Shelley Winter in 1940, when a student at the New Theater School at Brooklyn. In 1947 she added the 's' to her second name. She went to Hollywood in 1942
**John WINTON**
John PRATT
1931–
British author
**Estelle WINWOOD**
Estelle GOODWIN
1883–
American actress
**Norman WISDOM**
Norman WISDEN
1918–
British slapstick comedian; in films since 1953
**Ernie WISE**
Ernest WISEMAN
1925–
British comedian. He formed a comedy team with Eric Morecambe in 1943

172

**Donald WOLFIT**
Donald WOOLFITT
1902–1968
British actor
**Stevie WONDER**
Stephen JUDKINS
1952–
American pop singer
**Anna May WONG**
Wong Liu TSONG
1907–1961
American actress
**Mary WOOD**
Veronica BAMFIELD
1908–
British author
**Natalie WOOD**
Natasha GURDIN
1938–
American actress, in films since
1943. Her name was changed for
the film *Tomorrow is Forever*
(1946) by production executives,
William Goetz and Leo Spitz, in
memory of the director Sam
Wood, and her first name was
anglicised to Natalie
**Papernose WOODENSCONCE,
Esq.**
Robert Barnabas BROUGH
1828–1860
British author and playwright
**Martin WORTH**
Martin WIGGLESWORTH
1926–
British author
**John WRAY**
John MALLOY
1890–1940

American actor
**Martha WRIGHT**
Martha WIEDERRECHT
1926–
American singer
**Saul WRIGHT**
T. T. WILSON
1840–1905
American author
**Gideon WURDZ**
Charles Wayland TOWNE
1895–
American author
**John WYCLIFFE**
H. BEDFORD-JONES
1887–1949
American author
**Jane WYMAN**
Sarah Jane FAULKS
1914–
American actress
**Patrick WYMARK**
Patrick CHEESMAN
1926–1970
British actor
**Ed WYNN**
Isaiah Edwin LEOPOLD
1886–1966
American vaudeville comedian.
He divided his middle name to
form his stage name
**Dana WYNTER**
Dagmar WYNTER
1929–
British actress
**Diana WYNYARD**
Dorothy COX
1906–1964
British actress

# X

**X, AUTHOR OF NOTHING, AND PROPERLY REPRESENTED BY THE ABOVE UNKNOWN QUANTITY**
Major George RANKEN
1838–1855
British soldier and author

**XARIFFA**
Mary Ashley TOWNSEND
1832–1901
American poet

**XO-HO**
Horace WALPOLE
1717–1797
English writer

# Y

**YLG**
Yehuda Leib GORDON
1830–1892
Hebrew novelist

**Y.Y.**
Robert LYND
1879–1949
Irish essayist. He used this pen-name for articles in the *New Statesman*

**Pat YANKEE**
Patricia WEIGUM
1929–
American blues singer

**Dornford YATES**
Major Cecil William MERCER
1888–1960
British novelist

**Peyo YAVOROV**
Peyo KRACHOLOV
1878–1914
Bulgarian poet and dramatist

**YEHOASH**
Solomon BLOOMGARDEN
1870–1927
American poet who wrote in Yiddish

**YELLOW BIRD**
John RIDGE
1827–1867
American Cherokee Indian poet. This pen-name is a translation of his Indian name, Cheesquatalawny

**Charles YELLOWPLUSH**
William Makepeace THACKERAY
1811–1863
British author

**Andrew YORK**
Christopher NICOLE
1930–
British author

**Jeremy YORK**
John CREASEY
1908–1973
British writer. Creasey wrote 20 suspense stories under this pseudonym

**Bud YORKIN**
Alan YORKIN
1926–
American film director

**Alan YOUNG**
Angus YOUNG
1919–
British-born Canadian comic actor

**Gig YOUNG**
Byron BARR
1913–
American actor

**Loretta YOUNG**
Gretchen YOUNG
1913–
American actress

**Robert YOUNG**
Robert PAYNE
1911–
British author
**Stephen YOUNG**
Stephen LEVY
1939–
Canadian actor
**The YOUNGER LADY OF THE THWAITE CONISTON**
John RUSKIN
1819–1900
British art critic and author

# Z

**Z**
Ezra POUND
1885–1972
American poet. He used this initial for a magazine article in 1913
**ZADKIEL**
Richard James MORRISON
1794–1874
British clairvoyant. He published a popular almanac
**ZAPATA**
François Marie AROUET
1694–1778
French philosopher and writer better known as Voltaire
**ZAPHANIEL**
George Alexander STEVENS
1731–1784
English writer and lecturer

**Gabriela ZAPOLSKA**
Gabriela KORWON-PIOTROWSKA
1857–1921
Polish dramatist
**Franco ZEFFIRELLI**
Franco Zeffirelli CORSI
1922–
Italian theatrical and operatic director
**ZOG**
Ahmed ZOGU
1895–1961
Albanian king
**Vera ZORINA**
Eva Brigitta HARTWIG
1917–
Norwegian ballet dancer

# List of Real Names

# A

William ABBOTT
 Bud ABBOTT
Frank ABELSON
 Frankie VAUGHAN
Martin ABRAHAM
 Chink MARTIN
Leon ABRAMSON
 Lee ABRAMS
Raymond ABRAMSON
 Ray ABRAMS
Judah ABRAVANEL
 Leone EBREO
ABÚ-'L KÁSIM MANSÚR
 FIRDAUSI
Sophia ABUZA
 Sophie TUCKER
Rauff de Ryther Duan ACKLOM
 David MANNERS
Betty May ADAMS
 Julie ADAMS
Franklin P. ADAMS
 F.P.A.
Helen ADAMS
 Nancy BARNES
Henry Brooks ADAMS
 Francis Snow COMPTON
Samuel ADAMS
 ALFRED
 An AMERICAN
 A CHATTERER
 DETERMINATUS
 SINCERUS
 A TORY
William Taylor ADAMS
 Irving BROWN
 Clingham HUNTER, M.D.

OLD STAGER
 Oliver OPTIC
Nick ADAMSCHOCK
 Nick ADAMS
Moslih ADDIN
 SADI, SAADI or SA'ADI
Joseph ADDISON
 C.L.I.O.
 The OLD WHIG
 Peter PUZZLE
Paul ADER
 James ALLEN
Jane Sterling ADRIANCE
 Jan STERLING
Walter L. AGNEW
 Stanley FIELDS
Andrea d'AGNOLO
 Andrea DEL SARTO
William Harrison AINSWORTH
 W. Harassing PAINSWORTH
Timothy AIVERUM
 Timmie ROGERS
Elizabeth AKERS
 Florence PERCY
AKUTAGAWA RYUNOSUKE
 GAKI
Leopoldo ALAS
 CLARIN
Rosemarie ALBACH-RETTY
 Romy SCHNEIDER
Harry ALBERSHART
 Rocky LANE
Hardy ALBRECHT
 Hardy ALBRIGHT
John Sidney ALCOTT
 Sidney OLCOTT

**Louisa May ALCOTT**
A. M. BARNARD
Tribulation PERIWINKLE
**Charles ALDEN**
Ted RAY
**Isabella ALDEN**
PANSY
**Alfred ALDERDICE**
Tom DRAKE
**Edward Geoffrey ALDINGTON**
Richard ALDINGTON
**Konstantin Sergeyevich ALEKSEEV**
Konstantin STANISLAVSKI
**Odysseus ALEPOUDELIS**
Odysseus ELYTIS
**Janet A LEXANDER**
Janet McNEIL
**Joan ALEXANDER**
Joan PEPPER
**John M. ALEXANDER**
Johnny ACE
**William ALEXANDER**
AMICUS
**Marie ALGOOD**
Marie O'NEILL
**Durante ALIGHIERI**
DANTE
**Argentine ALINGTON**
Hugh TALBOT
**John S. ALLDRIDGE**
John STRATTEN
**Barbara Jo ALLEN**
Vera VAGUE
**Benjamin ALLEN**
JUBA
OSANDER
**Forrest C. ALLEN**
Phog ALLEN
**Fuller ALLEN**
Blind Boy FULLER
**Henry ALLEN**
Clay FISHER
Will HENRY
**John E. ALLEN**
Paul M. DANFORTH
**J. E. ALLEN**
Judith EVELYN
**Terry Diener ALLEN**
Don Bala ALLEN

**Terry and Don ALLEN**
T. D. ALLEN
**Anthony ALLESSANDRINI**
Tony ALESS
**Jean ALMEREYDA**
Jean VIGO
**Aleksandr ALOYKHIN**
Alexander ALEKHINE
**Alida Maria ALTENBURGER**
Alida VALLI
**John ALTWERGER**
Georgie AULD
**Rosita ALVERIO**
Rita MORENO
**Eric AMBLER and Charles RODDA**
Eliot REED
**Angelo AMBROGINI**
POLITIAN
**AMENHOTEP IV**
AKHNATON I
**Kingsley AMIS**
Robert MARKHAM
**Frances ANDERSON**
Judith ANDERSON
**Gary ANDERSON**
Gary U.S. BONDS
**Mrs. J.C.O'G. ANDERSON**
Stella BENSON
**Kathryn ANDERSON**
Kathryn FORBES
**Poul ANDERSON**
A. A. CRAIG
Michael KARAGEORGE
Winston P. SANDERS
**Vivian ANDERSON**
Vivian OAKLAND
**William ANDERSON**
Lief ERICKSON
**Eliza ANDREWS**
Elezy HAY
**George ANDREWS**
George ARLISS
**Mrs. H. M. ANDREWS**
née Cicily FAIRFIELD
Rebecca WEST
**William Forrest ANDREWS**
Steve FORREST

Nicole ANDRIEUX
 Nicole COURCEL
Ardis ANKERSON
 Brenda MARSHALL
Walter ANNICHIARICO
 Walter CHIARI
Barbara ANTHONY
 Antonia BARBER
Ray ANTONINI
 Ray ANTHONY
Marcus Aurelius ANTONINUS
 CARACALLA
Paul ANTSCHEL
 Paul CELAN
John ANWYL
 BODFAN
Augusta APPLE
 Lila LEE
St. Thomas AQUINAS
 Melinto LEUTRONIO
Fernando ARAMBILLET
 Fernando REY
Doroteo ARANGO
 Pancho VILLA
Roscoe 'Fatty' ARBUCKLE
 Will B. GOOD
 William GOODRICH
ARISTOCLES
 PLATO
Hymen ARLUCK
 Harold ARLEN
Harold Hunter ARMSTRONG
 Henry G. AIKMAN
Paul ARMSTRONG
 RIGHT CROSS
George ARNOLD
 Graham ALLEN
 PIERROT
Matthew ARNOLD
 'A'
 A.M.
 Arminius VON
 THUNDERTENTRONCLE
Sidney J. ARNONDRIN
 Sidney J. ARODIN
Siegfried ARON
 Sig ARNO
Max ARONSON
 G. M. ANDERSON

François Marie AROUET
 (see VOLTAIRE)
Cliff ARQUETTE
 Charley WEAVER
Alfred ARRINGTON
 Charles SUMMERFIELD
Arthur Jacob ARSHAWSKY
 Artie SHAW
Robert ARTHAUD
 Robert ARTHUR
Jimmie ARTIS
 Sir Adolf HITLER
Florence ARTO
 Florence VIDOR
Renee ASCHERSON
 Renee ASHERSON
Marvin ASHBAUGH
 Marvin ASH
Henry Spencer ASHBEE
 Pisanus FRAXI
Frederick Charles ASHFORD
 Frederick CHARLES
Basil N. ASHMORE
 Roy MARLIN
Winifred ASHTON
 Clemence DANE
Sylvia ASHTON-WARNER
 Sylvia HENDERSON
Isaac ASIMOV
 Dr. A.
 Paul FRENCH
Peggy ASKINS
 Evelyn HOME
Kridor ASLANIAN
 Grégoire ASLAN
Dolores ASÚNSOLO MARTINEZ
 Dolores DEL RIO
Gertrude ATHERTON
 Frank LIN
Richard Tupper ATWATER
 RIQ
Louis AUCHINCLOSS
 Andrew LEE
Signe AUEN
 Seena OWEN
Anton Alexander Graf von
AUERSPERG
 Anastasius GRÜN

Paul H. AURANDT
Paul HARVEY
James AURNESS
James ARNESS
Peter AURNESS
Peter GRAVES
Fred AUSTERLITZ
Fred ASTAIRE
Francis AVALLONE
Frankie AVALON

Harold AVERY
Harold WESTRIDGE
Richard Charles AWDRY
Richard CHARLES
Alan AYCKBOURN
Ronald ALLEN
Lewis AYER
Lew AYRES
Charles AZNAVURJAN
Charles AZNAVOUR

# B

Joan BABBO
Joni JAMES
Edward BABCOCK
James VAN HEUSEN
Jean BACKUS
David MONTROSS
Mary BACON
Dolores MARBOURG
Rev. Samuel BADCOCK
JUSTINOPHILUS
Jacob BAER
Buddy BAER
George BAGBY
Moses ADAMS
Helen F. BAGG
Jarvis HALL
Lal BAHADOUR
Lal Bahadour SHASTRI
Dulcie BAILEY
Dulcie GRAY
Gordon BAILEY
Keith GORDON
Harriette BAKER
Mrs. Madeline LESLIE
Laura N. BAKER
Nelson MINIER
Norma Jean BAKER
Marilyn MONROE
Ray. S. BAKER
David GRAYSON
Georgi BALANCHIVADZE

George BALANCHINE
Nigel BALCHIN
Mark SPADE
Dorothy BALDWIN
Clara JONES
William BALFOUR
Raymond RUSSELL
Israel BALINE
Irving BERLIN
Doris Bell BALL
Josephine BELL
James BALLANTYNE
ALDIBORONTIPHOSCO-
PHORNIO
R. M. BALLANTYNE
COMUS
Ralph ROVER
Ensign SOPHT
Maturin M. BALLOU
Lieut. MURRAY
Penelope BALOGH
Petronella FOX
Catherine BALOTTA
Kaye BALLARD
Honoré de BALZAC
Lord RHOONE
Ludwig BAMBERGER
Ludwig BERGER
Veronica BAMFIELD
Mary WOOD
Kamuzu BANDA
Hastings BANDA

182

Sacha BARABIEV
  Sy BARTLETT
**Giorgio BARBARELLI**
  GIORGIONE
**Margaret Fairless BARBER**
  Michael FAIRLESS
**R. H. BARBOUR and L. H.**
**BICKFORD**
  Richard Stillman POWELL
**David BARCLAY**
  Dave O'BRIEN
**John BARCLAY**
  Jonathan DAWPLUCKER, Esq.
**Donato di Betto BARDI**
  DONATELLO
**Arthur Owen BARFIELD**
  G. A. L. BURGEON
**Benjamin BARKER**
  Egbert Augustus COWSLIP, Esq.
**Dudley BARKER**
  Lionel BLACK
**Michael J. BARKER**
  Jack BARKER
**Ronald E. BARKER**
  E. B. RONALD
**Will BARKER**
  Doug DEMAREST
**Edith BARNES**
  Edith MASON
**Gitelle BARNES**
  Binnie BARNES
**Irene BARNES**
  Irene VANBRUGH
**Violet BARNES**
  Violet VANBRUGH
**Alan Gabriel BARNSLEY**
  Gabriel FIELDING
**Byron BARR**
  Gig YOUNG
**Dave BARRACLOUGH**
  Dave PEARSON
**Hugh G. BARRETT**
  Walter BELLMAN
**J. M. BARRIE**
  Gavin OGILVY
**Frances BARROW**
  AUNT FANNY
**Joseph Louis BARROW**
  Joe LOUIS

**Georgetta BARRY**
  Andrea KING
**Patrick BARRY**
  Barry SULLIVAN
**Eric BARTHOLOMEW**
  Eric MORECAMBE
**Alice BARTLETT**
  Birch ARNOLD
**William F. BARTLETT**
  William CARLETON
**Lob BARUCH**
  Ludwig BORNE
**Afro BASALDELLA**
  AFRO
**Elias BASNA**
  CICERO
**Clara May BASS**
  Claire May OVERY
**Louis BATTENBERG**
  Louis MOUNTBATTEN, Earl
  Mountbatten of Burma
**Esther G. BATTISCOMBE**
  Gina HARWOOD
**Gladys BATTYE**
  Margaret LYNN
**H. E. BATES**
  FLYING OFFICER X
**Harriet BATES**
  Eleanor PUTNAM
**Leonie BATHIAT**
  ARLETTY
**Esther G. BATTISCOMBE**
  Gina HARWOOD
**Georg BAUER**
  Georgius AGRICOLA
**L. Frank BAUM**
  Floyd AKENS
  Schuyler STAUNTON
  Edith VAN DYNE
**James BAUMGARNER**
  James GARNER
**Sir Arnold BAX**
  Dermot O'BYRNE
**John BAYLISS**
  John CLIFFORD
**Clifford BAYNES**
  STAINLESS STEPHEN
**Gwyneth G. BEADEL**
  Glenda GORDON

Aubrey BEARDSLEY
A.B.
John McIntosh BEATTIE
John WARWICK
Jerome BEATTY
Lawrence McCANN
David BEATY
Paul STANTON
Shirley BEATY
Shirley MACLAINE
Warren BEATY
Warren BEATTY
Mary Annette BEAUCHAMP
ELIZABETH
Helen Gould BECK
Sally RAND
William BECKFORD
Jacquetta Agneta Mariana
JENKS, of Belgrove Priory in
Wales
The Right Hon. Lady Harriet
MARLOW
Samuel BECKNER
Belle Z. BUBB
H. BEDFORD-JONES
John WYCLIFFE
Henry Ward BEECHER
ONE WHO KEEPS HIS EYES
AND EARS OPEN
William BEEDLE, Jr.
William HOLDEN
Clarence BEEKS
King PLEASURE
Israel BEER
Paul Julius REUTER
Sir Max BEERBOHM
DIOGENES
MAX
QUIZ
Lionel BEGLEITER
Lionel BART
Sir John Hay BEITH
Ian HAY
Jean BEKESSY
Hans HABE
Archie BELANEY
GREY OWL
Louis BELASSONI
Louis BELLSON

Lynda BELCHER
Lyn PAUL
George F. BELDAM
Rex BELL
Elizabeth BELLAMY
Kamba THORPE
Marie BELLON-DOWNEY
Marie BELL
Anne-José BENARD
Cécile AUBRY
Ray BENARD
Ray 'Crash' CORRIGAN
Robert BENCHLEY
Guy FAWKES
Gladys BENDIT
John PRESLAND
Anthony BENEDETTO
Tony BENNETT
Riccard BENEDETTO
Richard BENEDICT
Ruth BENEDICT
Ann SINGLETON
Victoria BENEDICTSSON
Ernst AHLGREN
Israel BEN ELIEZER
BAAL-SCHEM-TOV
Manuel BENITEZ
El CORDOBÉS
Joseph BEN MATTHIAS
Flavius JOSEPHUS
Arnold BENNETT
Sampson KING
Jacob TONSON
Geoffrey M. BENNETT
SEA-LION
Jeremy BENTHAM
Philip BEAUCHAMP
Gamaliel SMITH
James W. BENTLEY
James CLAUGHTON-JAMES
NOSTALGIA
Peggie BENTON
Shifty BURKE
James BERESFORD
Timothy TESTY and Samuel
SENSITIVE
Marcus BERESFORD
Marc BRANDEL

Gene BERG
  Gene NELSON
Solomon BERG
  Steven HILL
Maurice Jean de BERGER
  Maurice BEJART
Ingmar BERGMAN
  Ernest RIFFE
Stephanie BERINDEY
  Steffi DUNA
George BERKELEY
  Ulysses COSMOPOLITE
Elaine BERLIN
  Elaine MAY
Milton BERLINGER
  Milton BERLE
Sara BERNARD
  Sarah BERNHARDT
Benjamin BERNSTEIN
  Ben BLUE
Morris BERNSTEIN
  Morris LOUIS
Sheldon BERSHAD
  Sheldon LEONARD
Emily Marie BERTELSON
  Marie WINDSOR
George BESSELO
  George REEVES
Rayleigh B. A. BEST
  Breton AMIS
Alexandre BESTOUJEFF
  MARLINSKY THE COSSACK
Dawn BETHEL
  Sheree NORTH
Aneurin BEVAN
  CELTICUS
Hanne Karin BEYER
  Anna KARINA
Marie Henri BEYLE
  STENDHAL
Mario BIANCHI
  Monty BANKS
Frederick BICKEL
  Frederic MARCH
Richard BICKERS
  Mark CHARLES
  Riccard CITTAFINO
  Philip DUKES
  Gerhardt MULLER

David RICHARDS
  Richard TOWNSEND
L. H. BICKFORD and R. H.
BARBOUR
  Richard Stillman POWELL
Phyllis BICKLE
  Phyllis CALVERT
Preston BIDEN
  Preston STURGES
Robert BIEN
  Robert WARWICK
Ambrose BIERCE
  Dod GRILE
  URSUS
Natalie BIERLE
  Tala BIRELL
John BIGELOW
  Jackie COOPER
Patricia BIGG
  Patricia AINSWORTH
Ronald BIGGS
  Ronald FURMINGER
  Michael HAYNES
William BIGLOW
  Roger ROUNDELAY
Domenico BIGORDI
  Domenico GHIRLANDAIO
Denise BILLECARD
  Denise DARCEL
Gaspare BIONDOLILLO
  Jack LA RUE
Cyril Kenneth BIRD
  FOUGASSE
Dennis Leslie BIRD
  John NOEL
Frederic M. BIRD
  Robert TIMSOL
Nathan BIRNBAUM
  George BURNS
Aileen BISBEE
  Aileen PRINGLE
Stanley BISHOP
  Icarus Walter EDGAR
Albert BITZIUS
  Jeremias GOTTHELF
Marjorie BITZER
  Lynn BARI
Alexandre César Léopold BIZET
  Georges BIZET

185

Dorothy BLACK
  Kitty BLACK
Susan BLACK
  Susan BEAUMONT
Veronica BLACKETT
  Veronica HEATH
William BLACKWOOD
  OLD EBONY
Edward BLAIKLOCK
  GRAMMATICUS
Dorothy BLAIR
  Ray D. BOLITHO
Eric Arthur BLAIR
  George ORWELL
Hume BLAKE
  Hume CRONYN
Lillie BLAKE
  TIGER LILY
William BLAKE
  AUGUR
  PICTOR IGNOTUS
Karoline BLAMAUER
  Lotte LENYA
Bela Lugosi BLASKO
  Bela LUGOSI
Alexander BLIEDUNG
  John BEAL
Baroness Karen BLIXEN-
FINECKE
  Pierre ANDREZEL
  Isak DINESEN
  OSCEOLA
Herbert L. BLOCK
  HERBLOCK
Gertrude BLOEDE
  Stuart STERNE
John BLOFELD
  CHU FENG
Anthony BLOOMFIELD
  John WESTGATE
Solomon BLOOMGARDEN
  YEHOASH
Claire BLUME
  Claire BLOOM
Harold BLUNDELL
  George BELLAIRS
Ethel BLYTHE
  Ethel BARRYMORE

Herbert BLYTHE
  Maurice BARRYMORE
John BLYTHE
  John BARRYMORE
Lionel BLYTHE
  Lionel BARRYMORE
Vernon BLYTHE
  Vernon CASTLE
Jeff BOATFIELD
  Jeff JEFFRIES
Oscar BOETTICHER
  Budd BOETTICHER
Elizabeth BOGER
  Betsy BLAIR
Mervin BOGUE
  Ish KABIBBLE
Lilian BOHNY
  Billie DOVE
Maria BOLDAO Y CASTILLA
  MARGO
Sister Mary Angela BOLSTER
  Evelyn BOLSTER
Walter BOND
  Walter FITZGERALD
Beulah BONDY
  Beulah BONDI
William H. BONNEY
  BILLY THE KID
Salvatore BONO
  SONNY
Elaine BOOKBINDER
  Elkie BROOKS
Charles Eugene BOONE
  Pat BOONE
Fanny BORACH
  Fanny BRICE
Ermes BORGNINE
  Ernest BORGNINE
Hal BORLAND
  Ward WEST
Jez Cruz BOSEN
  James CRUZE
Dorothy BOUCHIER
  Chili BOUCHIER
Mohammed BOUKHAROUBA
  Houri BOUMEDIENNE
Jeanne Marie BOURGEOIS
  MISTINGUETT

186

**Paul BOURQUIN**
Richard AMBERLEY
**Frederick W. BOWDITCH**
Kane RICHMOND
**John BOWEN and Jeremy**
**BULLMORE**
Justin BLAKE
**Ralph BOWMAN**
John ARCHER
**Martin BOYD**
Martin MILLS
**Estelle BOYLAN**
Estelle TAYLOR
**John BOYLE**
Goliah ENGLISH
Reginald FITZWORM
Michael KRAWBRIDGE
Moses ORTHODOX
**C. S. BOYLES**
Will C. BROWN
**Parnell BRADBURY**
Stephen DERMOTT
**Robert BRADBURY**
Bob STEELE
**Rev. Thomas BRADBURY**
T.B.
**Sarah BRADFORD**
COUSIN CICELY
**Charles BRADLAUGH**
ICONOCLAST
**Mary BRADLEY**
COUSIN ALICE
**Warren BRADLEY**
Glance GAYLORD
**Odette BRAILLY**
ODETTE
**Ailsa BRAMBLEBY**
Jennifer CRAIG
**Harry BRATSBURG**
Harry MORGAN
**Helen BRAWNER and F. Van**
**Wyck MASON**
Geoffrey COFFIN
**Vivian BRECKENFELD**
Vivian BRECK
**Wellman BREAUX**
Wellman BRAUD
**Edward BREITENBERGER**
Edd BYRNES

**John BRENNAN**
John WELCOME
**Clemens BRENTANO**
MARIA
**George K. A. BREST**
Geroge K. ARTHUR
**Clare BRETON-SMITH**
Elinor CALDWELL
**Robert BRIDGES**
DROCH
**Charles F. BRIGGS**
Harry FRANCO
**Helen Virginia BRIGGS**
Virginia BRUCE
**Gertrude BRIGHAM**
Viktor FLAMBEAU
**Gerald BRIGHT**
GERALDO
**Ernest BRIMMER**
Richard DIX
**Son BRIMMER**
Will SHADE
**Smylla BRIND**
Vanessa BROWN
**Henry BRINTON**
Alex FRASER
**Herman BRIX**
Bruce BENNETT
**Dora BROADBENT**
Dora BRYAN
**Amanda BRODBENT**
Amanda BARRIE
**John Henry BRODRIBB**
Henry IRVING
**Denis BROGAN**
Maurice BARRINGTON
**Lev Davidovich BRONSTEIN**
Leon TROTSKY
**Anne BRONTË**
Acton BELL
**Charlotte BRONTË**
Currer BELL
**Emily Jane BRONTË**
Ellis BELL
**Clifford BROOK**
Clive BROOK
**James G. BROOKS**
FLORIO

Vivian BROOKS
  Osmington MILLS
Robert Barnabas BROUGH
  Papernose WOODENSCONCE,
  Esq.
Gwethalyn G. BROWN
  Gwethalyn GRAHAM
H. Clark BROWN
  Donald THISTLE
Helen BROWN
  Helen Hayes
James BROWN
  James HALL
Mary BROWN
  Vanessa BLAKE
Robert BROWN
  WASHBOARD SAM
Theron BROWN
  Park LUDLOW
W. J. C. BROWN
  Jamieson BROWN
William P. BROWN
  Capt. William B. PERRY
Zenith J. BROWN
  Leslie FORD
  David FROME
Charles Farrer BROWNE
  Artemus WARD
George W. BROWNE
  Victor ST. CLAIR
Hablot Knight BROWNE
  PHIZ
Rilma BROWNE
  Stanley CASTLE
Elizabeth Barrett BROWNING
  A.A.
Mrs. John BROWNING
  Jean MADEIRA
Josip BROZ
  Marshal TITO
Elliot L. BROZA
  Elliot LAWRENCE
Wallace BRUCE
  Thursty McQUILL
Cornelia BRUCH
  Cornell BORCHERS
Spangler Arlington BRUGH
  Robert TAYLOR

Patricia BRUMECK
  Betsy PALMER
George BRUMMELL
  Beau BRUMMELL
George BRUNIES
  Georg BRUNIS
Rita BRUNSTROM
  Jane CARR
Robert BRYANS
  Robert HARBINSON
Vincert BUCCI
  Vinnie BURKE
Susan and John BUCHAN
  CADMUS and HARMONIA
Charles BUCHINSKI
  Charles BRONSON
Pearl BUCK
  John SEDGES
Jeremy BULLMORE and John
BOWEN
  Justin BLAKE
Michelagniolo di Ludovico
BUONARROTI
  MICHELANGELO
Suzanne BURCE
  Jane POWELL
David BURG
  Alexander DOHLBERG
George BURGESS
  Burgess MEREDITH
Nellie Paulina BURGIN
  Polly BERGEN
Edmund BURKE
  SECOND CHILDHOOD
John F. BURKE
  Jonathan GEORGE
  Joanna JONES
Chester BURNETT
  HOWLIN' WOLF
Robert BURNS
  SYLVANDER
Agnes BURR
  Barbara BOYD
William BURROUGHS
  William LEE
Dallas BURROWS
  Orson BEAN

**Sir Richard BURTON**
  Frank BAKER, D.O.N.
**Louis BUSH**
  Joe Fingers CARR
**Samuel BUTLER**
  John CANNE
**Isaac BUTT**
  Edward Stevenson O'BRIEN
**David BUTTERFIELD**

  David BLAIR
**Amy BYERS**
  Ann BARRY
**Witter BYNNER**
  Emanuel MORGAN
**Reg BYRD**
  Professor LONGHAIR
**George Gordon BYRON**
  Horace HORNEM

# C

**Michalis CACOGHIANNIS**
  Michael CACOYANNIS
**Paolo CAGLIARI**
  VERONESE
**Alan CALDWELL**
  Rory STORM
**Janet Taylor CALDWELL**
  Taylor CALDWELL
**Cora CALHOUN**
  Lovie AUSTIN
**Martin CALINIFF**
  Michael CALLAN
**Thomas Henry CALLARD**
  Sutherland ROSS
**John CALVIN**
  ALCUINUS
  LUCANIUS
**Candido CAMERO**
  CANDIDO
**Mrs. Alan CAMERON**
  Elizabeth BOWEN
**Clementina CAMPBELL**
  Cleo LAINE
**Gabrielle Margaret-Vere CAMPBELL**
  Marjorie BOWEN
  George R. PREEDY
  Joseph SHEARING
**John Lorne CAMPBELL**
  FEAR CHANAIDH
**Sidney CAMPION**
  Geoffrey SWAYNE
**Albert CAMUS**

  Louis NEUVILLE
**Antonio CANALE**
  CANALETTO
**Leonard CANEGATA**
  Canada LEE
**Margarita CANSINO**
  Rita HAYWORTH
**Maria CAPDEVILLE**
  Mona MARIS
**Alfred Gerald CAPLIN**
  Al CAPP
**Alfredo CAPURRO**
  Alfred DRAKE
**Neville CARDUS**
  CRICKETER
**Harold James CAREW-SLATER**
  James CAREY
**Mrs. John CARLETON**
  Janet Buchanan ADAM SMITH
**Thomas CARLYLE**
  Herr TEUFELSDRÖCKH
**Gareth CARMODY**
  Gary CONWAY
**Suzanne CARNAHAN**
  Susan PETERS
**Raymond CARNEGIE**
  Sacha CARNEGIE
**Pierre Augustin CARON**
  BEAUMARCHAIS
**Harlean CARPENTIER**
  Jean HARLOW
**Margaret CARR**
  Martin CARROLL

Richmond CARRADINE
John CARRADINE
John Peter RICHMOND
Lilliane CARRÉ
Lili DAMITA
Mathilde CARRÉ
The CAT
Charles Edmund CARRINGTON
Charles EDMONDS
Daniel CARROLL
Danny LA RUE
Bryan CARTER
Nick CARTER
Ernest Frank CARTER
Frank GIFFIN
John F. CARTER
Jay FRANKLIN
Jacopo CARUCCI
Jacopo di PONTORMO
Joyce CARY
Thomas JOYCE
John CASCALES
Johnny RICHARDS
Camille Auguste Marie CASELEYR
Jack DANVERS
Christina CASEMENT
Christina MACLEAN
James CASEY
Jimmy JAMES
John CASEY
Sean O'CASEY
Ronald CASSILL
Owen AHERNE
Frederick CASSON
Baden BEATTY
Walden Robert CASSOTTO
Bobby DARIN
Lee CASTALDO
Lee CASTLE
Francesco CASTIGLIA
Frank COSTELLO
Max CATTO
Simon KENT
Monica CECIARELLI
Monica VITTI
Teresa de CEPEDA Y AHUMADA
Saint THERESA (or TERESA)
OF AVILA

Peter CERAGIOLI
Pete JOLLY
Al CERNICK
Guy MITCHELL
Jacinto CHABANIA
Jerry BLAKE
Herbert CHALKE
Hereth BLACKER
Mary CHALLANS
Mary RENAULT
Alexander CHALMERS
Ferdinando FIDGET
John S. CHALONER
Jon CHALON
Appolonia CHALUPEK
Pola NEGRI
Aiden CHAMBERS
Malcolm BLACKLIN
Jessie Ralph CHAMBERS
Jessie RALPH
Sir William CHAMBERS
TAN CHAU QUA OF QUANG
CHEW FU, Gent.
Edwin Ross CHAMPLIN
Clarence FAIRCHILD
Arthur CHANDLER
George WHITLEY
Naomi CHANDOR
Louise GRAY
Creighton CHANEY
Lon CHANEY, Jr.
John CHAPMAN
Johnny APPLESEED
John and Mary CHAPMAN
Maristan CHAPMAN
Jane SELKIRK
Raymond CHAPMAN
Simon NASH
George S. CHAPPELL
Walter E. PRAPROCK
Suzanne CHARPENTIER
ANNABELLA
Émile CHARTIER
ALAIN
Micheline CHASSAGNE
Micheline PRESLE
Thomas CHATTERTON
DECIMUS

PROBUS
  T. ROWLEY
**William Andrew CHATTO**
  Joseph FUME
**Lily Claudette CHAUCHOIN**
  Claudette COLBERT
**Christine CHAUNDLER**
  Peter MARTIN
**Emperatriz CHAVARRI**
  Yma SUMAC
**Sidney CHAYEFSKY**
  Paddy CHAYEFSKY
**Patrick CHEESMAN**
  Patrick WYMARK
**Leonard M. CHEETHAM**
  Leonard MUDIE
**Clarence CHEROCK**
  Shorty SHEROCK
**Philip Dormer Stanhope, Earl of CHESTERFIELD**
  Adam FITZADAM
**G. K. CHESTERTON**
  ARION
**Sir Joseph Lister CHEYNE**
  R. MUNROE
**Lilian Mary CHISHOLM**
  Anne LORRAINE
**Sir Thomas Willes CHITTY**
  Thomas HINDE
**Betty CHOATE**
  Betty FURNESS
**René CHOMETTE**
  René CLAIR
**Charles CHORLEY**
  Timothy TUGMUTTON, Esq.
**Dr. Elizabeth CHOW**
  Han SUYIN
**Robert CHUDNICK**
  Red RODNEY
**Aaron CHWATT**
  Red BUTTONS
**Antek CIERPLIKOWSKI**
  ANTOINE
**Andrea di CIONE**
  Andrea ORCAGNA
**Andrea CIONI**
  Andrea del VERROCCHIO
**Enid CITOVICH**
  Enid BALDRY

**Nathaniel CLAP**
  A MINISTER OF THE GOSPEL
**Henry CLAPP**
  FIGARO
**Louise CLAPPE**
  Dame SHIRLEY
**Charles CLARK**
  Max ADELER
**Charles CLARK**
  W. J. HAMILTON
**Charles CLARK**
  SNARLEY CHARLEY
**Charlotte M. CLARK**
  Charles M. CLAY
**Dorothy CLARK and Isabella McMEEKIN**
  Clark McMEEKIN
**Brenda CLARKE**
  Brenda HONEYMAN
**John CLARKE**
  Bryan FORBES
**Mrs. Mary CLARKE**
  Harry Wandsworth SHORTFELLOW
**Pauline CLARKE**
  Helen CLARE
**Rebecca CLARKE**
  Sophie MAY
**Robert CLARKE**
  Robert INDIANA
**William CLARKE**
  Sir Alexander BUSTAMANTE
**Cassius Marcellus CLAY**
  MUHAMMAD ALI
**Augustus S. CLAYTON**
  David CROCKETT
**W. Paul CLEGG**
  Keith VALE
**Samuel Langhorne CLEMENS**
  Mark TWAIN
**Titus Flavius CLEMENS**
  CLEMENT OF ALEXANDRIA
**Joseph COAD**
  Gregory GREENDRAKE
**Sylvanus COBB**
  Austin C. BURDICK
  Walter B. DUNLAP
**William COBBETT**
  An AMERICAN

A BROTHER OF THE BIRCH
Peter PORCUPINE
Dick RETORT
A SUBALTERN
**Arnette COBBS**
Arnett COBB
**Richard COBDEN**
A MANCHESTER
MANUFACTURER
**Robert COCHRAN**
Steve COCHRAN
**Claud COCKBURN**
James HELVICK
Frank PITCAIRN
**Alfredo COCOZZA**
Mario LANZA
**John CODMAN**
Captain RINGBOLT
**Joaquim COELHO**
Julio DINIS
**Robert B. COFFIN**
Berry GRAY
**Robert Stevenson COFFIN**
The BOSTON BARD
**Frank COGHLAN**
Junior COGHLAN
**Alfred COHEN**
Alan DALE
**Elizabeth COHEN**
Betty COMDEN
**Ellen COHEN**
Mama CASS
**Morris COHEN**
Two Gun COHEN
**Pierre COHEN**
Pierre CHENAL
**S. David COHEN**
David BLUE
**Theodore Charles COHEN**
Teddy CHARLES
**Janet COLE**
Kim HUNTER
**Lois Dwight COLE**
Lynn AVERY
Nancy DUDLEY
Allan DWIGHT
Anne LATTIN
**Maurice COLE**
Kenny EVERETT

**Samuel Taylor COLERIDGE**
C.
**Nathaniel Adams COLES**
Nat King COLE
**Sidonie Gabrielle COLETTE**
COLETTE
**Lucy Ann COLLIER**
Ann MILLER
**Edwin COLLINGS**
John BLACKWELL
**Mildred COLLINS**
Joan COLLINS
**Brenda COLLOMS**
Brenda HUGHES
**Claire COLOMBAT**
Barbara LAAGE
**Ruggiero COLUMBO**
Russ COLUMBO
**Lillian COMBER**
Lillian BECKWITH
**Pierno COMO**
Perry COMO
**Emanuele CONEGLIANO**
Lorenzo DA PONTE
**Celia Logan CONNELLY**
L. FAIRFAX
**Thomas CONNER**
Sean CONNERY
**Cyril CONNOLLY**
PALINURUS
**Kevin CONNOR**
Chuck CONNORS
**Sir William CONNOR**
CASSANDRA
**Sister Mary CONSOLATA**
Consolata CARROLL
**Fernand CONTANDIN**
FERNANDEL
**Nicholas CONTE**
Richard CONTE
**David COOK**
David ESSEX
**Robert COOK**
Robin COOK
**Will COOK**
Wade EVERETT
James KEENE
**William COOK**
John Milton EDWARDS

Catherine **COOKSON**
Catherine FAWCETT
Charles W. **COOLIDGE**
Skip MORR
Joyce **COOMBS**
Joyce HALES
Laurette **COONEY**
Laurette TAYLOR
Edward Ashley **COOPER**
Edward ASHLEY
Frank **COOPER**
Gary COOPER
James Fenimore **COOPER**
An AMERICAN
Cornelius LITTLEPAGE
Amabel PENFEATHER
A TRAVELLING BACHELOR
John Cobb **COOPER III**
John COBB
William **COOPER**
Harry Summerfield HOFF
Allan **COPELON**
Allan SHERMAN
Carolyn **COPP**
Carolyn LEE
Barbara Carole **COPPERSMITH**
Barbara CARROLL
Benoît Constant **COQUELIN**
COQUELIN AÎNÉ
Mia **CORAK**
Mia SLAVENSKA
Paula **CORDAY**
Rita CORDAY
Raymond **CORDIAUX**
Raymond CORDY
Kathleen **CORKREY**
Carol RAYE
Charles **CORRELL**
(*see* Freeman F. GOSDEN)
Franco Zeffirelli **CORSI**
Franco ZEFFIRELLI
Desmond **CORY**
Theo CALLAS
John Russell **CORYELL**
Nick CARTER
Bertha M. CLAY
Tyman CURRIO

Lillian R. **DE AYTON**
Julia **EDWARDS**
Geraldine **FLEMING**
Margaret **GRANT**
Barbara **HOWARD**
Harry Dubois **MILMAN**
Milton **QUARTERLY**
Lucy May **RUSSELL**
Louis **COTE**
Lew CODY
Gordon **COTLER**
Alex GORDON
Audrey **COTTER**
Audrey MEADOWS
Jane **COTTER**
Jayne MEADOWS
Josephine **COTTLE**
Gale STORM
Felicity **COULSON**
Emery BONETT
John **COULSON**
John BONETT
Don **COURT**
Ken MURRAY
Émile **COURTE**
Émile COHL
Claude **COWAN**
Claude DAMPIER
Odessa **COWAN**
Ina HUTTON
Noël **COWARD**
Hernia WHITTLEBOT
Frances **COWEN**
Frances MUNTHE
Jules **COWLES**
Chester CONKLIN
Anthony Berkeley **COX**
Anthony BERKELEY
Francis ILES
Dorothy **COX**
Diana WYNYARD
John **COX**
John HOWARD
Nathan **COX**
Rod CAMERON
Edna May **COX-OLIVER**
Edna May OLIVER

Clarence CRABBE
 Buster CRABBE
Vincent Eugene CRADDOCK
 Gene VINCENT
Edward CRAIG
 Edward CARRICK
Pearl Mary CRAIGIE
 John Oliver HOBBS
William CRANCH
 Lucius Junius BRUTUS
Stephen CRANE
 Johnston SMITH
Imelda CRAWFORD
 Anne CRAWFORD
John CREASEY
 Gordon ASHE
 Norman DEANE
 Michael HALLIDAY
 Kyle HUNT
 Peter MANTON
 J. J. MARRIC
 Richard MARTIN
 Anthony MORTON
 Ken RANGER
 William K. REILLY
 Tex RILEY
 Jeremy YORK
Irene CREESE
 Rene RAY
Kyle Samuel CRICHTON
 Robert FORSYTHE
Michael CRICHTON
 Jeffrey HUDSON
Henry Hawley CRIPPEN and
Ethel LE NEVE
 Mr. and Master ROBINSON
S. E. CRISP
 CRISPIE

Louis Francis CRISTILLO
 Lou COSTELLO
Dorothy CRITCHLOW
 Jane DAWSON
John CROALL
 John STUART
Dino CROCETTI
 Dean MARTIN
Jane Cunningham CROLY
 Jennie JUNE
Olga CRONK
 Claire WINDSOR
Hugh P. CROSBIE
 John CARRICK
 Provan CROSBIE
Harry Lillis CROSBY
 Bing CROSBY
Eliza Emma CROUCH
 Cora PEARL
Glynn CROUDACE
 Peter MONNOW
Lady Bettina CROWE
 Peter LUM
Edwige CUNATI
 Edwige FEUILLÈRE
Pierre CUQ
 Pierre MONDY
Lt. Com. Bryan CURLING
 HOTSPUR
George Ticknor CURTIS
 Peter BOYLSTON
Antonio Furst de CURTIS-
GAGLIARDI
 TOTO
Shmuel CZACZKES
 Shmuel Yosef AGNON
Barbara CZUKOR
 Barbara BRITTON

# D

Nathan DABOLL
 Edmund FREEBETTER
Alphonso D'ABRUZZO
 Robert ALDA

Simon DACH
 CHASMINDO
Antonio DA COSTA
 O. ALEIJADINHO

194

Donald Barry D'ACOSTA
 Don BARRY
Gabriel D'ACOSTA
 Uriel ACOSTA
Joan DA COSTA
 Joan SHAW
Bob DADE
 Bob ASTOR
Karl DAEN
 Karl DANE
Catherine DAILEY
 Cass DALEY
Margaret DALE
 Margaret J. MILLER
John and Barbara DALRYMPLE-HAY
 John HAY
William DALTON
 Julian ELTINGE
Frederick DANIELS
 Austin FRIARS
Victor DANIELS
 CHIEF THUNDERCLOUD
Virginia DANIELS
 Bebe DANIELS
Frederic DANNAY and Manfred B. LEE
 Barnaby ROSS
 Ellery QUEEN
Louise DANTZLER
 Mary BRIEN
Iva Ikuko Toguri D'AQUINO
 TOKYO ROSE
Aldo DA RE
 Aldo RAY
Manetta DARNELL
 Linda DARNELL
Sabu DASTAGIR
 SABU
Burnu DAVENPORT
 ACQUANETTA
Hans DAVIDSOHN
 Jakob VAN HODDIS
David M. DAVIES
 David MARGERSON
Ivor DAVIES
 Ivor NOVELLO
Nigel DAVIES
 Justin DE VILLENEUVE

Charles Augustus DAVIS
 J. DOWNING
Frederick Clyde DAVIS
 Stephen RANSOME
Frederick W. DAVIS
 Scott CAMPBELL
 Nicholas CARTER
Ruth Elizabeth DAVIS
 Bette DAVIS
Frank Cyril DAVISON
 Pierre COALFLEET
Robert Shaen DAWE
 Robert SHAYNE
Florence DAWSON
 Florence DESMOND
Margaret DAY
 Margaret LOCKWOOD
C. DAY-LEWIS
 Nicholas BLAKE
Reginald DAYMORE
 Reginald DENNY
Borden DEAL
 Lee BORDEN
Luis DE ALONSO
 Gilbert ROLAND
Etienne DE BUJAC
 Bruce CABOT
Malcolm DECKER
 Peter DECKER
Maria de Carmo Miranda DE CUNHA
 Carmen MIRANDA
Jean DEE
 Frances DEE
Barbara DEEKS
 Barbara WINDSOR
Felix DE FONTAINE
 PERSONNE
Boniface Ferdinand Leonardo DE FRANCO
 Buddy DE FRANCO
Michael DE FREITAS
 Abdul MALIK
 MICHAEL X
Guy DEGHY
 Harold FROY
Lou DEGNI
 Mark FOREST

Roland DE GOSTRIE
  Roy William NEILL
Dorothy DE GUICHE
  Dorothy GISH
Lillian DE GUICHE
  Lillian GISH
Joan DE HAVILLAND
  Joan FONTAINE
John DEIGHTON
  Chris FARLOWE
Eduard Douwes DEKKER
  MULTATULI
Jeanne DE LA FONTE
  Renée ADORÉE
Walter DE LA MARE
  Walter RAMAL
Alonso DELANO
  The OLD BLOCK
Louise DE LA RAMÉE
  OUIDA
Roderick La Rocque DE LA ROUR
  Rod LA ROCQUE
Cateau DE LEEUW
  Jessica LYON
Adelaida DELGADO
  Adele MARA
Issur Danielovitch DEMSKY
  Kirk DOUGLAS
Zerby DENBY
  Kim DARBY
Mary A. DENISON
  Clara VANCE
Louis DENNINGER
  Richard DENNING
Harold DENNIS-JONES
  Paul HAMILTON
  Dennis HESSING
A. A. DENT
  Anthony AMPLEGIRTH
Jane Gaskell DENVIL
  Jane GASKELL
George Horatio DERBY
  John PHOENIX
  John P. SQUIBOB
August DERLETH
  Stephen GRENDON
Peggy DERN
  Georgia CRAIG

Carolina LEE
  Joan SHERMAN
Avodis DEROUNIAN
  John Roy CARLSON
Maria DE SANTO SILAS
  Maria MONTEZ
Peter DEUEL
  Pete DUEL
Joseph Anthony DEUSTER
  Joseph ANTHONY
Joaquim DE VASCONCELOS
  Teixeira DE PASCOAIS
Mary DE VERE
  Madeline BRIDGES
Gene DEVLAN
  Gene FOWLER
Autrey DE WALT
  Junior WALKER
Bert DE WAYNE MORRIS
  Wayne MORRIS
Frederick DEY
  Nicholas CARTER
  Varick VANARDY
Rodrigo DIAZ DE VIVAR
  CAMPEADOR
  El CID
Corinne DIBOS
  Corinne CALVET
William B. DICK
  Joshua Jedediah JINKS
  Leger D. MAYNE
Charles DICKENS
  BOZ
  Charles John HUFFAM
  Timothy SPARKES
  TIBBS
Maria Magdalena DIETRICH
  Marlene DIETRICH
Noreen DILCOCK
  Jill CHRISTIAN
Charles DIMITRY
  Tobias GUARNERIUS
Dion DI MUCCI
  DION
Benjamin DISRAELI
  BEAKITORIUS
Rudolf DITZEN
  Hans FALLADA

196

Vincent DI VITTORIO
 Vinnie DEAN
Arthur DIXON
 Felix WHYE
Charles Lutwidge DODGSON
 Lewis CARROLL
Isaiah DOMACHEVITSKY
 Isaiah BERSHADSKY
Albert DOMINIQUE
 Don ALBERT
Edson Arantes DO NASCIMENTO
 PELE
Padre Manuel DO NASCIMENTO
 Filinto ELISIO
Théophile DONDEY
 Philothée O'NEDDY
Florence Hariette Zena DONES
 Zena DARE
Phyllis DONES
 Phyllis DARE
Augustine DONNELLY
 Bullen BEAR
Paolo di DONO
 Paolo UCCELLO
Anita DOOLEY
 Nita NALDI
Hilda DOOLITTLE
 H.D.
Angela DORIAN
 Victoria VETRI
Catherine DORLÉAC
 Catherine DENEUVE
Capt. Henry DORLING
 TAFFRAIL
Dolores DORN-HEFT
 Dolores DORN
Arnold DORSEY
 Engelbert HUMPERDINCK
Sarah DORSEY
 FILIA
Joseph DOTO
 Joey ADONIS
Walter Hampden DOUGHERTY
 Walter HAMPDEN
Lord Alfred DOUGLAS
 BELGIAN HARE
Norman DOUGLAS
 NORMYX

Marian DOURAS
 Marion DAVIES
Michael Delaney DOWD, Jr.
 Mike DOUGLAS
Richard DOYLE
 Dick KITKAT
Harry Sinclair DRAGO
 Kirk DEMING
 Will ERMINE
 Bliss LOMAX
 J. Wesley PUTNAM
 Grant SINCLAIR
Janis DREMANN
 Janis CARTER
Davis DRESSER
 Brett HALLIDAY
Emma DREW
 Georgina BARRYMORE
Jean-Paul DREYFUS
 Jean-Paul LE CHANOIS
Marion DRISCOLL
 Molly McGEE
Phyllis DRIVER
 Phyllis DILLER
François DROUINEAU
 Frank VILLARD
Humphrey DRUMMOND
 Humphrey ap EVANS
Aurore DUDEVANT, née DUPIN
 George SAND
Walter DUDLEY
 Bide DUDLEY
Denise DUGGAN
 Denise EGERTON
Michael DUMBLE-SMITH
 Michael CRAWFORD
Renault Renaldo DUNCAN
 Duncan RENALDO
W. C. DUNKINFIELD
 Charles BOGLE
 Otis CRIBLECOBLIS
 W. C. FIELDS
 Mahatma Kane JEEVES
Marie Blackford DUNN
 Marie PRÉVOST
Aurore DUPIN
 George SAND
Edna Mae DURBIN
 Deanna DURBIN

Francis DURGIN
　Rory CALHOUN
Trent DURKIN
　Junior DURKIN
Lawrence DURRELL
　Charles NORDEN
Paul DURST
　Peter BANNON
　John SHANE

Michele DUSIAK
　Michele LEE

Reginald DWIGHT
　Elton JOHN

Iosif Vissarionovich
DZHUGASHVILI
　KOBA
　Joseph STALIN

# E

Deloreese EARLY
　Della REESE
Dale EASTON
　Greg McCLURE
Helen EASTWOOD
　Olive BAXTER
Christian EBSEN
　Buddy EBSEN
William ECKSTEIN
　Billy ECKSTINE
Gertrude EDELSTEIN
　Gertrude BERG
Alfred EDGAR
　Barre LYNDON
Sybil EDMONDSON
　Sybil ARMSTRONG
Herbert C. EDWARDS
　Bertram EDWARDS
Norma EGSTROM
　Peggy LEE
Willy EICHBERGER
　Carl ESMOND
Harry EINSTEIN
　PARKYAKARKUS
Ben EISENBERG
　Ben ROBERTS
Edward Kennedy ELLINGTON
　Duke ELLINGTON
Gordon ELLIOTT
　Wild Bill ELLIOTT
Arthur ELLIOTT-CANNON
　Nicholas FORDE
George ELLIS
　Sir Gregory GANDER, Kt.

Magdalen ELLIS
　Joan LORRING
Molly ELLIS
　Diana NAPIER
Jeanette ELPHICK
　Victoria SHAW
Mary ELSAS
　Mary ELLIS
Emma EMBURY
　IANTHE
Kurt EMRICH
　Peter BAMM
Charles ENDICOTT
　Junius AMERICANUS
Peter King ENGLE
　Peter WHITNEY
Thomas D. ENGLISH
　Montmorency Sneerlip SNAGS,
　Esq.
Edith ENKE
　Edie ADAMS
William Berkeley ENOS
　Busby BERKELEY
Desiderius ERASMUS
　ROTTERDAMENSIS
James ERCOLANI
　James DARREN
Marisol ESCOBAR
　MARISOL
Jose ESTEVES, Jr.
　Joe LOCO
Marie ETHERINGTON
　Marie TEMPEST

Elisabeth ETTEL
  Elisabeth BERGNER
Joan EUNSON
  Joan EVANS
Elizabeth EVANS
  Elizabeth RISDON
Ernest EVANS
  Chubby CHECKER

Mary Ann EVANS
  George ELIOT
William EVANS
  Yusef LATEEF
Albert EVANS-JONES
  CYNAN
William EVERSON
  Brother ANTONINUS

# F

Nanette FABARES
  Nanette FABRAY
Cecilia de FABER
  Fernán CABALLERO
Sara FABRICIUS
  Cora SANDEL
Ina FAGAN
  Ina CLAIRE
Eleanor FAIRBURN
  Catherine CARFAX
Conrad FALK
  Robert CONRAD
Eugenia FALKENBURG
  Jinx FALKENBURG
Louis FARIGOULE
  Jules ROMAINS
Vito FARINOLA
  Vic DAMONE
Eve FARJEON
  Sarah JEFFERSON
Howard FAST
  E. V. CUNNINGHAM
  Walter ERIKSON
Virginia FAULKNER
  Princess Tulip MURPHY
Sarah Jane FAULKS
  Jane WYMAN
Frederick FAUST
  George Owen BAXTER
  Max BRAND
  M.B.
Charles FEATHERS
  Charlie MORGAN
Robert A. FEDER
  Robert ARTHUR

Stefania FEDERKIEWICZ
  Stefanie POWERS
Katherine FEENEY
  Sally FORREST
Marc FELD
  Marc BOLAN
Gerald FELDMAN
  Jerry FIELDING
Ian FELLOWES-GORDON
  Ian GORDON
Joan FELT
  Joan CARROLL
Mary McNeil FENOLLOSA
  Sidney McCALL
Pasquale FERZETTI
  Gabriele FERZETTI
Beverly FESSENDEN
  Beverly GARLAND
Thomas G. FESSENDEN
  Simon SPUNKEY
Lion FEUCHTWANGER
  J. G. WETCHEEK
Walter FEUCHTWANGER
  Walter WANGER
Emil FEURSTEIN
  Avigdor HAMEIRI
Arthur Davison FICKE
  Anne KNISH
Roberta FICKER
  Suzanne FARRELL
Margaret FIELD
  Virginia FIELD
Henry FIELDING
  Joseph ANDREWS

Giorgio FIGLIA
 George WALLINGTON
Joseph FILIPELLI
 Flip PHILLIPS
Alessandro FILIPEPI
 Sandro BOTTICELLI
Gloria Stuart FINCH
 Gloria STUART
Muriel FINDLAY
 Muriel ANGELUS
Tomasso di Christaforo FINI
 MASOLINO DA PANICALE
Merton FINK
 Matthew FINCH
George FINKIL
 E. M. PENNANCE
Tula FINKLEA
 Cyd CHARISSE
Harry FINKLEMAN
 Ziggy ELMAN
Robert Douglas FINLAYSON
 Robert DOUGLAS
Martha FINLEY
 Martha FARQUHARSON
Brendan FINUCANE
 Paddy FINUCANE
Robert L. FISH
 Robert L. PIKE
Arnold FISHKIND
 Arnold FISHKIN
Patrick FITZGERALD
 Creighton HALE
Margaret FITZPATRICK
 Gail PATRICK
Maureen FITZSIMMONS
 Maureen O'HARA
Martin FLACHSENHARR
 Marty FLAX
Edward FLANAGAN
 Dennis O'KEEFE
Florence FLANAGAN
 Florrie FORDE
Janet FLANNER
 GENET
Arthur FLEGENHEIMER
 Dutch SCHULTZ
Anthony FLEISCHER
 Hans HOFMEYER

Walter FLEISCHMANN
 Anthony DEXTER
Harry FLETCHER
 John GARDEN
Julia FLETCHER
 George FLEMING
Hellmuth FLIEGEL
 Stefan HEYM
Diana FLUCK
 Diana DORS
Leona FLUGARTH
 Shirley MASON
Violet FLUGRATH
 Viola DANA
Janet FLYNN
 Gina MALO
Mary M. FLYNN
 Margaret LIVINGSTONE
Ernest FOCKE
 Ernest PAUL
Daniel FOE
 A BRITISH OFFICER IN THE
 SERVICE OF THE CZAR
 CAPTAIN TOM
 Captain George CARLETON
 Robinson CRUSOE
 DANIEL THE PROPHET
 Daniel DEFOE
 HELIOSTROPOLIS, Etc.
 A JOBBER
 JUNIOR RECTOR OF ST.
 MICHAEL
 THE MAN IN THE MOON
 ONE OF THE PEOPLE
 CALLED QUAKERS
 A SCOTS GENTLEMAN IN
 THE SWEDISH SERVICE
 A SHROPSHIRE GENTLEMAN
 William SMITHIES
William FOLKARD
 Maurice ELVEY
Michael FOOT
 CASSIUS
Nicholas FORAN
 Dick FORAN
Meriel FORBES-ROBERTSON
 Meriel FORBES
Consuelo FORD
 Althea URN

Corey FORD
John RIDDELL
Gwyllyn FORD
Glenn FORD
Thelma Booth FORD
Shirley BOOTH
Feodora FORDE
Jane BAXTER
Carl FOREMAN
Derek FRYE
George FORMBY
George HOY
Fabian FORTE
FABIAN
Mabel FORTESCUE
Mabel NORMAND
Charles FOSDICK
Harry CASTLEMON
Lawrence FOTINAKIS
Larry FOTINE
Robert FOULICY
Robert DHERY
Henri-Alain FOURNIER
ALAIN-FOURNIER
Clara Ann FOWLER
Patti PAGE
Kenneth FOWLER
Clark BROOKER
Charles FOX
Richard JEREMY
Mona FOX
Mona BRAND
Heinrich FRAENKEL
ASSIAC
Karl Herbert FRAHM
Willy BRANDT
Mary Jane FRAHSE
Jane FRAZEE
Caterina di FRANCAVILLA
Catherine BOYLE
Samuel Ward FRANCIS
A SINGULAR MAN
Stephen D. FRANCIS
Hank JANSON
Claude FRANC-NOHAIN
Claude DAUPHIN
Concetta FRANCONERA
Connie FRANCIS

Benjamin FRANKLIN
A.B.
Anthony AFTERWIT
The BUSYBODY
Silence DOGWOOD
FATHER ABRAHAM
HISTORICUS
The LEFT HAND
MEDIUS
PHILOMATH
Richard SAUNDERS
Cilia SINGLE
A TRADESMAN OF
PHILADELPHIA
Harold FRASER
Snub POLLARD
Jacques FRÉDÉRIX
Jacques FEYDER
Nicolas FREELING
F.R.E. NICHOLAS
Monica FREEMAN
Mona FREEMAN
Anita Louise FREMAULT
Anita LOUISE
Philip FRENEAU
Tomo CHEEKI
Robert SLENDER
John FREUND
John FORSYTHE
Lewis FRIEDLANDER
Lew LANDERS
Esther FRIEDMAN
Ann LANDERS
Eve R. FRIEDMAN
Robert TIBBER
Rosemary TIBBER
Pauline FRIEDMAN
Abigail VAN BUREN
Theodore FRIEDMAN
Ted LEWIS
William FRIEDMAN
William FOX
Samile Diane FRIESEN
Dyan CANNON
Marie FRYE
Marie McDONALD
Jean Muir FULLERTON
Jean MUIR

Blanche FUMOLEAU
  Gaby MORLAY
Vince FURNIER
  Alice COOPER
Elda FURRY

Hedda HOPPER
Martin FUSS
  Ross HUNTER
James FYFE
  Monte REY

# G

Clark GABLE
  Clarke GABEL
Sari GABOR
  Zsa Zsa GABOR
Paul GADD
  Gary GLITTER
  Paul RAVEN
Laura GAINER
  Janet GAYNOR
Robert GAINES
  Rowland SUMMERSALES
John Kenneth GALBRAITH
  Mark EPERNAY
  Herschel McLANDRESS
Richard GALLAGHER
  Skeets GALLAGHER
Amelita GALLI
  Amelita GALLI-CURCI
John GALSWORTHY
  John SINJOHN
John GALT
  Archibald JOBBRY
Judy GAMBLE
  Judy CAMPBELL
Victoria GAMEZ
  Victoria DE LOS ANGELES
Arturo GARCIA
  Arturo DE CORDOVA
Felix Rubén GARCÍA
SARMIENTO
  Rubén DARÍO
Alfred George GARDINER
  ALPHA OF THE PLOUGH
Erle Stanley GARDNER
  A. A. FAIR
Julius GARFINKLE
  John GARFIELD

Art GARFUNKEL and Paul
SIMON
  Tom and JERRY
David GARNETT
  Leda BURKE
Ralph GAROFALO
  Ralph GARI
James GARRETSON
  John DARBY
Henry GARROWAY
  Henry STEPHENSON
Edith GASSION
  Edith PIAF
Dorothy GATLEY
  Ann HARDING
Bernice GAUNT
  Shirley ROSS
Siddhartha GAUTAMA
  BUDDHA
Françoise GAUTCH
  Françoise ARNOUL
John GAWSWORTH
  T. I. FYTTON-ARMSTRONG
Christine GEACH
  Anne LOWING
Hilde GEIRINGER
  Hilde GUEDEN
Ella GEISMAN
  June ALLYSON
Samuel GELBFISCH
  Samuel GOLDWYN
Art GELIAN
  Tab HUNTER
Claude GELLÉE
  Claude LORRAINE
Louis GENDRE
  Louis JOURDAN

Manfred GEORG
Manfred GEORGE
Steve GEORGIOU
Cat STEVENS
Leslie March GERAGHTY
Garry MARSH
Harry GERGUSON
Mike ROMANOFF
Claudius Caesar Drusus
GERMANICUS
NERO
Leslie GETTMAN
Leslie BROOKS
Katherine GIBBS
Kay FRANCIS
Charles GIBSON
Richard SUDBURY
Edward GIBSON
Hoot GIBSON
John GIESY
Charles DUSTIN
James N. GIFFORD
Eliot BREWSTER
Carol HOLLISTON
Warren HOWARD
Griffith JAMES
John SAXON
Jolanda GIGLIOTTI
DALIDA
Maria GILBERT
Lola MONTEZ
Ruth GILBERT
Ruth AINSWORTH
William Schwenck GILBERT
BAB
Tomline LA TOUR
Beth GILCHRIST
John Prescott EARL
Elizabeth GILLEASE
Elizabeth ALLEN
Caroline GILMAN
Mrs. Clarissa PACKARD
Rufus H. GILMORE
Rufus HAMILTON
Elizabeth GILZEAN
Elizabeth HOUGHTON
Mary HUNTON
Asher GINZBERG
Achad HAAM

Gabrielle GIRARD
Daniele DELORME
William P. GISLINGHAM
Will P. KELLINO
Also GIURLANI
Aldo PALAZZESCHI
William Ewart GLADSTONE
Bartholomew BOUVERIE
ETONIAN
GLADIOLUS
Mr. GRESHAM
WILLIAM
William GLASCOCK
An OFFICER OF RANK
Gerald M. GLASKIN
Neville JACKSON
John GLASSCO
Jean DE SAINT LUC
Hideki OKADA
Miles UNDERWOOD
Rupert GLEADOW
Justin CASE
Duncan GLEN
Ronald EADIE
Edgar GLOSSUP
Eddie DEAN
Oliver GLOUX
Gustave AIMARD
Alexsander GLOWACKI
Boleslaw PRUS
Josephine Lawrence GODDARD
Jody LAWRANCE
Armand GODET
GOD
Lucila GODOY DE ALCAYAGA
Gabriela MISTRAL
Edward GODWIN
Henry Edward Gordon CRAIG
George GOETZ
V. F. CALVERTON
John GOFFAGE
Chips RAFFERTY
Nikolai Vasilievich GOGOL
V. ALOF
Odette GOIMBAULT
Mary ODETTE
Dora GOLDBERG
Nora BAYES

**Israel GOLDBERG**
Rufus LEARSI

**Avrom Hirsch GOLDBOGEN**
Mike TODD

**Emanuel GOLDENBERG**
Edward G. ROBINSON

**Harry GOLDENHURST**
Harry GOLDEN

**Don GOLDFIELD**
Don GOLDIE

**Louise GOLDING**
Louise DAVIES

**William GOLDMAN**
Harry LONGBAUGH

**Max GOLDMANN**
Max REINHARDT

**Oliver GOLDSMITH**
The CITIZEN OF THE
WORLD

**Elliott GOLDSTEIN**
Elliot GOULD

**Robert GOLDSTON**
Robert CONROY

**John GOLENOR**
James GAVIN

**Arnold von GOLSSENAU**
Ludwig RENN

**José Victoriano GONZÁLEZ**
Juan GRIS

**Theodosia GOODMAN**
Theda BARA

**Sandra GOODRICH**
Sandie SHAW

**Estelle GOODWIN**
Estelle WINWOOD

**Odette GORDON**
ODETTA

**Patricia GORDON**
Joan HOWARD

**Yehuda Leib GORDON**
YLG

**Joseph GOREED**
Joe WILLIAMS

**Anna Andreyevna GORENKO**
Anna AKHMATOVA

**Joannes GORIS**
Marinx GIJSEN

**Freeman F. GOSDEN and Charles
CORRELL**
AMOS 'N' ANDY

**Jan GOSSAERT**
Jan MABUSE

**Mathis GOTHARDT**
Matthias GRÜNEWALD

**Joseph GOTTLIEB**
Joey BISHOP

**Ralph GOTTLIEBSEN**
O. R. SCOTT

**Joseph GOUCHER**
Eddie DOWLING

**Charles GOULD**
Charles K. FELDMAN

**Anthony GOURDINE**
LITTLE ANTHONY

**Mary GOVAN**
Mary ALLERTON
J. N. DARBY

**Barbara GOWING**
Barbara KAYE

**Ronald GRABOWSKI**
Ronnie GREB

**Charles GRACI**
Charlie GRACIE

**Florence GRAHAM**
Elizabeth ARDEN

**James A. Maxtone GRAHAM**
James ANSTRUTHER

**St. Edward S. GRAHAM**
Stuart CLOETE

**Katherine GRANDSTAFF**
Kathryn GRANT

**Irving GRANICH**
Michael GOLD

**Seafield GRANT**
Louis HAYWARD

**Reginald GRASDORF**
Reginald PURDELL

**Robert GRAVES**
John DOYLE

**Donald GRAY**
Charles GRAY

**Dorothy GRAY**
Dorothy K. HAYNES

**Elizabeth GRAYSON**
Eunice GAYSON**

Michael GREAVES
 Michael CALLUM
Horace GREELEY
 Godek GOODWILL
Clifford GREEN
 Tom BERKLEY
David GREEN
 David BEN-GURION
Dorothy GREEN
 Dorothy AUCHTERLONIE
Ian GREEN
 Gil EVANS
Lorne GREEN
 Lorne GREENE
Mae GREEN
 Jean PARKER
Maxwell GREEN
 CABBY WITH A CAMERA
Peter GREEN
 Denis DELANEY
Mutz GREENBAUM
 Max GREENE
Gladys GREENE
 Jean ARTHUR
Sarah GREENE
 Sally Platt McLEAN
Sammy GREENFIELD
 Sidney GEORGE
 George SIDNEY
Julia GREENWOOD
 Francis ASKHAM
Michael GREGSON
 Michael CRAIG
Clive GREIG
 Colin CLIVE
Maysie GREIG
 Jennifer AMES
Katherina Houston GRIBBIN
 Renée HOUSTON
Christopher Murray GRIEVE
 Hugh MacDIARMID
Debralee GRIFFIN
 Debra PAGET
Frank GRIFFIN
 Charles ATKIN
Charles GRIFFITHS
 Ralph BOLD
Rev. Jack GRIFFITHS
 Jack GRIFFITH

Christoffel von
GRIMMELSHAUSEN
 ACEEEFFGHHIILLMMNN-
 OORRSSSTUV
Eugène GRINDAL
 Paul ÉLUARD
Arnold GRISHAVER
 Buddy ARNOLD
Brian GRITT
 Edward DRIVER
Alison GROOM
 Alison SKIPWORTH
Yitzroch Loiza GROSSBERG
 Larry RIVERS
Ira GROSSEL
 Jeff CHANDLER
Arthur GROSSMAN
 Arthur FREED
Antocz GROSZEWSKI
 Anton GROT
Hugh GROTIUS
 Sibrandus LUBERTUS
Victor GRUENBAUM
 Victor GRUEN
Sam GRUNDY
 Wallace FORD
Tomasso GUARDATI
 Masuccio SALERNITANO
Julius GUBENKO
 Terry GIBBS
Michael GUBITOSI
 Robert BLAKE
Jacques GUENOD
 Jim GERALD
Albert GUERISSE
 Pat O'LEARY
Rudolpho GUGLIEMI
 Rudolph VALENTINO
Tomasso GUIDI
 MASACCIO
Nelly GUILLERM
 Violette VERDY
Raymond GUION
 Gene RAYMOND
Frances GUMM
 Judy GARLAND
Gladys GUNN
 Gladys HENSON

Natasha GURDIN
Natalie WOOD
Greta GUSTAFSON
Greta GARBO
Thomas Anstey GUTHRIE
F. ANSTEY

Irene GUYONVARCH
Irene PEARL
Stanislav GVOTH
Stan MIKITA
Stefan GYERGYAY
Steve GERAY

# H

Martti HAAVIO
P. MUSTAPHA
Leonard HACKER
Buddy HACKETT
Stetia HAGAN
John HAWKINS
Ilona HAJMASSY
Ilona MASSEY
Gyula HALASZ
BRASSAI
Marie HALE
Maurice RUTLEDGE
Thomas Chandler HALIBURTON
Sam SLICK of Slickville
Frederick HALL
Patrick HALL
Henry HALL
Huntz HALL
Howard HALL
Charles SUMNER
Josef HALL
Upton CLOSE
Samuel HALL
BUCKSKIN SAM
Gloria HALLWARD
Gloria GRAHAME
Frank HALSEY
Frank A. McALISTER
Constance HALVERSTADT
Constance CUMMINGS
Herbert HAMBLEN
Frederick Benton WILLIAMS
Alexander HAMILTON
An AMERICAN
CAMILLUS
CATO
Lucius CRASSUS

PACIFICUS
PUBLIUS
SCIPIO
John HAMILTON
Sterling HAYDEN
Fay HAMMERTON
Dorothy CLYDE
Fay HOLDEN
Henrietta HAMMOND
Henri DAUGE
Robert Lowery HANKS
Robert LOWERY
Clifford HANLEY
Henry CALVIN
James HANLEY
Patric SHONE
Reverend James Owen HANNAY
George A. BIRMINGHAM
Ellen HANSEN
Ellen CORBY
Winifred HANSON
Winnie LIGHTNER
Friedrich Leopold von
HARDENBERG
NOVALIS
Laura HARDIE
Constance COLLIER
Louis HARDIN
MOONDOG
Muriel HARDING
Olga PETROVA
Marjorie HARDY
Bobby HARDY
Robert HARE
Eldred GRAYSON
Georg HÄRING
Willibald ALEXIS

Henry HARLAND
  Sidney LUSKA
Jakob HARMENSEN
  Jacobus ARMINIUS
Derek HARRIS
  John DEREK
George Washington HARRIS
  SUGARTAIL
William B. HARRIS
  Billy BEVAN
William P. HARRIS
  Peter HARRIS
Frieda HARRISON
  Suzy KENDALL
Mary HART
  Lynne ROBERTS
Robert Alton HART
  Robert ALTON
William Sterling HART
  Robert STERLING
Vivian HARTLEY
  Vivien LEIGH
Samuel HARTMAN
  Don HARTMAN
Charles HARTRE
  Charles HAWTREY
Henry HARTSHORNE
  Corinne L'ESTRANGE
Eva Brigitta HARTWIG
  Vera ZORINA
Inez HARVUOT
  Irene MANNING
Joseph HASLEWOOD
  Gridiron GABBLE, Gent.,
  Godson to Mother Goose
Major Jock HASWELL
  George FOSTER
Gyozo HATAR
  MEDVECZKY
Jonathan HATLEY
  Jonathan HALE
Sigrid Gurie HAUKELID
  Sigrid GURIE
Marty HAUSMAN
  Marty HOLMES
Jacques HAUSSMANN
  John HOUSEMAN
Sir Anthony Hope HAWKINS
  Anthony HOPE

Jelacy HAWKINS
  Screamin' Jay HAWKINS
Francis Lister HAWKS
  Uncle PHILIP
Helen HAY
  Helen HAYE
Kintaro HAYAKAWA
  Sessue HAYAKAWA
Isaac Israel HAYES
  John HARDY, Mariner
Mary Jane HAYES
  Allison HAYES
Michael HAYES
  Mickie MOST
Joan HAYTHORNTHWAITE
  Joan HAYTHORN
William HAZLITT
  PHANTASTES
  RATIONALIS
  Boswell REDIVIVUS
  Edward SEARCH
Travers HEAGERTY
  Henry TRAVERS
Patrick HEALEY-KAY
  Anton DOLIN
Gerald HEARD
  H. F. HEARD
Lafcadio HEARN
  Ozias MIDWINTER
Frederick HEATH
  Johnny KIDD
Zelma HEDRICK
  Kathryn GRAYSON
Dorothy HEERMANCE
  June COLLYER
Emmett Evan HEFLIN
  Van HEFLIN
Elaine HEIGHINGTON
  HAVINGTON
Eddie Albert HEIMBERGER
  Eddie ALBERT
Jerome HEINZ
  Jerome HINES
Don HELFMAN
  Don ELLIOTT
Margot HEMINGWAY
  Margaux HEMINGWAY
Lisle HENDERSON
  Lyle TALBOT

George **HENDLEMAN**
George HANDY
**Henrietta HENKLE**
Henrietta BUCKMASTER
**Nella HENNEY**
Henry MARSHALL
**Paul Von HENREID**
Paul HENREID
**Veronica HENRIQUES**
Veronica GOSLING
**Carl HENTY-DODD**
Simon DEE
**Sandra Lee HENVILLE**
BABY SANDY
**Audrey HEPBURN-RUSTON**
Audrey HEPBURN
**Sir Alan Patrick HERBERT**
A.P.H.
**Henry W. HERBERT**
Frank FORESTER
**Eileen HERLIHY**
Eileen HERLIE
**Mildred HERMAN**
Melissa HAYDEN
**Anthony HERN**
Andrew HOPE
**Reed HERRING**
Reed HADLEY
**Lazar HERRMANN**
Leo LANIA
**Norbert N. HERST**
ALERTUS
**Irene HERWICK**
Irene HERVEY
**Emile HERZOG**
André MAUROIS
**Hermann HESSE**
Emil SINCLAIR
**Melvyn HESSELBERG**
Melvyn DOUGLAS
**Cecil Rolph HEWITT**
C. H. ROLPH
**Rev. Joseph T. HEWLETT**
Peter PRIGGINS
**John HIBBS**
John BLYTH
**Myrthas Helen HICKMAN**
Helen WESTCOTT

**Dolores HICKS**
Dolores HART
**Thomas HICKS**
Tommy STEELE
**Ida HIGMAN**
Margaret BARRY
**Benson E. HILL**
Polexenes Digit SNIFT
**Grace HILL**
Marcia MACDONALD
**George S. HILLARD**
Sylvanus DASHWOOD
An IDLER
Silas STANDFAST
**B. C. HILLIAM**
FLOTSAM
**Brian HINES**
Denny LAINE
**Milton HINES**
Soupy SALES
**Agnes HINKLE**
Agnes AYRES
**Hugh HIPPLE**
Hugh MARLOWE
**Gillian HIRST**
Gillian BAXTER
**Reginald HITCHCOCK**
Rex INGRAM
**Peter HOAR**
Simon AMBERLEY
**Thomas Terry HOAR-STEVENS**
TERRY-THOMAS
**George HOBART**
Hugh McHUGH
**Doris HODGES**
Charlotte HUNT
**Isabel HODGKINSON**
Isabel DEAN
**Norman HOEFFER**
Norman FOSTER
**Pim HOFDORP**
Will GEERLINK
**Syd HOFF**
HOFF
**David HOFFMAN**
Anthony GRUMBLER, Esq. of
Grumbleton Hall
**Susan HOFFMAN**
VIVA

Peter HOFLER
  Jesse THOOR
Ray HOGAN
  Clay RINGOLD
Grace HOGARTH
  Amelia GAY
William HOGARTH
  Giles GRINAGAIN
Charlie May HOGUE
  Charlie May SIMON
Theophrastus Bombast Von
HOHENHEIM
  PARACELSUS
Martha HOLDEN
  AMBER
Josiah Gilbert HOLLAND
  Timothy TITCOMB
Webb Parmalee HOLLENBECK
  Clifton WEBB
Joe HOLLIDAY
  Jack DALE
Peter Fenwick HOLMES
  Peter FENWICK
Oliver Wendell HOLMES
  The AUTOCRAT OF THE
  BREAKFAST TABLE
  The POET AT THE
  BREAKFAST TABLE
  The PROFESSOR AT THE
  BREAKFAST TABLE
Charles HOLT
  Tim HOLT
Marie HOLT
  Marie BURKE
Catherine HOLZMAN
  Kitty CARLISLE
Elizabeth HOLZMAN
  Libby HOLMAN
Mary HOMES
  Millie MAYFIELD
Theodore Edward HOOK
  Alfred ALLENDALE
  Vicesimus BLENKINSOP
  Richard JONES
  Mrs. RAMSBOTTOM
  TEKELI
Lois HOOKER
  Lois MAXWELL

Margaret HOOKHAM
  Margot FONTEYN
Leslie Townes HOPE
  Packey EAST
  Bob HOPE
Joseph HOPKINSON
  Peter GRIEVOUS, Esq.,
  A.B.C.D.E.
Tom HOPKINSON
  Thomas PEMBROKE
  VINDICATOR
Kirby HORN
  Kirby GRANT
John HORNBY
  Calvin BRENT
  Joseph GRACE
Leslie HORNBY
  TWIGGY
Geoffrey HORNE
  Gil NORTH
John HORNIHOLD
  J . . . H . . . . .
Juanita HORTON
  Bessie LOVE
Cyril Henry HOSKINS
  Dr. Carl KUON SUO
  Tuesday LOBSANG RAMPA
Iris HOSTETTER
  Iris ADRIAN
Walter HOUGHSTON
  Walter HUSTON
Vanig HOUSEPLAN
  Turk VAN LAKE
June HOVICK
  June HAVOC
Rose Louise HOVICK
  Gypsy Rose LEE
Augustus HOWARD
  Gus McNAUGHTON
Francis HOWARD
  Frankie HOWERD
Patrick HOWARTH
  C. D. E. FRANCIS
William HOWE
  Mohammed PASHA
John HOYSRADT
  John HOYT
Lafayette Ronald HUBBARD
  Tom ESTERBROOK

209

Rene LAFAYETTE
Kurt VON RACHEN
**Paul HUBSCHMID**
Paul CHRISTIAN
**Winnifred Shaughnessy De Wolfe**
**HUDNUT**
Natasha RAMBOVA
**Ford Madox HUEFFER**
Ford Madox FORD
**Barbara HUFFMAN**
Barbara EDEN
**Jeremy HUGGINS**
Jeremy BRETT
**Thomas HUGHES**
A LAYMAN
An OLD BOY
VACUUS VIATOR
**Walter D. HUGHES**
DERVENTIO
**Victor HUGO**
HIERRO
**Joan HULBERT**
Primrose ROSTRON
**Betty HUMPHREYS**
B. V. H. SCHNEIDER
**Elsie HUMPHRIES**
Mary FORRESTER
**Leslie George HUMPHRYS**
Geoffrey HUMPHRYS
**Orton HUNGERFORD**
Ty HARDIN

**Dorothy HUNT**
Doris COLLYER
**E. Howard HUNT**
John BAXTER
Gordon DAVIS
Robert DIETRICH
David ST. JOHN
**Eleanor HUNT**
Joyce COMPTON
**Marcia HUNT**
Marsha HUNT
**Suzanne HUNT**
BADGERY
**Norma HUNTER-BLAIR**
Alison HUNTER
**Jerome HURWITZ**
Jerome LLOYD
**John HUS**
Paul CONSTANTIUS
**Jules HUSSON**
CHAMPFLEURY
**Roelof HUYSMANN**
Rodolphus AGRICOLA
**Samuel HYAMS**
Dennis HOEY
**Edith HYDE**
PANDORA
**John HYMAN**
Johnny WIGGS

# I

**Dolores IBÁRRURI**
La PASIONARIA
**Zoë IDALIE**
Zoë OLDENBOURG
**Peter INGLE-FINCH**
Peter FINCH
**Concetta INGOLIA**
Connie STEVENS
**Hammond INNES**
Ralph HAMMOND

**INSHATATHEANBA**
Suzette LA FLESCHE
**William Henry IRELAND**
Charles CLIFFORD
Henry FIELDING
Anser PEN-DRAGON, Esq.
Satiricus SCULPTOR, Esq.
**Peter IRVING**
Percival G
**Washington IRVING**
Friar Antonio AGAPIDO

An AMERICAN GENTLEMAN
Anthony EVERGREEN
Diedrich KNICKERBOCKER
Jonathan OLDSTYLE, Gent.
**William IRVING**
Pindar COCKLOFT, Esq.
**Arnold ISAACS**
SCAASI
**Edward Israel ISKOWITZ**

Eddie CANTOR
**Phyllis ISLEY**
Jennifer JONES
**Anne ITALIANO**
Anne BANCROFT
**Dimitar IVANOV**
ELIN PELIN
**Beryl IVORY**
Beryl BAXTER

# J

**Frederick JACKSON**
Victor THORNE
**Helen Hunt JACKSON**
H.H.
Saxe HOLM
**Henry JACKSON**
Henry ARMSTRONG
**Amos JACOBS**
Danny THOMAS
**Rosetta JACOBS**
Piper LAURIE
**Lucas JACOBSZ**
LUCAS VAN LEYDEN
**Lee JACOBY**
Lee J. COBB
**Donna Mae JADEN**
Janis PAIGE
**Gabriel JAFFE**
Vivian POOLE
**Charles JAGELKA**
Chuck WAYNE
**Jessie JAMES**
Johnnie HOWARD
**(Margaret) Storm JAMESON**
James HILL
William LAMB
**Theodor Emil JANENZ**
Emil JANNINGS
**Margaret JANVIER**
Margaret VANDEGRIFT
**Cora JARRETT**
Faraday KEENE
**Charles Édouard JEANNERET**
Le CORBUSIER

**Mitzi JEDLICKA**
Maria JERITZA
**Arthur Stanley JEFFERSON**
Stan LAUREL
**Thomas JEFFERSON**
Oliver FAIRPLAY
**Dean JEFFRIES**
Dean JAGGER
**Greg JEFFRIES**
Geoffrey COLLINS
**Roderick Graeme JEFFRIES**
Roderick GRAEME
**Oliver JELLY**
Alfred FOSSE
**Harold JENKINS**
Conway TWITTY
**Richard JENKINS**
Richard BURTON
**Wendy JENKINS**
Wendy BARRIE
**Will F. JENKINS**
Murray LEINSTER
**George C. JENKS**
Nick CARTER
W. B. LAWSON
**Doris JENSEN**
Colleen GRAY
**Gladys JEPSON-TURNER**
BELITA
**Douglas William JERROLD**
The Late Captain Barabbas
WHITEFEATHER
**Bernard JEWRY**
Shane FENTON
Alvin STARDUST

**Wong Tung JIM**
  James Wong HOWE
**Constantine JOANIDES**
  Michael CONSTANTINE
**Anna JOHNSON**
  Hope DARING
**Annabel JOHNSON**
  A. E. JOHNSON
**Carol Diahann JOHNSON**
  Diahann CARROLL
**Charles La Vere JOHNSON**
  Charles LA VERE
**Frank JOHNSON**
  Frankie DARRO
**George M. JOHNSON**
  George METCALF
**James JOHNSON**
  Raymond ST. JACQUES
**La Raine JOHNSON**
  Laraine DAY
**Lawrence JOHNSON**
  Laurence NAISMITH
**Marguerite JOHNSON**
  Maya ANGELOU
**Marion JOHNSON**
  Georgina MASSON
**Merle JOHNSON**
  Troy DONAHUE
**Victor Hugo JOHNSON**
  John BELL
**Dr. Samuel JOHNSON**
  The GREAT CHAM OF
  LITERATURE
  An IMPARTIAL HAND
  PROBUS BRITANNICUS
  S.J.
  T
**Angus JOHNSTONE WILSON**
  Angus WILSON
**Charles JONES**
  Buck JONES
**Charles M. JONES**
  Chuck JONES
**David JONES**
  David BOWIE
**Eddie JONES**
  Slim GUITAR

**Felix JONES**
  Felix AYLMER
**Franklin Albert JONES**
  BUBBA FREE JOHN
**Harry A. JONES**
  Hal JONES
**Henry JONES**
  CAVENDISH
**James A. JONES**
  MURGATROYD
**Lady JONES**
  Enid BAGNOLD
  A LADY OF QUALITY
**Lindley Armstrong JONES**
  Spike JONES
**Nora JONES**
  Rosamund JOHN
**Ruth JONES**
  Dinah WASHINGTON
**Ruth Gordon JONES**
  Ruth GORDON
**Virginia JONES**
  Virginia MAYO
**William JONES**
  Billy DE WOLFE
**James Edward JORDAN**
  Fibber McGEE
**Robert Dwyer JOYCE**
  FEARDANA
  MERULAN
**William JOYCE**
  Lord HAW-HAW
**Samuel JUDAH**
  Terenlius PHLOGOBOMBOS
**Nadine JUDD**
  Nadia NERINA
**Peter JUDGE**
  F. J. McCORMICK
**Stephen JUDKINS**
  Stevie WONDER
**Edward JUDSON**
  Ned BUNTLINE
**Emily JUDSON**
  Fanny FOSTER
**Helen JURGENS**
  Helen TWELVETREES
**William JUSTICE**
  Richard TRAVIS

# K

Isser KAC
  Kurt KATCH
Romain KACEW
  Romain GARY
Rudolph KAGEY
  Kurt STEEL
Bob KAHAKALAU
  Bob CARTER
Arnold KAISER
  Norman KERRY
Geza KAISER
  Charles KORVIN
Bernice KAMIAT
  Cara WILLIAMS
Simone KAMINKER
  Simone SIGNORET
David Daniel KAMINSKY
  Danny KAYE
Melvyn KAMINSKY
  Mel BROOKS
Oleksander KANDYBA
  Oleksander OLES
Yvonne KAPP
  Yvonne CLOUD
Doris KAPPELHOFF
  Doris DAY
Walter KARIG
  Keats PATRICK
Philip KARLSTEIN
  Phil KARLSON
William KATT
  Bill WILLIAMS
Joel KATZ
  Joel GREY
Dennis KAUFMAN
  Dziga VERTOV
Seymour KAUFMAN
  Cy COLEMAN
Dorothy KAUMEYER
  Dorothy LAMOUR
Hilda KAY
  Jan HILLIARD
Arline KAZANJIAN
  Arlene FRANCIS
Elia KAZANJOGLOUS
  Elia KAZAN

Sheila KEATLEY
  Margaret AVON
Joseph Francis KEATON
  Buster KEATON
Rose KEEFER
  Rose HOBART
Harold KEEL
  Howard KEEL
Frederick KEEN
  Frederick KERR
Tom KEENE
  George DURYEA
  Richard POWERS
Robert KEITH
  Brian KEITH
Ethel KELLER
  Barbara KAY
  Lucia WHITNEY
Arthur Gordon KELLEY
  Art LINKLETTER
Edward KELLOGG
  WHITEHOOK
Vernon KELLOGG
  Max VERNON
John P. KENNEDY
  Solomon SECONDTHOUGHTS
Elizabeth KENO
  Mitzi GREEN
Louise KERLIN
  Louise DRESSER
Deborah KERR-TRIMMER
  Deborah KERR
John H. D. KERSHAW
  Hugh D'ALLENGER
Mihaly KERTÉSZ
  Michael CURTIZ
Samuel KETTELL
  Sampson SHORT-AND-FAT
  Timo TITTERWELL
Abdullah Jaffa Bey KHAN
  Robert JOFFREY
Noor Inayat KHAN
  MADELEINE
Taidje KHAN, Jr.
  Yul BRYNNER

Howard KHAURY
TINY TIM
Raymond N. KIENZLE
Nicholas RAY
Sören KIERKEGAARD
ANTI-CLIMACUS
Hilarius BOGBINDER
Constantin CONSTANTIUS
Johannes DE SILENTIO
Victor EREMITA
H.H.
Virgilius HAUFNIENSIS
Nicolaus NOTABENE
Margaret KIES
Margaret LINDSAY
Sidney KIESCHNER
Sidney KINGSLEY
Hedwig KIESLER
Hedy LAMARR
Kitty KILLINGSWORTH
Kitty NOBLE
Leslie KING, Jr.
Gerald FORD
Moira KING
Moira SHEARER
Riley B. KING
B.B. KING
William KING
Tom BOGGS
Donald KINLEYSIDE
Donald DOUGLAS
Clark KINNAIRD
Hargis EARLYWINE
Ellen KIRK
Henry HAYES
Phillis KIRKEGAARD
Phillis KIRK
Caroline KIRKLAND
Mrs. Mary CLAVERS
James KIRKUP
Andrew JAMES
TERATHA JUN
TSUYUKI SHIGERU
Joyce I. KIRKWOOD
Joyce I. CORLETT
Conrad KIRNON
Connie KAY
Maude KISKADDEN
Maude ADAMS

Heinz KISSINGER
Henry KISSINGER
Marvin KITMAN
William Randolph HIRSCH
Emmy KITTL
Emmy DESTINN
Eugene KLASS
Gene BARRY
Samuel KLAUSMAN
Larry PARKS
Carole KLEIN
Carole KING
Henry KLEINBACH
Henry BRANDON
Ingabor KLINCKERFUSS
Karen VERNE
Burton KLINE
Rufus DART II
Frank KLINE
Frank LATIMORE
Friedrich Gottlieb KLOPSTOCK
The GERMAN MILTON
Lillian KLOT
Georgia BROWN
Samuel KNAPP
ALI BEY
Ignatius Loyola ROBERTSON
Hildegarde KNEF
Hildegarde NEFF
Irwin KNIBERG
Alan KING
J. Forrest KNIGHT
Fuzzy KNIGHT
Gottfried KNILLER
Sir Godfrey KNELLER
Glen G. KNOBLAUGH
Glen GRAY
Reginald KNOWLES
Patric KNOWLES
Marie Adrienne KOENIG
Mae MURRAY
Helen KOFORD
Terry MOORE
Fritz KOHN
Fritz KORTNER
Jan Amos KOMENSKÝ
COMENIUS
Virginia KOMISS
Virginia GRAHAM

Ludwik KONDRATOWICZ
  Wladyslaw SYROKOMLA
Allen Stewart KONIGSBERG
  Woody ALLEN
N. I. KORNEICHUK
  Korney CHUKOVSKY
Gerthe KORNSTADT
  Dita PARLO
Gabriela KORWON-
PIOTROWSKA
  Gabriela ZAPOLSKA
Teodor Jozef Konrad
KORZENIOWSKI
  Joseph CONRAD
Larysa KOSACH
  Lesya UKRAINKA
Jerzy KOSINSKI
  Joseph NOVAK
Sophia KOSOW
  Sylvia SIDNEY
Hermann KOSTERLITZ
  Henry KOSTER
Wilhelm Apollinaris de
KOSTROWITSKY
  Guillaume APOLLINAIRE
Peyo KRACHOLOV
  Peyo YAVOROV
Hugh KRAMPKE
  Hugh O'BRIAN
Jacob KRANTZ

Ricardo CORTEZ
Stanley KRANTZ
  Stanley CORTEZ
Violet KRAUTH
  Marion MARSH
Sergei Mikhailovich
KRAVCHINSKY
  STEPNIAK
Warren KRECH
  Warren WILLIAM
Gerhard KREMER
  Gerhadus MERCATOR
David KRIEDT
  David VAN KRIEDT
Jiddu KRISHNAMURTI
  ALCYONE
Caroline KROUT
  Caroline BROWN
Benjamin KUBELSKY
  Jack BENNY
Robert KUHN
  Bob KEENE
Nadia KUJNIR-HERESCU
  Nadia GRAY
K'UNG FU-TZU
  CONFUCIUS
Dikran KUYUMJIAN
  Michael ARLEN
Hryhoriy KVITKA
  OSNOVYANENKO

# L

Gerard LABRUNIE
  Gérard DE NERVAL
  Gérard NERVAL
Pearl LACK
  Pearl LANG
Joanne LA COCK
  Joanne DRU
Joseph B. LADD
  AROUET
Julian LA FAYE
  John CARROLL
Christine LAFFEATY
  Netta CARSTENS
Martha LAFFERTY
  Janet BLAIR

John LAFFIN
  Carl DEKKER
Ann LA HIFF
  Nancy CARROLL
Irving LAHRHEIM
  Bert LAHR
Harriette LAKE
  Ann SOTHERN
Charles LAMB
  BURTON JUNIOR
  CRITO
  EDAX
  ELIA
  An EYE-WITNESS
  HOSPITA

A LONDONER
MORITURUS
**Richmal C. LAMBURN**
Richmal CROMPTON
**Ferdinand Joseph LA MENTHE**
Jelly Roll MORTON
**M. A. LANDAU**
Marl Aleksandrovich ALDANOV
**Melville de Lancey LANDON**
Eli PERKINS
**Reginald LANE**
Angel LANE
**Lucille LANGEHANKE**
Mary ASTOR
**Ronald LANGINGER**
Ronny LANG
**Claude LANGMANN**
Claude BERRI
**George T. LANNIGAN**
George Washington AESOP
**Carol LARAIA**
Carol LAWRENCE
**William F. LARKINS**
Gerry LONG
**Romulo LARRALDE**
Romney BRENT
**Suzan LARSEN**
Susanna FOSTER
**Signe LARSSON**
Signe HASSO
**Dianne LARUSKA**
Dianne FOSTER
**Jesse Louis LASKY**
Frances SMEED
**Pierre Jules LAUDENBACH**
Pierre FRESNAY
**John LAUSEN**
Yank LAWSON
**D. H. LAWRENCE**
L. H. DAVIDSON
Lawrence H. DAVISON
GRANTORTO
**Elizabeth S. LAWRENCE**
E. S. BRADBURNE
**Joyce LAWRENCE**
Joyce CAREY
**T. E. LAWRENCE**
John Hume ROSS
T. E. SHAW

**Alexandre LAWRENCE-KLASEN**
Gertrude LAWRENCE
**Marie LAWRIE**
LULU
**Betty LEABO**
Brenda JOYCE
**Archibald LEACH**
Cary GRANT
**Leonard LEBITSKY**
Jack E. LEONARD
**Huddie LEDBETTER**
LEADBELLY
**Rudolf LEDER**
Stephen HERMLIN
**Evelyn LEDERER**
Sue CAROL
**Arthur LEE**
Junius AMERICANUS
**Manfred B. LEE and Frederic DANNAY**
Barnaby ROSS
Ellery QUEEN
**Palmer LEE**
Gregg PALMER
**James LEE-RICHARDSON**
Desmond DUNNE
**Antoinette LEES**
Andrea LEEDS
**Germaine LEFEBURE**
CAPUCINE
**Laura LEFEVRE**
Zenobia BIRD
**Pinkus LEFF**
Pinky LEE
**Aléxis Saint-Léger LÉGER**
ST. JOHN PERSE
**Sidney LEIBOWITZ**
Steve LAWRENCE
**Donovan LEITCH**
DONOVAN
**William LENCEL**
Charles GRANT
**Jason Gregory LENHART**
Paul GREGORY
**Irene LENTZ**
IRENE
**Daniel LEONARD**
MASSACHUSETTENSIS

216

**Helen LEONARD**
  Lilian RUSSELL
**Isaiah Edwin LEOPOLD**
  Ed WYNN
**Alice LEPPERT**
  Alice FAYE
**Mrs. Richard LERT**
  Vicki BAUM
**Katherine LESTER**
  Katherine DE MILLE
**Lucille LE SUEUR**
  Joan CRAWFORD
**Hazel LETOUT**
  Hazel DAWN
**George M. LETZ**
  George MONTGOMERY
**Ivo LEVI**
  Yves MONTAND
**Gabriel LEVIELLE**
  Max LINDER
**Bernard LEVIN**
  Felix BATTLE
  A. E. CHERRYMAN
**Joseph LEVITCH**
  Jerry LEWIS
**Burton LEVY**
  Burton LANE
**Frederick LEVY**
  Conway TEARLE
**Herbert I. LEVY**
  Herbert I. LEEDS
**Marion LEVY**
  Paulette GODDARD
**Paul LEVY**
  Paul BERN
**Stephen LEVY**
  Stephen YOUNG
**Ivan LEVYTSKY**
  NECHUY
**Georg LEWIN**
  Herwath WALDEN
**Anthony C. LEWING**
  Mark BANNERMAN
**Barbara Geddes LEWIS**
  Barbara BEL GEDDES
**Clifford and Mary LEWIS**
  Judith M. BERRISFORD
**Sinclair LEWIS**
  Tom GRAHAM

**François L'HÉRMITE**
  TRISTAN
**Wladziu Valentino LIBERACE**
  LIBERACE
**Joe LICHTMAN**
  Joe LAYTON
**Thomas LIEBER**
  Thomas ERASTUS
**A. LIFSHITS**
  A. VOLODIN
**Marta LILETTS**
  Lil DAGOVER
**Goran LILJA**
  Georg STJERNHJELM
**Joseph Conrad LIND**
  Peter Lind HAYES
**Ragnar LIND**
  Jeffery LYNN
**Louis Bert LINDLEY**
  Slim PICKINS
**Florence LINDON-TRAVERS**
  Linden TRAVERS
**Jack LINDSAY**
  Richard PRESTON
**Kathleen LINDSAY**
  Margaret CAMERON
**Paul LINEBARGER**
  Felix C. FORREST
  Carmichael SMITH
**Elizabeth LININGTON**
  Anne BLAISDELL
  Lesley EGAN
  Egan O'NEILL
**Otto Elmo LINKENHELTER**
  Elmo LINCOLN
**Carl LINNÉ**
  Carolus LINNAEUS
**Mildred LINTON**
  Karen MORLEY
**LIN YU-YUNG**
  LIN PIAO
**Sara LIPPENCOTT**
  Grace GREENWOOD
**Jacques LIPSCHITZ**
  Jacques LIPCHITZ
**Edward LITTLE**
  Edward LEXY
**Malcolm LITTLE**
  MALCOLM X

Carlos LLERAS RESTREPO
 Cleofas PEREZ
Frederick LLEWELLYN
 Freddie BARTHOLOMEW
Mary LLOYD
 Mary MERRALL
Charles LOCHER
 Jon HALL
Donald LOCHER
 Don TERRY
David Ross LOCKE
 Petroleum Vesuvius NASBY
Ingersoll LOCKWOOD
 Irwin LONGMAN
Ralph Ingersoll LOCKWOOD
 Mr. SMITH
Dolores LOEHR
 Diana LYNN
Heidi LOEWENGARD
 Martha ALBRAND
Laszlo LOEWENSTEIN
 Peter LORRE
Igor LOIEWSKI
 Igor CASSINI
 Cholly KNICKERBOCKER
Evan LOMBINO
 Hunt COLLING
 Evan HUNTER
 Ed McBAIN
 Richard MARSTEN
Vilma LONCHIT
 Vilma BANKY
Harry LONGBAUGH
 The SUNDANCE KID
Henry Wadsworth LONGFELLOW
 An AMERICAN
 Joshua COFFIN
 Hans HAMMERGAFFERSTEIN
Roger LONGRIGG
 Ivor DRUMMOND
 Rosalind ERSKINE

Stephen LONGSTREET
 Thomas BURTON
 Paul HAGGARD
 David ORMSBEE
Phillips LORD
 Seth PARKER
Maxwell LORIMER
 Max WALL
Joseph LOSEY
 Victor HANBURY
Marilyn LOUIS
 Rhonda FLEMING
Frank LO VECCHIO
 Frankie LAINE
Samuel LOVER
 Ben TROVATO
John LOWE
 John LODER
James Russell LOWELL
 Hosea BIGLOW
 ELMWOOD
 Columbus NYE
 Homer WILBUR
 Homer WILSON
Charles Salvatore LUCANIA
 Lucky LUCIANO
Hayden LUCID
 Russell HAYDEN
Pal LUKACS
 Paul LUKAS
Arthur Milton LUNT
 Milton ROSMER
Henry LUPINO
 Lupino LANE
Irene LUTHER
 Irene RICH
Robert LYND
 Y.Y.
Dennis LYNDS
 Michael COLLINS

# M

Golda MABOVITZ
  Golda MEIR
Margaret H. McALPINE
  Ann CARMICHAEL
Thomas Babington MACAULAY
  CID HAMET BENENGELI
  Tristram MERTON
  Richard QUONGTI
Fannie MACAULEY
  Frances LITTLE
Marden McBROOM
  David BRUCE
James D. McCABE
  Edward Winslow MARTIN
Colin McCALLUM
  Charles COBORN
Justine McCARTHY
  Kay KENDALL
Barbara McCORQUODALE
  Barbara CARTLAND
Johnston McCULLEY
  Raley BRIEN
  George DRAYNE
  Frederic PHELPS
  Rowena RALEY
  Harrington STRONG
George Barr McCUTCHEON
  Richard GREAVES
Ellas McDANIEL
  Bo DIDDLEY
James P. McDONALD
  Preston JACKSON
Marion Lorne MacDOUGAL
  Marion LORNE
Katherine McDOWELL
  Sherwood BONNER
Malcolm McEACHRAN
  JETSAM
William Blake McEDWARDS
  Blake EDWARDS
Jane McELHENEY
  Ada CLARE
Arthur McEVOY
  Frank RANDLE
George Emmett McFARLAND
  Spanky McFARLAND

Cornelius McGILLICUDDY
  Connie MACK
Fabia Drake McGLINCHY
  Fabia DRAKE
Alfred McGONEGAL
  Alan JENKINS
Robert MACGREGOR
  Rob ROY
Bernard F. McGUINNESS
  Brian McGUINNESS
Milton R. MACHLIN
  W. M. JASON
Maureen McILWRAITH
  Mollie HUNTER
Rufus Alan McKAHAN
  Alan HALE
Henry S. McKEAN
  John SMITH
Florence McKECHNIE
  Florence ELDRIDGE
Wayne McKEEKAN
  David WAYNE
Ann McKIM
  Ann DVORAK
Henry H. McKINNIES
  Jeffrey HUNTER
Charles McKINNON
  Vivian DONALD
J. Fairfax McLAUGHLIN
  PASQUINO
Joseph McLAUGHLIN
  Joseph LOCKE
Edmund McLAVERTY
  Edmund BREON
C. M. S. McLELLAN
  Hugh MORTON
Jean McLEOD
  Catherine AIRLIE
Ellen McLEOD
  Ella ANDERSON
Paul MacMAHON
  Paul GILBERT
Guy McMASTER
  John MACGROM
Virginia McMATH
  Ginger ROGERS

**Isabella McMEEKIN and Dorothy CLARK**
 Clark McMEEKIN
**James McMILLAN**
 CORIOLANUS
**Ursula McMINN**
 Ursula JEANS
**Horace McNALLY**
 Stephen McNALLY
**H. C. McNEILE**
 SAPPER
**Mildred McNEILLY**
 James DEWEY
 Glenn KELLY
**Dorothy McNULTY**
 Penny SINGLETON
**Thelma McQUEEN**
 Butterfly McQUEEN
**Virginia McSWEENEY**
 Virginia VALLI
**Martha MACVICAR**
 Martha VICKERS
**Angela MADISON**
 Angela BANNER
**Louis MADISON**
 Kid SHOTS
**William MAGINN**
 Dionysius DUGGAN
 Blaise FITZTRAVESTY
 Giles MIDDLESTITCH
 Morty Macnamara MULLIGAN
 SODA WATER
 MANUFACTURER
**Albertus MAGNUS**
 Albertus GROTUS
 Albertus LAVINGENSIS
**Leonide MAGUILEVSKY**
 Leonide MOGUY
**Edward MAINWARING**
 Ed STEWART
**George MAIR**
 Kooshti BOK
**Charles MAJOR**
 Edwin CASKODEN
**Curzio MALAPARTE**
 Kurt SUCKERT
**James Ferdinand MALLINCKRODT**
 John THINKINGMACHINE

**Lady MALLOWAN**
 Agatha CHRISTIE
 Mary WESTMACOTT
**John MALLOY**
 John WRAY
**Edmond MALONE**
 STULTIFEX ACADEMICUS
**Dorothy MALONEY**
 Dorothy MALONE
**Joseph MANDEL**
 Joe MAY
**Lionel MANDER**
 Miles MANDER
**Frederick Feike MANFRED**
 Feike FEIKEMA
**Arthur MANN**
 A. R. THURMAN
**Giacomo MANZONI**
 Giacomo MANZU
**Jean MARAIS-VILLAIN**
 Jean MARAIS
**MARCUS ANNIUS VERUS**
 MARCUS AURELIUS
 ANTONINUS
**Kurt W. MAREK**
 C. W. CERAM
**David MARGULOIS**
 David MERRICK
**Vincent MARKOWSKY**
 Tom TYLER
**Lilian MARKS**
 Alicia MARKOVA
**Charles MARKS and Joseph SELTZER**
 SMITH and DALE
**Sadye MARKS**
 Mary LIVINGSTONE
**Edythe MARRINER**
 Susan HAYWARD
**Robert B. MARSHALL**
 Edmund CRISPIN
**Fernand MARTENS**
 Fernand GRAVET
**Robert B. MARTIN**
 Robert BERNARD
**Violet MARTIN**
 Martin ROSS
**Luis MARTÍNEZ-DELGADO**
 LUIMARDEL

José MARTINEZ RUIZ
 AZORÌN
 CANDIDO
Adolph MARX
 Harpo MARX
Julius MARX
 Groucho MARX
Leonard MARX
 Chico MARX
F. Van Wyck MASON and
Helen BRAWNER
 Geoffrey COFFIN
Michael MASON
 Cameron BLAKE
Salvatore MASSARO
 Eddie LANG
Kelly R. MASTERS
 Zachary BALL
Walter MATASSCHANSKAYA-
SKY
 Walter MATTHAU
Sylvia MATHESON
 Max MUNDY
Albert MATHEWS
 Paul SIOGVOLK
Cornelius MATHEWS
 The LATE BEN SMITH
Pauline MATTHEWS
 Kiki DEE
Harvey MATUSOW
 Omar MULDOON
Emma MATZO
 Lizabeth SCOTT
Christian MAUDET
 CHRISTIAN-JAQUE
Robin MAUGHAM
 David GRIFFIN
Emmaline MAULTSBY
 Debby MOORE
Mathew Fontaine MAURY
 Harry BLUFF
Osborne Henry MAVOR
 James BRIDIE
Marvel MAXWELL
 Marilyn MAXWELL
Victoria MAYA
 Linda CRISTAL
Jane MAYER and Clara SPIEGEL
 Clare JAYNES

Ann Todd MAYFIELD
 Ann TODD
Horace and Henry MAYHEW and
Robert BROUGH
 Rigdum FUNNIDUS
Giulio MAZARINI
 Jules MAZARIN
Mikhail MAZURWSKI
 Mike MAZURKI
Girolamo Francesco Maria
MAZZOLA
 PARMIGIANO or
 PARMIGIANINO
Sidney MEAD
 MOKO
James MEADOR
 James CRAIG
Henry MEECHAM
 ARISTEAS
Leon MEGERDICHIAN
 Leon MERIAN
Ulrich MEGERLE
 ABRAHAM-A-SANTA-CLARA
Ramjankhan MEHBOOBKHAN
 MEHBOOB
Joseph MEIBES
 John ERICSON
Grenville MELLEN
 Reginald REVERIE
John Calvin MELLETT
 Jonathan BROOKS
Leonard MELLING
 LUMINUS
MELLOS
 Ilias VENEZIS
Pavel MEL'NIKOV
 Andrei PECHERSKY
William B. MELONEY
 Margaret GRANT
Mrs. W. B. MELONEY
 Rose FRANKEN
H. L. MENCKEN and George Jean
NATHAN
 Owen HATTERAS
Rustam MENTA
 Roger HARTMAN
Major Cecil William MERCER
 Dornford YATES

221

Prosper MÉRIMÉE
Clara GAZUL
Barbara MERTZ
Barbara MICHAELS
Milton MESIROW
Mezz MEZZROW
André MESRITZ
André MORELL
Samuel G. MESSER
Robert MIDDLETON
Robert Preston MESSERVEY
Robert PRESTON
Kenneth W. METHOLD
Alexander CADE
Ricardo METZETTI
Richard TALMADGE
David MEYER
David JANSSEN
Laurence MEYNELL
Valerie BAXTER
Sidney BEDFORD
Robert ETON
Stephen A. TRING
Janet Beecher MEYSENBURG
Janet BEECHER
Leonid MIASSINE
Leonide MASSINE
Marianna MICHALSKA
Gilda GRAY
Maurice MICKLEWHITE
Michael CAINE
Peggy MIDDLETON
Yvonne DE CARLO
Ella MIGHELS
Aurora ESMERALDA
Maria MIKKOLA
Malia TALVIO
Kenneth MILLAR
John Ross MACDONALD
Edna St. Vincent MILLAY
Nancy BOYD
Cincinnatus MILLER
Joaquin MILLER
Eschal MILLER
Nan GREY
Gary MILLER
Michael DUNN

Susan MILLER
Susan SAINT JAMES
Warren MILLER
Amanda VAIL
William MILLER
Stephen BOYD
Wright W. MILLER
Mark NORTH
Martin MILLS
Martin BOYD
David MINTZ
David KNIGHT
Donald Grant MITCHELL
Ik MARVEL
Helen MITCHELL
Nellie MELBA
Isabel MITCHELL
Josephine PLAIN
James MITCHELL
Lewis Grassic GIBBON
Mrs. Merrian MODELL
Evelyn PIPER
Robert MODINI
Robert STACK
Paul MOERSCHBACHER
Paul MOER
Jelal-ed-din-MOHAMMED
AKBAR
Zahir ed-din MOHAMMED
BABER
Jean MOKIEJESWKI
Jean-Pierre MOCKY
Joan MOLINSKY
Joan RIVERS
Alexis MONCOURGE
Jean GABIN
Bernice Hale MONRO
Binnie HALE
Robert Hale MONRO
Sonnie HALE
Luigi MONTAGNA
Bull MONTANA
François de MONTCORBIER
François VILLON
Eurreal MONTGOMERY
LITTLE BROTHER
Henry MONTGOMERY
Robert MONTGOMERY

James **MONTGOMERY**
Paul POSITIVE
Gabriel SILVERTONGUE, Gent.
Leslie A. **MONTGOMERY**
Lynn DOYLE
Robert D. **MONTGOMERY**
Kent DOUGLASS
Douglass MONTGOMERY
Rutherford **MONTGOMERY**
Al AVERY
Ron **MOODNICK**
Ron MOODY
Michael **MOORCOCK**
James COLVIN
Clara **MOORE**
Clara MORETON
Mrs. H. O. WARD
George **MOORE**
The PAGAN
Idora **MOORE**
Betsy HAMILTON
James **MOORE**
Slim HARPO
Thomas **MOORE**
Thomas BROWN
Tom CRIB
An IRISHMAN
Thomas LITTLE Esq.
Mr. MINUS
Anacreon MOORE
ONE OF THE FANCY
T***Y M***E
Trismagistur RUSTIFUSTIUS
George **MOORE-MARRIOTT**
Moore MARRIOTT
Gabrielle **MOPPERT**
Gabrielle DORZIAT
Mario **MORENO**
CANTINFLAS
Thomas **MORFIT**
Garry MOORE
Murray **MORGAN**
Cromwell MURRAY
McKinley **MORGANFIELD**
Muddy WATERS
Eileen **MORISON**
Patricia MORISON
Grigori **MORMENKO**
Grigori ALEXANDROV

Stanley **MORNER**
Dennis MORGAN
Alvin **MORRIS**
Tony MARTIN
Joseph Christopher Columbus
**MORRIS**
Chris COLUMBUS
Frank **MORRISON**
Mickey SPILLANE
Janette **MORRISON**
Janet LEIGH
Kathleen **MORRISON**
Coleen MOORE
Marion **MORRISON**
John WAYNE
Paul Fix **MORRISON**
Paul FIX
Richard James **MORRISON**
ZADKIEL
Penelope **MORTIMER**
Ann TEMPLE
J. B. **MORTON**
BEACHCOMBER
Nathaniel **MOSCOVITCH**
Noel MADISON
Robert **MOSELEY**
Guy MADISON
Lawrence **MOSELY**
Snub MOSLEY
Samuel **MOSTEL**
Zero MOSTEL
Maryse **MOURER**
Martine CAROL
Michail Christodoulou **MOUSKOS**
MAKARIOS III
Phoebe Annie Oakley **MOZEE**
Annie OAKLEY
Helen **MUDGETT**
Pat MORAN
Marvin **MUELLER**
Marvin MILLER
John Henry **MUENZENBERGER**
Johnny MINCE
Edward **MUGGERIDGE**
Eadweard MUYBRIDGE
Margaret E. **MUGGESON**
Margaret DICKINSON
Rafael **MUGICA**
Gabriel CELAYA

Edwin MUIR
  Edward MOORE
Marie MUIR
  Monica BLAKE
Donna MULLENGER
  Donna REED
Rudolph MULLER
  Martin MILLER
Juan MUNDANSCHAFFTER
  Carlos THOMPSON
Hector Hugh MUNRO
  SAKI
Patrice MUNSIL
  Patrice MUNSEL

Constance MUNSTON
  Beatrice LILLIE
Jules MURAIRE
  RAIMU
Mabel MURPHY
  Anna S. LEE
Egbert Roscoe MURROW
  Edward R. MURROW
Kathleen Middleton MURRY
  Matilda BERRY
  Katherine MANSFIELD
Mary MUSSI
  Josephine EDGAR
Mary Cathart MYERS
  Mary Cathart BORER

# N

Vladimir NABOKOV
  SIRIN
Alan NAPIER-CLAVERING
  Alan NAPIER
Filippo NAPOLI
  Phil NAPOLEON
George Jean NATHAN and H. L. MENCKEN
  Owen HATTERAS
John NEAL
  John O'CATARACT
  SOMEBODY, M.D.C.
Harold NEBERROTH
  Alan CURTIS
Julien NEIL
  Martin ASHE
Beverly NEILL
  Amanda BLAKE
Terence NELHAMS
  Adam FAITH
Eric NELSON
  Jerry FULLER
  Rick NELSON
Barbara NEVILLE
  Edward CANDY
John NEWBERY
  Mrs. Mary MIDNIGHT
Charles NEWELL
  Captain Robert BARNACLE

Robert Henry NEWELL
  Orpheus C. KERR
Bernard NEWMAN
  Don BETTERIDGE
Julia NEWMEYER
  Julie NEWMAR
D. B. NEWTON
  Dwight BENNETT
  Clement HARDIN
  Ford LOGAN
Eliza NICHOLSON
  Pearl RIVERS
Miss Susan D. NICKERSON
  A LADY OF BOSTON
Philip H. NICKLIN
  Peregrine PROLIX
Eric NICOL
  JABEZ
Christopher NICOLE
  Peter GRANGE
  Andrew YORK
Federico NOBILE
  Fred NIBLO
Luciel NOEL
  NOEL-NOEL
George B. NOLAN
  George BRENT
Thomas NOON
  Tommy NOONAN

Virginia NOONAN
 Sally O'NEIL
Peter NOONE
 HERMAN
Hans Erich Maria Stroheim von
NORDENWALL
 Erich VON STROHEIM
Alexander NORRIS
 Max NOSSECK
Olive NORTON
 T. R. NOON
Kenneth NORVILLE
 Red NORVO
Nevil Shute NORWAY
 Nevil SHUTE

Michel de NOTREDAME
 NOSTRADAMUS
Marilyn NOVAK
 Kim NOVAK
Rita NOVELLA
 Dona DRAKE
 Rita RIO
Olga de Kireef NOVIKOFF
 O.K.
Allen NUMANO
 A. L. A. CORENANDA
Anthony NUMKENA
 Earl HOLLIMAN
Lily NUTT
 Clive ARDEN

# O

Louis OBEE
 Sonia DRESDEL
Angela O'BRIEN
 Margaret O'BRIEN
Conor Cruise O'BRIEN
 Donat O'DONNELL
Howard Vincent O'BRIEN
 Clyde PERRIN
Jane O'BRIEN
 Jane BRYAN
John O'BRIEN
 John T. RAYMOND
Mary O'BRIEN
 Dusty SPRINGFIELD
Patrica O'BRIEN
 Patrica ELLIS
Marie M. O'CARROLL
 Madeleine CARROLL
Constance OCKLEMAN
 Constance KEANE
 Veronica LAKE
Alma O'CONNOR
 Ann GILLIS
Patrick J. O'CONNOR
 Padraid FIAAC
Michael O'DONOVAN
 Frank O'CONNOR

Louella OETTINGER
 Louella PARSONS
Francis O'FEENEY
 Francis FORD
Sean O'FEENEY
 John FORD
Lewis Delaney OFFIELD
 Jack OAKIE
Leo H. OGNALL
 Harry CARMICHAEL
Kreker OHANIAN
 Michael CONNORS
Kieron O'HANRAHAN
 Kieron MOORE
Hyacinth Hazel O'HIGGINS
 Hy HAZELL
OHIYESA
 Charles EASTMAN
Peter OHM
 Peter VAUGHAN
Joan Lucille OLANDER
 Mamie VAN DOREN
Berna Eli OLDFIELD
 Barney OLDFIELD
Lilian OLDLAND
 Mary NEWLAND
John OLESON
 John QUALEN

Ann-Margaret OLSSON
ANN-MARGRET
David O'MAHONEY
Dave ALLEN
Jacques O'MAHONEY
Jock MAHONEY
Lady O'MALLEY
Ann BRIDGE
Palmina OMICCIOLI
Elenora ROSSI-DRAGO
Henry Ustick ONDERDONK
H.U.O.
Anny ONDRAKOVA
Anny ONDRA
Oliver ONIONS
George OLIVER
Brian O'NOLAN
MYLES NA GOPALEEN
Flann O'BRIEN
Jill OPPENHEIM
Jill ST. JOHN
Max OPPENHEIMER
Max OPHULS
Maggie O'REED
Martha RAYE
Eve ORME
Irene DAY
Richard ORNSTEIN
Richard OSWALD
Ruth O'ROURKE
Ruth HUSSEY

Michael OROWITZ
Michael LANDON
Carmen ORRICO
John SAXON
Laughton OSBORN
Charles Erskine WHITE, D.D.
Dorothy OSBORNE
Gladys ARTHUR
Geoffrey OSTERGAARD
Gaston GEORGE
Paula OSTERMAN
Raquel TORRES
Isabel OSTRANDER
Robert Orr CHIPPERFIELD
David FOX
Pamela OSTRER
Pamela KELLINO
Eugene O'SULLIVAN
Gene GERRARD
Mischa OUNSKOWSKY
Mischa AUER
Ronald Le Roy OVERACKER
Baby LE ROY
Wayne D. OVERHOLSER
John S. DANIELS
Joseph WAYNE
Wayne D. OVERHOUSE
Dan J. STEVENS
Jack OWEN
Jack DYKES

# P

John Arthur PAGE
Robert PAIGE
José PAIGE
Don ALVARADO
Djanira PAIVA
DJANIRA
Elizabeth PAJAUD
Lizzie MILES
PAL
LASSIE
Walter PALANUIK
Jack PALANCE

Simon S. PALESTRANT
Stephen EDWARD
S. P. STEVENS
Paul E. STRAND
Claude PALMER
Claude ALLISTER
John Leslie PALMER and
Hilary St. George SAUNDERS
Francis BEEDING
Madelyn PALMER
GEOFFREY

Vera Jane PALMER
  Jayne MANSFIELD
Dandhu PANTH
  NANA SAHIB
Alfred PAOLELLA
  Teddy POWELL
Iannis
PAPADIAMANTOPOULOS
  Jean MORÉAS
Anthony PAPALEO
  Anthony FRANCIOSA
George Frederick PARDON
  QUIET GEORGE
Marion PARES
  Judith CAMPBELL
Dawn PARIS
  Dawn O'DAY
  Ann SHIRLEY
Cecilia PARKER
  Suzy PARKER
Robert Le Roy PARKER
  Butch CASSIDY
Frank PARKES
  Kwesi DOMPO
Charles PARROTT
  Charley CHASE
Hugh Jones PARRY
  James CROSS
Patrick PARSONS
  Patrick HOLT
Mustafa Kemal PASHA
  Kemal ATATÜRK
Mike PASTERNAK
  Emperor ROSKO
William Gilbert PATTEN
  Burt L. STANDISH
Jules PAUFICHET
  Jules BERRY
John PAUL
  John Paul JONES
James Kirke PAULDING
  Launcelot LANGSTAFF
Robert PAYNE
  Richard CARGOE
  Howard HORNE
  Robert YOUNG
Thomas Love PEACOCK
  Peter PEPPERCORN

Brian PEARCE
  Leonard HUSSEY
Hal PEARY
  Great GILDERSLEEVE
George Washington PECK
  Cantell A. BIGLEY
Julie PECK
  Julie LONDON
Santo J. PECORARO
  Santo J. PECORA
Carl PEDERSON
  Carl BRISSON
Hazel PEEL
  HAYMAN
Jozsef PEHM
  Jozsef MINDSZENTY
Maria Lilli PEISER
  Lilli PALMER
Carlo PELLEGRINI
  APE
Mort PELOVITZ
  Mort HERBERT
Vladimir PENIAKOFF
  POPSKI
Richard PENNIMAN
  LITTLE RICHARD
Cenni di PEPO
  Giovanni CIMABUE
Joan PEPPER
  Joan ALEXANDER
Jacob PERELMUTH
  Jan PEERCE
Thomas PERKINS
  Thomas WAYNE
Gerald PERREAU-SAUSSINE
  Peter MILES
Ghislaine PERREAU-SAUSSINE
  Gigi PERREAU
Lincoln PERRY
  Stepin FECHIT
Rufus PERRYMAN
  SPECKLED RED
Betty Joan PERSKE
  Lauren BACALL
Truman PERSONS
  Truman CAPOTE
Isabella Augusta PERSSE
  Lady GREGORY

Harry Arnold PERSSON
 Harry ARNOLD
Michael Igor PESCHKOWSKY
 Mike NICHOLS
Aleksei Maksimovich PESHKOV
 Maxim GORKY
Antonio PESTRITTO
 Tony PASTOR
Roberta PETERMAN
 Roberta PETERS
Curtis Arnoux PETERS
 Peter ARNO
Jane Alice PETERS
 Carole LOMBARD
Maureen PETERS
 Veronica BLACK
Beatrice PETERSON
 Hillary BROOKE
Corinna PETERSON
 Corinna COCHRANE
Anne-Marie PETIT
 Pascale PETIT
Rhonda PETRIE
 Eileen-Marie DUELL
Michele PEZZA
 FRA DIAVOLO
Elizabeth PHELPS
 Leigh NORTH
Judson Pentecost PHILIPS
 Hugh PENTECOST
Dennis PHILLIPS
 Peter CHESTER
John M. PHILLIPS
 January SEARLE
Tully Marshall PHILLIPS
 Tully MARSHALL
Thomas PICTON
 Paul PRESTON
Anna Maria PIERANGELI
 Pier ANGELI
Marisa PIERANGELI
 Marisa PAVAN
Virna PIERLISI
 Virna LISI
 Guido di PIETRI
 Fra ANGELICO
Rosamunde PILCHER
 Jane FRASER

François PILU
 François PERIER
Alberto PINCHERLE
 Alberto MORAVIA
Harold PINTER
 David BARON
Joe PINTER
 Joe PENNER
Jacqueline H. PINTO
 Jacqueline BLAIRMAN
Fortunio PINZA
 Ezio PINZA
Minerva PIOUS
 Mrs. MUSSBAUM
William PITT
 The CELEBRATED
 COMMONER
 The GREAT MAN
 WILLIAM THE FOURTH
William PITT, the Younger
 DEEP WILL
 Julius FLORUS
Vito PIZZO
 Vito PRICE
Sylvia PLATH
 Victoria LUCAS
Roger Vadim PLEMIANNIKOW
 Roger VADIM
Ernest PLUMLEY
 John CLEVEDON
Clare PLUMMER
 Clare EMSLEY
F. W. PLUMPE
 F. W. MURNAU
Edgar POE
 A BOSTONIAN
 Edgar Allan POE
Dorothy POLAND
 Alison FARELY
Lester POLFUS
 Les PAUL
Marina de POLIAKOFF-
BAIDAROV
 Marina VLADY
Militza de POLIAKOFF-
BAIDAROV
 Odile VERSOIS
Michael J. POLLACK
 Michael J. POLLARD

Byno POLUSKI
 Polly WARD
John POMPEO
 Johnny RAE
Andrea da PONTEDERA
 Andrea PISANO
Rosa PONZILLO
 Rosa PONSELLE
Elijah POOLE
 Elijah MUHAMMAD
Sherman POOLE
 Virginia GILMORE
Alexander POPE
 A
 APOTH
 Esdras BARNIVELT
 Dick DISTICH
 An EMINENT HAND
 An EYE-WITNESS
 Mr. Joseph GAY
 GNATHO
 Martinus SCRIBLERUS
 Bob SHORT
Aleksandr Serafimovich POPOV
 Aleksandr SERAFIMOVICH
Jean Baptiste POQUELIN
 MOLIÈRE
Bartolomeo della PORTA
 Fra BARTOLOMEO
Curtis PORTER
 Shafi HADI
Harold PORTER
 Holworthy HALL
William Sidney PORTER
 O. HENRY
Adrienne POSTER
 Adrienne POSTA
Heather POTTER
 Heather JENNER
Margaret POTTER
 Anne BETTERIDGE
 Margaret NEWMAN
Gilbert Emery Bensley POTTLE
 Gilbert EMERY
Ezra POUND
 William ATHELING
 M. D. ATKINS
 B. H. DIAS

FERREX
Henry HAWKINS
Weston LLEWMYS
Abel SANDERS
T.J.V.
A. VENISON
Bastien VON HELMHOLZ
Z
Clive POWELL
 Georgie FAME
Ollie POWELL
 Ollie POWERS
Vincent POWELL-SMITH
 Francis ELPHINSTONE
 JUSTICIAR
Mary Ellen POWERS
 Mala POWERS
Dennis PRATT
 Dennis KING
Eliza PRATT
 Ella FARMAN
John PRATT
 John WINTON
Theodore PRATT
 Timothy BRACE
William PRATT
 Boris KARLOFF
Barry PRENDERGAST
 John BARRY
Franz PRESSLER
 George FATTY
Irving PRESTOPNIK
 Irving FAZOLA
Violet PRETTY
 Anne HEYWOOD
Beverley PRICE
 Beverley RANDLE
Gertrude Malissa PRIDGETT
 Ma RAINEY
Joseph PRIESTLEY
 A LOVER OF PEACE AND
 TRUTH
 A LOVER OF THE GOSPEL
Dorothy PRIMA
 Keely SMITH
John PRINGLE
 John GILBERT

**Rebecca Marjorie PROOPS**
  Marjorie PROOPS
**David Law PROUDFIT**
  Peleg ARKWRIGHT
**Denis PULLEIN-THOMPSON**

Dennis CANNAN
**Lalage PULVERTAFT**
  Hilary MARCH
**Ken PURDY**
  Karl PRENTISS

# Q

**Eunice QUEDENS**
  Eve ARDEN
**Sir Arthur QUILLER-COUCH**
  Q
**Thomas QUINCEY**
  Thomas DE QUINCEY

An OPIUM EATER
**Maria C. QUIROGA**
  Maria CASARES
**Françoise QUOIREZ**
  Françoise SAGAN

# R

**Florence RABE**
  Florence BATES
**Jerome RABINOWITZ**
  Jerome ROBBINS
**Solomon RABINOWITZ**
  Sholom ALEICHEM
**Roy RADEBAUGH**
  Richard CROMWELL
**Emilio RADOCCHIA**
  Emil RICHARDS
**Netty RADVANYI**
  Anna SEGHERS
**Hugh C. RAE**
  Robert CRAWFORD
**Paula RAGUSA**
  Paula PRENTISS
**André RAIMBOURG**
  BOURVIL
**James RALPH**
  A. PRIMCOCK
**Vera RALSTON**
  Vera MILES
**Myriam RAMBERG**
  Marie RAMBERT
**Owen Nares RAMSAY**
  Owen NARES

**Major George RANKEN**
  X, AUTHOR OF NOTHING,
  AND PROPERLY REPRE-
  SENTED BY THE ABOVE
  UNKNOWN QUANTITY
**Gabriele RAPAGNETTA**
  Gabriele D'ANNUNZIO
**St. George Henry RATHBONE**
  Harrison ADAMS
  Duke DUNCAN
  Aleck FORBES
  Marline MANLY
  Harry ST. GEORGE
**George RAUBENHEIMER**
  George HARDING
**Ella RAUBES**
  Ella RAINES
**George RAUFT**
  George RAFT
**John RAVENSCROFT**
  John PEEL
**Clayton RAWSON**
  The GREAT MERLINI
  Stuart TOWNE
**Terry RAY**
  Ellen DREW

230

René RAYMOND
  James Hadley CHASE
Claire RAYNER
  Sheila BRANDON
  Ann LYNTON
John REA
  John RIDGELEY
John READ
  JAN
Thomas B. REAGAN
  Jim THOMAS
Malcolm REBERNACK
  Dr. JOHN
Ben Ray REDMAN
  Jeremy LORD
Isobel REED
  Isobel ELSOM
Myrtle REED
  Olive GREEN
Joan REES
  Ann BEDFORD
Alan REEVES-JONES
  Roger LUNCHBASKET
John Cowie REID
  CALIBAN
Patricia REID
  Kim STANLEY
Juliet REILLY
  Mary Miles MINTER
Elmer REIZENSTEIN
  Elmer RICE
Erich P. REMARK
  Erich Maria REMARQUE
Comtesse de RENEVILLE
  Mary MOTLEY
Neftalí Ricardo REYES
  Pablo NERUDA
Marie Frances REYNOLDS
  Debbie REYNOLDS
Adrienne RICCOBONI
  Adrienne CORRI
George RICE
  George O'HANLON
Joan RICE
  Jay HALLAM
Rosella RICE
  Chatty BROOKS
  Pipsissiway POTTS

Jean-Marius RICHARD
  CARLO-RIM
Ronald RICHARDS
  K. ALLEN
Ethel Henrietta RICHARDSON
  Henry Handel RICHARDSON
Jape RICHARDSON
  BIG BOPPER
Euphemia RICHMOND
  Effie JOHNSON
Johann RICHTER
  JEAN PAUL
Helen RICKERTS
  Helena CARTER
Alfons de RIDER
  Willem ELSSCHOT
John RIDGE
  YELLOW BIRD
Frances RIDSTE
  Carole LANDIS
Felicia RIESE
  Patricia ROC
Mary RIGGS
  Evelyn BRENT
James Whitcomb RILEY
  Benj. F. JOHNSON of Boone
Mildred RINKER
  Mildred BAILEY
Irene RIORDAN
  Irene RYAN
Lynne RIPLEY
  TWINKLE
Douglas RITCHIE
  Colonel BRITTON
Woodward RITTER
  Tex RITTER
Irene ROBERTS
  Roberta CARR
  Elizabeth HARLE
James ROBERTSHAW
  Michael GAUNT
John Wylie ROBERTSON
  Wylie WATSON
Marjorie ROBERTSON
  Anna NEAGLE
Ray Charles ROBINSON
  Ray CHARLES
Jacopo ROBUSTI
  TINTORETTO

Alfredo ROCHA
  Miguel TORGA
Jean de ROCHBRUNE
  Jean SOREL
Margaret ROCHE
  Maggi McNELLIS
Charles RODDA and Eric
AMBLER
  Eliot REED
Juan RODRIGUEZ
  Chi Chi RODRIGUEZ
Manuel RODRIGUEZ Y
SANCHEZ
  MANOLETE
Ivan ROE
  Richard SAVAGE
Vera-Ellen ROHE
  VERA-ELLEN
Frederick William Serafino Austin
Lewis Mary ROLFE
  Baron CORVO
Vera-Ellen ROME
  VERA-ELLEN
Lady Dorothy ROSE
  Dorothy CARRINGTON
Irving ROSE
  Ian RISK
Borge ROSENBAUM
  Victor BORGE
Harry ROSENBERG
  Arthur TRACY
Ina ROSENBERG
  Ina BALIN
Lev ROSENBERG
  Léon BAKST
Martin ROSENBLATT
  Ross MARTIN
Lev Borisovich ROSENFELD
  Lev Borisovich KAMENEV
Lyova ROSENTHAL
  Lee GRANT
Dennistoun ROSE-PRICE
  Dennis PRICE
Keith ROSS
  Ian KEITH
Sutherland ROSS
  T. H. CALLARD

Leo ROSTEN
  Leonard ROSS
Agnes ROTHERY
  Agnes EDWARDS
Mark ROTHKOVICH
  Mark ROTHKO
Simone ROUSSEL
  Michèle MORGAN
Bill ROWBOTHAM
  Bill OWEN
Schenor Zalman RUBASHEV
  Schenor Zalman SHAZAR
Harold RUBIN
  Harold ROBBINS
Edana RUDENSTEIN
  Edana ROMNEY
Antonio RUIZ SOLER
  ANTONIO
Pablo RUIZ Y PICASSO
  Pablo PICASSO
Helen RULFS
  Helen VINSON
Nedenia Hutton RUMBOUGH
  Dina MERRILL
Charles RUPPERT
  Charles DRAKE
John RUSKIN
  A GRADUATE OF OXFORD
  J.R.
  Kata PHUSIN
  The YOUNGER LADY OF THE
  THWAITE CONISTON
Charles Ellsworth RUSSELL
  Pee Wee RUSSELL
George RUSSELL
  AE
John RUSSELL
  Luke THRICE
Claudia RUSSELL-BROWN
  Anna RUSSELL
Lillian RUTSTEIN
  Lillian ROTH
Sally RUTTER
  Gale PAGE
John Joseph RYAN
  Jack LORD
Septimus RYOTT
  Stewart ROME

# S

John A. SABINI
  John ANTHONY
Sidney SADGROVE
  Lee TORRANCE
Melanie SAFKA
  MELANIE
Noel SAINSBURY
  Harvey D. RICHARDS
  Dorothy WAYNE
Dora Jesse SAINT
  Miss READ
Germaine SAISSET-SCHNEIDER
  Germaine DULAC
Liaquat Ali SALAAM
  Kenny CLARKE
Edward SALDANHA
  DIZZY SAL
Jean-Pierre SALOMONS
  Jean-Pierre AUMONT
Ramon SAMANIEGOS
  Ramon NOVARRO
Victor von SAMEK
  Vic OLIVER
Mrs. E. J. SAMUEL
  Edith SUMMERSKILL
Miriam SAMUELS
  Miriam KARLIN
Thomas SANDERS
  Tom CONWAY
James Elroy SANFORD
  Redd FOXX
Edward SANGER
  Herbert HOLMES
Valentina SANINA
  VALENTINA
Ines Isabella SANPIETRO
  Isa MIRANDA
Helen SANTOS
  GRIFFITHS
Raffaello SANZIO or SANTI
  RAPHAEL
Lucius Manlius SARGENT
  Ziba SPROULE
Thomas SARGENT
  Max MILLER

James SARRAPEDE
  Jimmy LYTELL
Alexander SARRUF
  Alex D'ARCY
Siegfried SASSOON
  Saul KAIN
Joseph SAUER
  Joseph SAWYER
Hilary St. George SAUNDERS and
John Leslie PALMER
  Francis BEEDING
Frederic SAUSER
  Blaise CENDRARS
Harry Lincoln SAYLER
  Ashton LAMAR
  Gordon STUART
  Elliott WHITNEY
Antonio SBARBARO
  Tony SPARGO
Milton SCHEINBLUM
  Mickey SHEEN
Jean Maurice SCHERER
  Eric ROHMER
Roy SCHERER
  Rock HUDSON
Marie SCHERR
  Marie CHER
Peter SCHILPEROORT
  Pat BRONX
Austin SCHILSKY
  Austin TREVOR
Gisele Eve SCHITTENHELM
  Brigitte HELM
Bruno Walter SCHLESINGER
  Bruno WALTER
Elke SCHLETZ
  Elke SOMMER
Josef SCHLIESSMAYER
  Oskar WERNER
William SCHLOSS
  William CASTLE
Kaspar SCHMIDT
  Max STIRNER
Ettore SCHMITZ
  Italo SVEVO

Gunther SCHNEIDER
Edward ARNOLD
Johannes SCHNEIDER
Johann AGRICOLA
Henry SCHNITTKIND
Henry THOMAS
Eduard SCHNITZER
EMIN PASHA
Henry SCHOOLCRAFT
Henry COLCRAFT
Gloria Jean SCHOONOVER
Gloria JEAN
Olive SCHREINER
Ralph IRON
Shirley SCHRIFT
Shelley WINTERS
Richard SCHULEFAND
Dick SHAWN
Cecil SCHWABE
Cecil PARKER
Bernard SCHWARTZ
Tony CURTIS
Richard SCHWARTZ
Dick SUTTON
Phillip SCHWARZERD
MELANCHTHON
Wilbur SCHWICHTENBERG
Will BRADLEY
Tony SCIACCA
Tony SCOTT
Sophia SCICOLONI
Sophia LOREN
David SCOFIELD
Paul SCOFIELD
Giovanna SCOGLIO
Gia SCALA
Sir Walter SCOTT
The ARISTO OF THE NORTH
The CALEDONIAN COMET
Jedediah CLEISHBOTHAM
Capt. CLUTTERBUCK
Chrystal CROFTANGRY
The Rev. Dr. DRYASDUST
The GREAT MAGICIAN
The GREAT UNKNOWN
A LAYMAN
Malachi MALAGROWTHER
MINSTREL OF THE BORDER
Peter PATTIESON

PAUL
SOMNABULUS
Laurence TEMPLETON
The VISIONARY
Mary Elfrieda SCRUGGS
Mary Lou WILLIAMS
Daphne SCRUTTON
Daphne ANDERSON
Elizabeth SEAMAN
Nellie BLY
Sonia SEEDO
Sonia FUCHS
Ruth SEID
Jo SINCLAIR
Mladen SEKULOVICH
Karl MALDEN
Charles SELBY
William MUGGINS
Tabitha TICKLETOOTH
Gilbert SELDES
Foster JOHNS
Archibald SELINGER
Archie PITT
Hildegarde SELL
HILDEGARDE
Isaiah SELLERS
Mark TWAIN
Joseph SELTZER and Charles MARKS
SMITH and DALE
Luis Philip SENARENS
Kit CLYDE
W. J. EARLE
Police Captain HOWARD
NONAME
Ned SPARLING
Jonathan SEWALL
Sir Roger DE COVERLEY
Henry SEYMOUR
HARTMANN
Thomas SEYMOUR
Walter FORDE
Aga Sultan Sir Mohamad SHAH
AGA KHAN III
Michel SHALHOUZ
Omar SHARIF
Henry SHALOFSKY
Hank SHAW

SHAMS ED-DÍN MUHAMMED
HÁFIZ
William SHARP
Fiona MACLEOD
Leon SHASH
Leon SASH
George Bernard SHAW
Corno DI BASSETTO
Henry Wheeler SHAW
Josh BILLINGS
John SHEEHAN
The IRISH WHISKEY
DRINKER
Lily SHEIL
Sheilah GRAHAM
Gail SHEKLES
Craig STEVENS
Samuel SHELLABARGER
John ESTEVEN
Peter LORING
Percy Bysshe SHELLEY
John FITZVICTOR
A GENTLEMAN OF OXFORD
A GENTLEMAN OF THE
UNIVERSITY OF OXFORD
MY AUNT MARGARET
NICHOLSON
The POETS OF POETS
S
VICTOR
Victoria SHENNAN
Ann SANGSTER
Michael SHEPLEY-SMITH
Michael SHEPLEY
Clara Lou SHERIDAN
Ann SHERIDAN
Richard Brinsley SHERIDAN
The MOST ARTFUL MAN
ALIVE
Josephine SHERWOOD
Josephine HULL
Mary Elizabeth Wilson
SHERWOOD
M.E.W.S.
William SHIELDS
Barry FITZGERALD
Levi SHKOLNIK
Levi ESHKOL

Alfred SHOENBERG
Al SHEAN
Frances Rose SHORE
Dinah SHORE
Annabelle SHORT
Annie ROSS
James SHORT
Jimmy LOGAN
Ralph Champion SHOTTER
Ralph MICHAEL
Paul SHOUVALOV
Paul SHERIFF
Joseph SHOVLIN
Michael WHALEN
Max SHOWALTER
Casey ADAMS
Frank SHOWELL STYLES
Glyn CARR
Jean SHUFFLEBOTTOM
Jeannie CARSON
Edward SHULMAN
Eddie SHU
Joe SHULMAN
Joe SAYE
Angelo SICILIANO
Charles ATLAS
Detlef SIERCK
Douglas SIRK
Dr. Frederick SIGFRED
Dr. Frank FREDERICKS
François SILLY
Gilbert BÉCAUD
Harold SILVERBLATT
Howard DA SILVA
Arthur SILVERLAKE
Arthur LAKE
Belle SILVERMAN
Beverly SILLS
Philip SILVERSMITH
Phil SILVERS
Herbert SILVETTE
Barnaby DOGBOLT
Georges SIMENON
Georges SIM
Mike SIMMONDS
Frank ESSEX
Yvonne SIMMS
SIMON

François SIMON
  Michel SIMON
William SIMONDS
  Walter AIMWELL
Norma SIMPSON
  Carol MARSH
Virginia SIMS
  Ginny SIMMS
Upton SINCLAIR
  Ensign Clarke FITCH, USN
Michael SINNOTT
  Mack SENNETT
Mildred Gillars SISK
  AXIS SALLY
Eva SJOKE
  Eva BARTOK
Richard SKELTON
  Red SKELTON
Larushka Mischa SKIKNE
  Laurence HARVEY
Kenneth SKINGLE
  Kenny GRAHAM
Vyacheslav Mikhalovich
SKRIABIN
  Vyacheslav Mikhailovich
  MOLOTOV
Elizabeth SLAUGHTER
  Betty BLYTHE
N. Carter SLAUGHTER
  Tod SLAUGHTER
David SLAVITT
  Henry SUTTON
John SLEEPER
  Hawser MARTINGALE
Patsy SLOOTS
  Susan SHAW
Leonard SLYE
  Roy ROGERS
  Dick WESTON
Charles SMART M.D.
  Polywarp OLDFELLOW M.D.
Hana SMEKALOVA
  Florence MARLY
Albert SMITH
  AL
Albert SMITH
  Jasper BUDDLE
Alfred Aloysius SMITH
  Trader HORN

Alma SMITH
  Alma RUBENS
David SMITH
  Johnston GRAHAM
Donald R. SMITH
  Robert ARMSTRONG
Dorothy SMITH
  Martha TRENT
Elizabeth SMITH
  Ernest HELFENSTEIN
Ernest Bramah SMITH
  Ernest BRAMAH
Frances Octavia SMITH
  Dale EVANS
George H. SMITH
  Uncle HENRY
  Farmer SMITH
Gladys Marie SMITH
  Mary PICKFORD
James SMITH
  P. J. PROBY
James Ellison SMITH
  James ELLISON
John SMITH
  Th. WATSON
June Johns SMITH
  June JOHNS
Laura Roundtree SMITH
  Caroline Silver JUNE
Mary SMITH
  Mary DREWERY
Mona SMITH
  Mona BARRIE
Phyllis SMITH
  Phyllis CURTIN
Reginald SMITH
  Marty WILDE
Robert SMITH
  Robert CHATTAN
Robert Charles SMITH
  Robert CHARLES
Robert Wilton SMITH
  Robb WILTON
Walker SMITH
  Sugar Ray ROBINSON
William J. T. SMITH
  Gul FERRAR
Mrs. Eliot-Burton SMITTER
  Lelia HADLEY

Joseph H. SMYTH
Joseph HILTON
Robert W. SNEDDON
Robert GUILLAUME
Lady SNOW
Pamela HANSFORD JOHNSON
Antonio da Fonseca SOARES
Frei Antonio DAS CHAGAS
Melvin SOKOLOFF
Mel LEWIS
Herbert SOLOMON
Herbie MANN
Edith SOMERVILLE
Geilles HERRING
Martin SORE
Martin AGRICOLA
Françoise SORYA
Anouk AIMÉE
Terry SOTHERN
Maxwell KENTON
Gwendoline SOUTAR
Sonia DEAN
Robert SOUTHEY
Espriella Manuel ALVAREZ
Solomon SOUTHWICK
Henry HOMESPUN
Lelio Francesco SOZZINI
SOCINUS
Edward SPARKMAN
Ned SPARKES
Raymond SPEARS
Jim SMILEY
William SPENCE
Jim BOWDEN
Floyd ROGERS
Avis S. SPENCER
Emma CARRA
Samuel SPEWACK
A. A. ABBOTT
Bart SPICER
Jay BARBETTE
Clara SPIEGEL and Jane MAYER
Clare JAYNES
Elizabeth SPILLIUS
Elizabeth BOTT
Aristokles SPIROU
ATHENAGORAS
Christopher St. John SPRIGG
Christopher CAULDWELL

Charles SPRINGALL
Charlie DRAKE
Joseph SPURIN-CALLEJA
Joseph CALLEIA
Ronald SQUIRL
Ronald SQUIRE
Leslie STAINER
Leslie HOWARD
Svetlana STALINA
Svetlana ALLILUYEVA
Theodoros STAMATELOS
Theodoros STAMOS
Dorothy STANDING
Kay HAMMOND
Edris STANNUS
Dame Ninette DE VALOIS
Grace STANSFIELD
Gracie FIELDS
John STANTON
Corry O'LANUS
Vivienne STAPLETON
Vivian BLAINE
Richard STARKEY
Ringo STARR
Kathryn STARKS
Kay STARR
Francis STEEGMULLER
David KEITH
Byron STEEL
Sir Richard STEELE
Isaac BICKERSTAFF
Ann STEELY
Cathy O'DONNELL
George STEIN
George E. STONE
Gertrude STEIN
Alice B. TOKLAS
Elsy STEINBERG
Elaine STEWART
Dr. Wilhelm STEKEL
Willy BOJAN
Dr. SERENUS
Charles STENGEL
Casey STENGEL
Anjuschka STENSKI
SUJAKEVITCH
Anna STEN
Inger STENSLAND
Inger STEVENS

**Ann S. STEPHENS**
Jonathan SLICK
**Josef STERN**
Josef VON STERNBERG
**Miroslava STERN**
MIROSLAVA
**Constance STEVENS**
Sally GRAY
**George Alexander STEVENS**
Sir Henry HUMM
A LADY
Wade WHIPPLE
ZAPHANIEL
**John STEVENS**
Steve BRODIE
**Mark STEVENS**
Stephen RICHARDS
**Ruby STEVENS**
Barbara STANWICK
**Onslow Ford STEVENSON**
Onslow STEVENS
**Robert Louis STEVENSON**
Le PICKLEUR
**Alfred Walter STEWART**
J. J. CONNINGTON
**Anna May STEWART**
Anita STEWART
**James STEWART**
Stewart GRANGER
**John STEWART**
Michael INNES
**Marie STEWART**
Marie DORO
**George Ford STITCH**
Ford STERLING
**Charles W. STODDARD**
Pip PEPPERPOD
**Ida Frances STOLOV**
Frances STELOFF
**Grace Zaring STONE**
Ethel VANCE
**Catherine STORR**
Helen LOURIE
**June STOVENOUR**
June HAVER
**Harriet Beecher STOWE**
Christopher CROWFIELD
**John Gary STRADER**
John GARY

**Leslie STRANDT**
Les STRAND
**Charles Sherwood STRATTON**
Tom THUMB
**Betty STREIDLER**
Betta ST. JOHN
**Peter Lee STRINGER**
Daniel BOONE
**Charles STRONG**
Nancy BARTLETT
Myron KEATS
William McCLELLAN
Kelvin McKAY
Chuck STANLEY
Charles STODDARD
Carl STURDY
**Latham C. STRONG**
Montague SHATT
**Geraldine STROOCK**
Geraldine BROOKS
**David STROTHER**
Port CRAYON
**Morton STUBBS**
Morton SELTEN
**Annie STUDDERT**
Annie RIXON
**Nikolay STUKALOV**
Nikolay POGODIN
**Kaarlo SULIN**
Kaarlo SARKIA
**Bonar SULLIVAN**
Bonar COLLEANO
**Elizabeth SULLIVAN**
Elsa LANCHESTER
**John F. SULLIVAN**
Fred ALLEN
**Raymond SULLIVAN**
Gilbert O'SULLIVAN
**Joan SUMMERFIELD**
Jean KENT
**Colleen SUMMERS**
Mary FORD
**George SUMMERVILLE**
Slim SUMMERVILLE
**Emanuel SVEDBERG**
Emanuel SWEDENBORG
**Madeleine SVOBODA**
Madeleine ROBINSON

238

Lubertus Jacobus SWAANSWIJK
  LUCEBERT
**Cormac SWAN**
  Shaun McCARTHY
  Philip TYNAN
**Homer D. L. SWEET**
  Parmenus SMARTWEED
**Josephine SWENSON**
  Gloria SWANSON
**Rev. William G. SWETT**
  Quicksilver SMALLTALK
**Jonathan SWIFT**
  A. B.
  Tom ASHE
  Isaac BICKERSTAFF
  M. B. DRAPIER
  An ENEMY OF THE PEACE
  Jack FRENCHMAN
  T. FRIBBLE
  Lemuel GULLIVER
  Gregory MISO-SARUM
  M. Flor O'SQUARR
  A PERSON OF HONOUR

T. N. PHILOMATH
PRESTO
Abel ROPER
S.P.A.M.
Martinus SCRIBLERUS
Tristram SHANDY
A SHOEBOY
STUDENT OF ASTROLOGY
T. TINKER
Dr. Andrew TRIPE
Simon WAGSTAFF, Esq.
**Algernon Charles SWINBURNE**
  Mrs. Horace MANNERS
**Carl SWITZER**
  Alfalfa SWITZER
**Anna Myrthle SWOYER**
  Nancy WALKER
**David SYMINGTON**
  James HALLIDAY
**Eugene Gero SZAKALL**
  S. Z. SAKALL
**Istvan SZEKELY**
  Steve SEKELY

# T

**Alice TAAFE**
  Alice TERRY
**Paul TABORI**
  Peter STAFFORD
  Christopher STEVENS
**Max-Gérard TANNENBAUM**
  Gérard OURY
**Beatrice TANNER**
  Mrs. Patrick CAMPBELL
**Edward Everett TANNER, III**
  Patrick DENNIS
  Virginia ROWANS
**Increase Niles TARBOX**
  UNCLE GEORGE
**Brenda Lee TARPLEY**
  Brenda LEE
**Margaret TATE**
  Dame Maggie TEYTE
**Laura TATHAM**
  Margaret PHIPPS

**Jacques TATISCHEFF**
  Jacques TATI
**F. Chase TAYLOR**
  Colonel STOOPNAGLE
**John TAYLOR**
  My-Heele MENDSOALE
  Sir Gregory NONSENCE
  THORNY AILO
  The WATER POET
**Marion Sayle TAYLOR**
  The VOICE OF EXPERIENCE
**Edward TEACH**
  BLACKBEARD
**Nahum TEATE**
  Nahum TATE
**Morton TECOSKY**
  Morton DA COSTA
**Saunders TEDDELL**
  Sonny TERRY
**Arthur Murray TEICHMAN**
  Arthur MURRAY

**Darwin TEILHET**
Cyrus FISHER
**Gabriel TÉLLEZ**
TIRSO DE MOLINA
**Irving TENNENBAUM**
Irving STONE
**Alfred TENNYSON**
ALCIBIADES
MERLIN
**Abram TERTZ**
Audrey Donatovich
SINYAVSKY
**Fyodor Kuz'mich TETERNIKOV**
Fyodor SOLOGUB
**John Salkeld TETLEY**
Michael ANTHONY
John ELSWORTH
**William Makepeace THACKERAY**
Mr. BROWN
Fitzroy CLARENCE
Frederick Haltamont DE
MONTMORENCY
Henry ESMOND, Esq.
George Savage FITZBOODLE,
Esq.
JEAMES OF BUCKLEY
SQUARE
Theresa MacWHORTER
MULLIGAN OF
KILBALLYMULLIGAN
ONE OF THEMSELVES
Arthur PENDENNIS
Harry ROLLICKER
Ikey SOLOMONS, Jr.
Lancelot WAGSTAFF
Theophile WAGSTAFF
Charles YELLOWPLUSH
**Nguyen That THANH**
HO CHI MINH
**THAYENDANEGEA**
Joseph BRANT
**Domenikos THEOTOCOPOULOS**
El GRECO
**Denis THEVENIN**
Georges DUHAMEL
**Anatole François THIBAULT**
Anatole FRANCE
**Philip THICKNESSE**
P.T. Esq.

**June Sylvia THIMBLETHORPE**
Sylvia THORPE
**Maurice THOMAS**
Maurice TOURNEUR
**Ross THOMAS**
Oliver BLEECK
**Ada THOMPSON**
Vivien MERCHANT
**Antony THOMPSON**
Antony ALBAN
**Ernest Seton THOMPSON**
Ernest Thompson SETON
**Estelle O'Brien Merle**
**THOMPSON**
Merle OBERON
**John THOMPSON**
John DALL
**Mortimer THOMPSON**
Q. K. Philander DOESTICKS
**Paul THOMPSON**
Paul ROTHA
**Betty THORNBURG**
Betty HUTTON
**Marion THORNBURG**
Marion HUTTON
**Argonne THORNTON**
Sadik HAKIM
**Rollo THORPE**
Richard THORPE
**Reuben TICKER**
Richard TUCKER
**Frances TIERNAN**
Christian REID
**Gerald TIERNEY**
Scott BRADY
**Shripad TIKEKAR**
Kartikeya MUSHAFIR
**Peter TILDSLEY**
Peter HADDON
**Gérard TISSERAND**
Gérard SOUZAY
**Janus Junius TOLAND**
John TOLAND
**Mary TOMLINSON**
Marjorie MAIN
**S. Yewell TOMPKINS**
Tom EWELL
**Haym TOPOL**
TOPOL

Elmore TORN
  Rip TORN
Joseph TORTORIELLO
  Joe TARTO
Arthur TOWLE
  Arthur LUCAN
Charles Wayland TOWNE
  Gideon WURDZ
Mary Ashley TOWNSEND
  XARIFFA
Secondo TRANQUILLI
  Ignazio SILONE
Nicholas TRAVASCIO
  Nick TRAVIS
Elleston TREVOR
  Roger FITZALAN
  Adam HALL
Marguerite Gwynne TRICE
  Anne GWYNNE
Eric TRIMMER
  Eric JAMESON
Michael TRIVOLIS
  MAKSIM THE GREEK

Anthony TROLLOPE
  ONE OF THE FIRM
Reginald TRUSCOTT-JONES
  Ray MILLAND
Wong Liu TSONG
  Anna May WONG
Arthur L. TUBBS
  Arthur SYLVESTER
James TUCKER
  David CRAIG
Bowen Charleston TUFTS
  Sonny TUFTS
Julia TURNER
  Lana TURNER
Lida L. TURNER
  Lida LARRIMORE
Violet Prudence Alan TURNER
  Prudence SUMMERHAYES
Judith TUVIM
  Judy HOLLIDAY
James TYTLER
  DON QUIXOTE, Jr.

# U

Douglas Elton ULMAN
  Douglas FAIRBANKS
Vladimir Ilyich ULYANOV
  Vladimir Ilyich LENIN
Charlotte UNDERWOOD
  Joan CHARLES
Unknown original names
  Harry HALYARD

JUNIUS
  Ben TRAVEN
George Putnam UPTON
  Peregrine PICKLE
Edward UPWARD
  Allen CHALMERS
Frank USHER
  Charles FRANKLIN

# V

Marie-Clementine VALADON
  Suzanne VALADON
Maurice VALADON
  Maurice UTRILLO
Guiseppe VALENTINO
  Joseph VALENTINE

Richard VALENZUELA
  Richie VALENS
Hubert Prior VALLEE
  Rudy VALLEE
Benjamin VALLENTINE
  FITZNOODLE

Frederic VALMAIN
Paul BAULAT
James CARTER
Derek Jules Gaspard Ulric Niven
VAN DEN BOGAERDE
Dirk BOGARDE
Pieter VAN DER FAES
Sir Peter LELY
Fritz VAN DUNGEN
Philip DORN
Worster VAN EPS
Willard PARKER
Cornelius VAN MATTEMORE
Richard ARLEN
Pietro VANNUCCI
PERUGINO
Robert VAN ORDEN
John SMITH
Donald VAN VLIET
CAPTAIN BEEFHART
Dominique VARAIGNE
Dominique SANDA
Alfred VARICK
Alfred DRAYTON
Mihaly VARKONYI
Victor VARCONI
Mahesh Prasad VARMA
MAHARISHI MAHESH YOGI
Peggy VARNADOW
Peggy DOW
Giuseppe VASATURO
Giuseppe AMATO
Arthur Treacher VEARY
Arthur TREACHER
Tiziaro VECELLI
TITIAN
Immanuel VELIKOVSKY
Immanuel RAM
Charles VENTURO
Charlie VENTURA
Jean VERHAGEN
Jean HAGEN
Pietro Martire VERMIGLI
Peter MARTYR
Johanna VERWER
Elizabeth JOHANSON
Julien VIAUD

Pierre LOTI
Metta Victoria VICTOR
Rose KENNEDY
Mrs. Mark PEABODY
Seeley REGESTER
SINGING SIBYL
Alexander VIESPI
Alex CORD
Edith VIGNAUD
Anne VERNON
Walter VINICOMBE
Wally PATCH
Daniel VINIELLO
Danny ALVIN
Ralph VITTI
Michael DANTE
John VOELKER
Robert TRAVER
Boris VOGAU
Boris Andreyevich PILNYAK
David VOGENITZ
David GEORGE
Carl Henry VOGT
Louis CALHERN
François Marie Arouet de
VOLTAIRE
Docteur AKAKIA
Rabbin AKIB
Une BELLE DAME
Un BÉNÉDICTIN
Milord BOLINGBROCKE
Marquis DE XIMENEZ
GEMELLUS
Le Docteur GOODHEART
M. IMHOF
Le Major KAISERLING
Curé MESLIER
Jean PLOKOF
Un QUAKER
SCARMENTADO
SORANUS
M. THOMSON
Catherine VADE
VOLTAIRE
ZAPATA
Vaclav VONAVKA
Vaclav REZAK

242

Francesca Mitzi VON GERBER
Mitzi GAYNOR
Betty VON GERLEAN
Kathleen HUGHES

Lelia VON KOERBER
Marie DRESSLER
Kurt VONNEGUT, Jr.
Kilgore TROUT

# W

Fred WACHENHEIMER
Fred W. FRIENDLY
Franz WACHSMANN
Franz WAXMAN
Miriam WADDINGTON
E. B. MERRIT
George WADE
George ROBEY
Gordon WAINWRIGHT
Ray GORDON
Meir WALACH
Maxim LITVINOV
Henry WALE
Henry OSCAR
Edmund WALKER
Jeremy KEMP
Peter WALKER
Christopher CORAM
Tom FERRIS
Ruby WALLACE
Ruby DEE
Jean WALLASEK
Jean WALLACE
Myron Leon WALLIK
Mike WALLACE
Horace WALPOLE
H***** W******
The Hon. Mr. H – – ce W – – LE
A MAN
William MARSHALL, Gent.
Onuphrio MURALTO
XO-HO
Sir Robert WALPOLE
Sir R–T W–LP–LE
BOB OF LYM
Bob BOOTY
FLIMNAP, the Lilliputian
Premier
Bob HUSH

IAGO
The KNIGHT
M. R. LYN
PUNCH
ROBIN
SIR BOB
Arthur WARD or WADE
Sax ROHMER
Andy WARHOLA
Andy WARHOL
Harold WARNOW
Raymond SCOTT
Dionne WARWICK
Dionne WARWICKE
Jack WATERS
Jack WARNER
Rosemary WATERS
Rosemary HORSTMANN
Joel WATFORD
Jon ESSEX
D. J. WATKINS-PITCHFORD
B.B.
Bernard WATNEY
Marcus J. DOLLEY
Julia WATSON
Jane DE VERE
Julia HAMILTON
Reatha WATSON
Barbara LA MARR
Vernon WATSON
Nosmo KING
Violet WATSON
Viola LYEL
Marilyn WATTS
Mara CORDAY
Dorothy WAYMAN
Theodate GEOFFREY
Eunice WAYMON
Nina SIMONE

243

Charles WAYNE
  Horace HAZELTINE
Daphne WAYNE
  Blanche SWEET
Anne WEALE
  Andrea BLAKE
Godfrey WEBB
  Norman ENGLAND
  Charles GODFREY
Harry WEBB
  Cliff RICHARD
Ruth WEBB
  Ruth MORRIS
Bayla WEGIER
  Bella DARVI
Elizabeth WEHNER
  Betty SMITH
Rex WEI
  Rex WILLIAMS
Patricia WEIGUM
  Pat YANKEE
Phyllis WEILER
  Phyllis BROOKS
Nathan WEINSTEIN
  Nathanael WEST
Chaim Reuben WEINTROP
  Bud FLANAGAN
Muni WEISENFREUND
  Paul MUNI
Louis WEISS
  Kent TAYLOR
Erich WEISS
  Harry HOUDINI
Susan Ker WELD
  Tuesday WELD
Julie WELLS
  Julie ANDREWS
H. G. WELLS
  Reginald BLISS
  Septimus BROWNE
  Jane CRABTREE
  D.P.
  Walker GLOCKENHAMMER
  S.S.
  TYRO
  H. G. WHEELS
Blanca Rosa WELTER
  Linda CHRISTIAN

Claire WEMLINGER
  Claire TREVOR
Rose WENGER
  Helen GIBSON
George WENZLAFF
  George WINSLOW
Gordon M. WERSCHKUL
  Gordon SCOTT
Fred WESTCOTT
  Fred KARNO
Donald E. WESTLAKE
  Richard STARK
Charles WESTOVER
  Del SHANNON
Karl Adrian WETTACH
  GROCK
Thomas T. WHALLEY
  A BEAUTIFUL AND
  UNFORTUNATE YOUNG
  LADY
Katherine WHITE
  Marie WILSON
Patricia WHITE
  Patricia WILDE
Priscilla WHITE
  Cilla BLACK
William Hale WHITE
  Mark RUTHERFORD
Walt WHITMAN
  ICHABOD
Hudson WHITTAKER
  TAMPA RED
Leonard P. O'Connor
WIBBERLEY
  Leonard HOLTON
Mary WICKENHAUSER
  Mary WICKES
Irene WICKER
  Ireene WICKER
Jesse WIEDENFELD
  Jesse WHITE
Martha WIEDERRECHT
  Martha WRIGHT
Ralf Harold WIGGER
  Ralf HAROLDE
Martin WIGGLESWORTH
  Martin WORTH

244

Reginald WILD
 Leonard EDWARDS
Oscar WILDE
 C.3.3.3.
Samuel WILDER
 Billy WILDER
Maybritt WILKENS
 May BRITT
Richard WILKES-HUNTER
 Shane DOUGLAS
Allen WILLIAMS
 Allen LANE
Marietta WILLIAMS
 Maxine SULLIVAN
Meurig WILLIAMS
 Michael CARRINGTON
Myrna WILLIAMS
 Myrna LOY
Thomas Lanier WILLIAMS
 Tennessee WILLIAMS
George A. A. WILLIS
 A.A.
 Anthony ARMSTRONG
Alfred WILLMORE
 Michael MacLIAMMOIR
Charles WILSON
 Joseph CREHAN
John Burgess WILSON
 Anthony BURGESS
 Joseph KELL
T. T. WILSON
 Saul WRIGHT
Cecil WIMHURST
 Nigel BRENT
Mavis WINDER
 Mavis ARETA
Karl WINKLER
 Theodor HELL
Robert WINNE
 Robert HUTTON
Joanna WINNIFRITH
 Anna LEE
Bernard WINOGRADSKY
 Bernard DELFONT
Lewis WINOGRADSKY
 Lew GRADE
Norman WISDEN
 Norman WISDOM
Ernest WISEMAN

Ernie WISE
Adolf WOHLBRUCK
 Anton WALBROOK
Ona WOLCOTT
 Ona MUNSON
Elizabeth WONG
 CHI LIEN
Ethel WOOD
 Ethel GRIFFIES
Gloria WOOD
 K. T. STEVENS
Matilda WOOD
 Bella DELAMARE
 Marie LLOYD
Irene WOODFORD
 Jane BARRIE
Josephine WOODRUFF
 Edwina BOOTH
Patti WOODWARD
 Jane DARWELL
Thomas Jones WOODWARD
 Tom JONES
Anna WOOLDRIDGE
 Abbey LINCOLN
Donald WOOLFITT
 Donald WOLFIT
William WORDSWORTH
 BARD OF RYDAL MOUNT
 The CUMBERLAND POET
Lambros WORLOOU
 Georges GUETARY
Philip WORNER
 Philip INCLEDON
Wilfrid WORSNOP
 Wilfrid LAWSON
Greta WOXHOLT
 Greta GYNT
Elinor WRIGHT
 Elinor LYON
Mary WRIGHT
 Mary BAWN
Paula WRIGHT
 Paula RAYMOND
Willard Huntingdon WRIGHT
 S.S. VAN DINE
Francis WUPPERMAN
 Frank MORGAN
Ronald WYCHERLEY

Billy FURY
Leon WYCOFF
Leon AMES
Oswald WYND
Gavin BLACK
John WYNDHAM

John BENYON
John Benyon HARRIS
Esme WYNN-TYSON
DIOTIMA and AMANDA
Dagmar WYNTER
Dana WYNTER

# X

XENOPHON
THEMISTOGENES OF
SYRACUSE

# Y

Donald YARMY
Don ADAMS
Mrs. Jess YATES
Heller TOREN
W. B. YEATS
D.E.D.I.
GANCONAGH
ROSICRUX
A STUDENT OF IRISH
LITERATURE
Forest Frederick YEO-THOMAS
WHITE RABBIT
Juan de YEPES Y ALVAREZ
St. JOHN OF THE CROSS
Leslie Charles YIN
Leslie CHARTERIS
Asa YOELSON
Al JOLSON

Henry YORKE
Henry GREEN
Alan YORKIN
Bud YORKIN
Nicolai YOSHKIN
Martin KOSLECK
Angus YOUNG
Alan YOUNG
Elizabeth YOUNG
Sally BLANE
Gretchen YOUNG
Loretta YOUNG
Elizabeth YOUNGER
Elizabeth HELY
Joe YULE
Mickey McGUIRE
Mickey ROONEY
John Gary YUSOLFSKY
Gary LOCKWOOD

# Z

Rev. F. N. ZABRISKIE
OLD COLONY
Łazar Ludwik ZAMENHOF
Dr. ESPERANTO

Bernard ZANVILLE
Dane CLARK
Leatrice Joy ZEIDLER
Leatrice JOY

**Margareta Gertruda ZELLE**
 MATA HARI
**Kamil ZEMAN**
 Ivan OLBRACHT
**George L. ZENON**
 George LEWIS
**Fanny ZILVERITCH**
 Franceska GAAL
**Sonia ZIM**
 Sonia BLEEKER
**Robert ZIMMERMAN**
 Bob DYLAN
**Ethel ZIMMERMANN**
 Ethel MERMAN

**Jillana ZIMMERMANN**
 JILLANA
**Ahmed ZOGU**
 ZOG
**Stuart ZONIS**
 Stuart DAMON
**Vincent Edward ZORRIO**
 Vince EDWARD
**Alexandra ZUCK**
 Sandra DEE
**Muni ZUDEKOFF**
 Buddy MORROW

# Quotations

'I *do* wish she would change her name.' – Louella Parsons (of actress Rita Gam)

'How could anyone called Levitch get laughs.' – Jerry Lewis (Joseph Levitch)

'Schwartz ain't a name to get you into the big time – not even George Bernard Schwartz.' – Hollywood producer Bob Goldstein to Tony Curtis (Bernard Schwartz)

'You wouldn't like to end up by being someone else, would you?' – Guy Mitchell (Al Cernick)

'I blushed when I was given that name.' – Rock Hudson (Roy Scherer)

'Beedle! It sounds like an insect.' – Paramount executive to William Holden (Beedle)

'Janet Cole could be anyone but "Kim Hunter" could go far as an actress.' – David O. Selznick

'Well, honey, you certainly picked a fancy one.' – Hollywood producer, when Joan Crawford (Lucille Le Sueur) correctly gave her original name

'Ailsa Craig! What a magnificent name for an actress!' – Ellen Terry

'Flowerbelle! What a euphonious appellation!' – W. C. Fields, when introduced to Mae West in *My Little Chickadee*

'A self-made man may prefer to use a self-made name.' – Judge Learned Hand, on granting permission to Samuel Goldfish to use the name Goldwyn

'The name Lily Shiel, to this day, horrifies me to a degree impossible to explain.' – Sheila Graham (Lily Shiel)

'My "X" replaced the white slavemaster name of "Little" which some blue-eyed devil named Little had imposed upon my paternal forebears.' – Malcolm X

'I wish I'd left it as it was – after all, Theodore Bickel did all right.' – Frederic March (F. Bickel)

'Horace Greeley said, "Go West, Young Man". So I did.' – Nathaniel West (Nathan Weinstein)

'The hyphen's the gap between my teeth.' – Terry-Thomas (Thomas Terry Hoar-Stevens)

'Broadbent is not a name for the stage.' – Noël Coward to Dora Bryan (Broadbent)

'Sam Johnson is hardly a name for a great writer.' – G. B. Shaw

'Well, I have, but then, of course, I'd have to *write* under another name if I did.' – George Orwell (Eric Blair) when asked if he had ever considered legally adopting his pen-name

'No, Groucho, is not my real name. I'm breaking it in for a friend.' – Groucho Marx (attr)

'Tell me Mr. Schwartz, why didn't you like the name "Curtis"?' – Oscar Brodney, Hollywood producer, on being introduced to Tony Curtis' father

'To possess a good cognomen is a long way on the road to success in life.' – Chamfort

'Imagine for a moment Napoleon I to have borne the name Jenkins, or Washington to have sustained the appellation of John Smith.' – Artemus Ward

'Bradford Dillman sounded like a distinguished, phoney, theatrical name so I kept it.' – Bradford Dillman

'I told him it had taken me most of my life to get used to the traumatic effects of being called Jack U. Lemmon, and that I was used to it now and I wasn't going to change it. . . .' – Jack Lemmon to Hollywood executive who wanted to change his name to 'Lennon'

# Bibliography

ABBATT, W., *The colloquial who's who: pseudonyms from 1600–1924*, New York, 1924

ANDERSSON, Per, *Pseudonymregister*, Lund, 1967

ATKINSON, Frank, *Dictionary of pseudonyms and pen-names*, London, 1975

BARBI, Torquato, *Opera anonime o pseudonime apparse fra il 1835 ed il 1907*, Florence, 1965

BAUER, Andrew, *Hawthorne dictionary of pseudonyms*, New York, 1971

BROWN, R. M., *The pseudonyms of God*, Philadelphia, 1972

COSTON, Henry, *Dictionaire des pseudonymes*, Paris, 1965

COURTNEY, W. P., *The secrets of our national literature*, New York, 1968

CUSHING, William, *Initials and pseudonyms: a dictionary of literary disguises*, New York, 1885

CUTOLO, Vicente, *Diccionario de alfonimos y seudónimos de la Argentina, 1800–1930*, Buenos Aires, 1962

ERDMAN, D. V. and FOGEL, E., *Evidence for authorship: essays on problems of attribution*, New York, 1966

FRATTAROLO, Renzo, *Anonimi e pseudonimi*, Rome, 1955

FREY, Albert R., *Sobriquets and nicknames*, Boston, 1888

GAINES, Pierce Welsh, *Political works of concealed authorship 1789–1809*, New Haven, 1959

HALKETT, Samuel and LAING, John, *Dictionary of anonymous and pseudonymous English literature*, London 1926–56

HALLIWELL, Leslie, *The Filmgoer's Companion*, London, 1965

HANAKOVIC, S., *Slovík pseudonymov slovenských spisovateľov*, Matica Slovenksa, 1961

HAYNES, John E., *Pseudonyms of authors*, New York, 1969

HEYM, R. G., *Bekannte unbekannte*, Berlin, 1960

HONCE, Charles, *Authors in falseface*, New York, 1939

MARBLE, A. R., *Pen-names and personalities*, New York, 1930

MORRIS, A. V., *A Bibliography of anonyms and pseudonyms*, Chicago, 1934

PÉREZ ORTIZ, Rubén, *Seudónimos colombianos*, Bogotá, 1961

PONCE DE LEÓN FREYRE, E., & ZAMORA LUCAS, F., *1500 seudónimos modernos de la literatura española 1900–1942*, Madrid, 1942

SCARONE, Arturo, *Diccionario de seudónimos del Uruguay*, Montevideo, 1941

SHARP, Harold S., *Handbook of pseudonyms and personal nicknames*, New York, 1972

SINT, Josef, *Pseudonymität im Altertum*, Innsbruck, 1960

STONEHILL, Charles A. *et al*, *Anonyma and pseudonyma*, London, 1926–27

TAYLOR, Archie and MOSHER, Fredric J., *The bibliographical history of anonyma and pseudonyma*, Chicago, 1951

THOMAS, Ralph, *Aggravating ladies: being a list of works published under the pseudonym of 'A LADY'*, London, 1880